Praise for *Just Promoted!*

"*Just Promoted!* provides sound strategies and tools that will help newly promoted employees hit the ground running in their new role and minimize their chances of derailment."

—Jon Peters, President,
The Institute for Management Studies

"A new leader does not get a second chance to make a first impression. This practical guide offers sage advice for a successful transition to a new leadership role."

—Madeline Bell, Chief Operating Officer,
Children's Hospital of Philadelphia

"*Just Promoted!* provides the knowledge, tools, and resources required by organizations today to maximize their investment in newly hired and promoted leaders. A must-read for all who care about 'leading for improvement' and positioning leaders for success."

—Judy Schueler, Vice President,
Organizational Development and
Chief Human Resources Officer,
University of Pennsylvania Health System

"*Just Promoted!* clearly details for the new leader potential pitfalls to avoid and strategies for success. Extremely practical, the book is straightforward and easy to use."

—Vincent A. Forlenza, President,
BD (Becton, Dickinson and Co.)

"Ed and Nila Betof team up to provide insightful analysis of those critical first months in a leadership role and will be an immense help to people who are tackling the challenge of new career roles, whether they're taking the helm of a major corporation or attaining a management position of a small team."

—Dr. Craig D. Weidemann,
Vice President for Outreach,
The Pennsylvania State University

Just Promoted!

A 12-Month Road Map for Success in Your New Leadership Role

SECOND EDITION

EDWARD BETOF, ED.D.
NILA BETOF, PH.D.

New York   Chicago   San Francisco   Lisbon   London   Madrid   Mexico City
Milan   New Delhi   San Juan   Seoul   Singapore   Sydney   Toronto

The **McGraw·Hill** Companies

The first edition of *Just Promoted!* was published in 1992 by McGraw-Hill, Inc., and was written by Edward Betof and Frederic Harwood.

1 2 3 4 5 6 7 8 9 0   DOC/DOC   1 9 8 7 6 5 4 3 2 1 0

ISBN   978-0-07-174525-3
MHID   0-07-174525-4

McGraw-Hill books are available at special quantity discounts to use as premiums and sales promotions or for use in corporate training programs. To contact a representative, please e-mail us at bulksales@mcgraw-hill.com.

This book is printed on acid-free paper.

To our Moms and Dads—
Jean and Martin Betof and Florence and Samuel Goodman—
who guided us through so many of our early transitions.

To our son Ari, daughter Allison, and daughter-in-law Shauna,
each of whom has already successfully made important life and leadership
transitions and will have so many more opportunities in the years to come.

To our granddaughters Anya and Kayla, whose energy, curiosity, and
zest for life bring us joy and pride every day.

CONTENTS

PREFACE

Just Promoted! was first published in 1992. The book was coauthored by Ed Betof and Fredric Harwood, and it has remained on the market for over 18 years. It has been used by thousands of professionals and leaders who were preparing for, or in the midst of, their own transition into new leadership roles. Human resources professionals and executive coaches have also made extensive use of the book as a resource in their work with transitioning leaders. We have been delighted to hear of the many examples of more senior executives using the book both for themselves and as a coaching aid as they helped those on their respective teams who were assuming new and greater leadership responsibilities.

This second edition of *Just Promoted!* builds on the principles of the earlier edition. However, much has changed in our world and the world of work since the early 1990s when *Just Promoted!* first became available. The updated material in this book addresses the many challenges of contemporary leadership and leadership transitions. The best ideas and activities from the first edition remain. However, there are many new elements in this edition. Almost 20 years of field-tested ideas and concepts developed since *Just Promoted!* was originally published are presented. These experiences were gained in many business, school, government, and not-for profit work settings. They have been taught in seminars and used extensively in coaching newly appointed and promoted leaders.

A major feature in this edition is the inclusion of a suite of Just Promoted Leader Tools that are presented throughout the book. These tools and the concepts they support really work. They are practical and have been used in many work settings and countries across the globe. These tools and concepts make leadership transitions a bit easier and greatly reduce the risk of career derailment during the 12 to 18 months when a newly promoted leader is tremendously challenged and very often working at a frenzied pace. With the help of past and current colleagues, we have personally enhanced our own ability to step into new leadership roles. We have also taught, consulted, and coached others with these tools and concepts. We share them with you for your use and with the goal of helping even more leaders make smooth and effective landings as they assume new, different, and broader responsibilities.

This book is about what happens in the first 12 months after you've been promoted to a new management or leadership role. You're moving up! It's about that exciting and challenging time in your professional life when your responsibilities change, expand, and usually become much more challenging for you. If it is your first management role, you will experience the strangeness of changing from an *us* to a *them*, when you opt for group over individual responsibility. For more experienced and more senior executives, every new role has its own challenges, often with higher stakes and implications. Whether you are a new manager or a more experienced leader, you are often tested to the limits of your ability and confidence during the weeks and months that follow your appointment. You will certainly stretch your professional and leadership comfort zones. This is a period of hazardous duty, and *Just Promoted!* is designed to help you at every turn.

For the first-time manager, this is a period of professional and personal change unlike any other in your career. In a relatively short time, no more than a few months, you will negotiate the rocky, treacherous channel that separates the knowledgeable, motivated, functional, or technical phase of your career from your new role as manager and leader of others. No longer responsible solely for the performance and quality of your own work, you now have to figure out how to help others achieve at least that same level of skill, motivation, and knowledge that earned you the promotion. No longer are you the effective or master professional; now you are in charge.

Whether you are new to management and leadership responsibility, or a veteran of numerous previous leadership roles and transitions, you will be observed and judged by your stakeholders with most every move you make and every decision you take. All leaders are watched. Newly promoted leaders are watched even more closely. There is great interest in everything you do . . . for some good and, unfortunately, not so good reasons. You will be judged on how well you manage this difficult transition. Your new responsibilities will test and challenge you as a person and as a professional. This period will likely have a lasting effect on your career and your personal brand as others assess your performance, your interactions, and your potential as a leader.

This book is designed to be a very practical resource for both new and experienced managers and leaders with titles such as *manager, group leader, depart-*

ment head, unit director, and *plant* or *general manager.* The book is also written for managers and leaders who are moving up in the government, education, or nonprofit sector with responsibilities, such as school principals,
superintendents, or program or executive directors. The processes for those
who assume new leadership responsibilities are similar even if the settings are
not. This book is also helpful for more experienced leaders and executives, who
can use it as a resource to guide and coach their managers and administrators
as they assume new responsibilities. Experienced leaders will also find this book
helpful as a reminder of what to do as they change roles and assignments.

When you move up, you are really making two transitions simultaneously.
Aspects of the first transition become obvious very quickly when you are
appointed or promoted to a new role. These are the organizational and leadership aspects of moving into a new position. You must quickly establish yourself in your new assignment and begin to work toward achieving meaningful
impact on your organization. On the surface, the obstacles and challenges may
or may not be obvious. Sometimes, the challenges may not seem especially
difficult or the hurdles particularly formidable. However, the barriers to success are ever present. There is much to do and much to plan for. This is a critical phase in your development as a leader, and your ability to perform can
make or break your career.

As you move up, you also have a second transition to make, a very personal
one. In their euphoria about getting the promotion, few leaders adequately plan
for the inevitable changes in their personal lives. In the last chapter we will
address the important interplay between work, personal, and home life. When
you take on a new leadership role, there is almost always a ripple effect on other
key aspects of your life. The more time, attention, and emotional engagement
you provide at work, the greater the likelihood that there is less of you to give
at home, to those you love. You will be less available to friends, and you will
have less free time and attention to give to your community, religious endeav-
ors, and even your personal health and fitness. Effectively managing this interplay between key elements of your life makes up the final section of this book.

In *Just Promoted!* we suggest effective, practical ways for you to succeed at
work and at home as you develop as a leader and specifically as you manage
the first year in each of your new leadership roles. This book is not a quick fix.
It is not a treatise on management or leadership philosophy; nor is it a single
set or cluster of isolated skills. Rather, it teaches from our own and from others' successes and errors when taking on new leadership responsibility.

We have drawn our suggestions from our own experiences and from the many with whom we have worked, interviewed, observed, taught, and coached. Their willingness to share has enriched this book with invaluable insight, and it has made it a useful tool for anyone who is fortunate to have been *Just Promoted!*

Ed Betof
Nila Betof

ACKNOWLEDGMENTS

We want to recognize several people whose ideas and work contributed to this second edition of *Just Promoted!*

Fredric Harwood, Ph.D., was the coauthor with Ed of the first edition of *Just Promoted!* The book was first published in April 1992. Ed and Fredric's collaboration resulted in a book that had a life span of 18 years in the marketplace. *Just Promoted!* helped launch the now-common practice of leadership onboarding. *Just Promoted!* also became the basis of a new type of structured executive coaching process called Newly Appointed Leader Coaching, which Ed developed and launched in 1993. We thank Fredric for his original work with the first edition and his support for our writing this second edition of *Just Promoted!*

Raymond Harrison, Ph.D., founder and managing director of Executive TransforMetrics, has been our friend and colleague for close to 20 years. From 1993 to 1997, Ed and Ray worked together as part of Manchester Consulting. Ray added invaluable ideas and techniques to Ed's original approaches to the Newly Appointed Leader Coaching process. Many of Ray's ideas have stood the test of time, and several of his concepts have been incorporated into this second edition of *Just Promoted!*

The Institute for Management Studies (IMS) has been highly supportive of Ed's work. Through the IMS, Ed has taught the program Navigating Your Leadership Transitions in many cities in the United States and Canada. For their support and sponsorship, we extend special thanks to Gordon Peters, Jon Peters, Cecile Morgan, Stephen Daniel, Joseph Paesani, Mark Pufundt, Kenneth and Robbie Verostick, Mark Antonucci, James F. Dowd III, Brendan Dowd, Jim Henderson, Mark Jesty, Charles Truza, Ginny Von der Schmidt, Robert Webster, William Woods, Lisa Read Peters, Carlos Hernandez, and Esther Killam. Special thanks to Joseph Toto, our friend and Ed's former colleague at BD for introducing Ed to IMS.

Special thanks as well to Jane Palmieri, editing manager, McGraw-Hill Professional, and MaryTherese Church, Editorial, McGraw-Hill Professional, who have provided invaluable editing and suggestions that have enabled us to publish this second edition of *Just Promoted!*

YOU'VE BEEN PROMOTED, NOW WHAT?

Far and away the best prize that life offers is the chance to work hard at work worth doing.

—Theodore Roosevelt

To successfully move up as a newly appointed leader, you will need to accomplish the following:

- Establish yourself in your new assignment.
- Achieve an impact on your organization.
- Manage the impact of moving up on your family and personal life.

In this chapter, there is useful information about the following:

- Great opportunities and hazardous duty: the two sides of being promoted
- The newly promoted leader dilemma
- Examples of the challenges that fuel the newly promoted leader dilemma
- Frequently cited issues that derail newly promoted leaders
- How to overcome the newly promoted leader dilemma: the 12 success practices for getting "up to speed" more quickly and effectively than ever before

This book is divided into three major parts:

Part I. Moving In: Establishing Yourself in Your New Role

Part II. Achieving an Impact on the Organization

Part III. Managing the Impact of Moving Up on Your Family and Personal Life

Also, each chapter in the book begins with an overview of the chapter.

JUST PROMOTED! NOW WHAT? AN INTRODUCTION TO THE FIRST 12 MONTHS IN YOUR NEW LEADERSHIP ROLE

Some people move into new management and leadership roles with the grace of Baryshnikov and the coordination of an Olympic Gold Medal skater. Others, most, experience the first year of their leadership role as if they were tap dancing on marbles. There's a lot of energy expended, a lot happening, but very little that is certain, stable, or efficient. The transition after being hired or promoted is a job in itself and must be tended as if your future depends on it. Many roles will require as much as a year or more to lay a solid foundation for long-term business or organizational results. During this same period you and your family may also need to regain a work/life integration and balance that you desire. This is especially true if your new role is a major change or expansion of responsibility requiring great uses of your time and energy, or if it is a relocation, expatriation, or repatriation. Yet the challenges of your new position demand that you must move quickly from the start to gain momentum and credibility.

Right from the beginning, including before your hire or promotion is announced, you must manage the events that occur around you during this period very well. Taking the right steps from the beginning and gaining early traction is vital for your success. Should you experience serious early missteps, it may be hard—and sometimes it is impossible—to recoup time, credibility, and progress lost.

There are many terms used to describe the first 12 months of leadership transition. Some call it the "perils of promotion," and others refer to it as "hazardous duty." Whatever it is called, it is a period of excellent opportunity for you and the business, organization, school, or team that you lead. It is also a period fraught with clear and not so clear challenges and dangers. Strikingly, evidence over the past two decades from several sources has suggested that when an individual is promoted or assumes a new or different leadership role, there is approximately a 40 to 44 percent likelihood of his or her demonstrating disappointing performance and/or being terminated or voluntarily leaving the position within 12 to18 months.[1]

During your first 12 months in a new role, either as a first-time manager or as a tested leader, you will often experience a wide range of thoughts, emotions, and reactions to events as they unfold as well as to what you are discovering about your business and organizational challenges. We have asked several thousand newly promoted leaders what they thought and how they felt shortly after they were notified that they had been selected for an important promotion or appointed to their new leadership responsibilities. Those we asked included first-time managers, leaders with relatively short managerial careers, and those with deep leadership experience. Most of these individuals expressed excitement, pride, happiness, and a feeling of relief that they had been selected. Quite a number also expressed their gratitude for having been chosen for the role. Interestingly, many of these very same individuals, and other leaders with whom we have had similar discussions, also expressed reservation, anxiousness, and sometimes deep concern about their ability to successfully step up after they had actually agreed to accept the promotion. It is common for the emotions of a leader to swing between elation and concern and back again during the difficult transition of assuming a new and challenging leadership role. Some used the adage "Be careful what you wish for" to communicate this self-doubt.

One leader recounted the story of the morning that an official announcement of his promotion was circulated by e-mail throughout his company. He immediately began receiving congratulations. He felt great about his new role and the recognition of his previous achievements. That afternoon, he had the first of three scheduled debriefs with the incumbent who had announced his retirement. After twenty minutes, one of his legs began to shake as he began to hear and learn about the role from the person who knew it best. Several minutes later, both legs began to shake in an up and down fashion. The incumbent, recognizing what he was seeing, suggested that "we can discuss more on Wednesday" and gently ended the meeting fifteen minutes early. Reality does have a way of setting in quickly when you realize that you have moved from being a what-if candidate for the role to which you aspired to that of the actual designee or brand-new incumbent.

This early phase of your leadership transition can be quite sobering and eye-opening. But, in its own way, this period can also help you establish your personal hopes and aspirations for building a truly winning organization. In fact, great excitement and a sense of pride are the dominant reactions by leaders once they know that they are moving up and have been asked to take on a new role and new responsibilities. They express a readiness to "bring it on."

The many leaders we have taught and coached have provided the inspiration for two caricatures that depict the range of thoughts, feelings, and reactions that are typical of newly promoted leaders in the days and weeks following their promotion. This is the first of the caricatures:

Just Promoted!

Once the announcement of your promotion has been made and you begin to prepare or have actually stepped into your new role, an additional set of dynamics typically comes into play. Members of your team or organization will want to determine how, if at all, their personal situations will be affected. Others will also wish to know if their business, function, or team will experience major changes. These kinds of questions, and many others, are all very natural and even predictable. In Chapter 2, specific communication suggestions are provided to help ease concern and help you shape the initial positive impressions you desire to have with others. However, you should anticipate that right away, as the new leader, you will be asked questions, many questions. Even though it is not rational or logical, people will often have every expectation that you will be up to speed the day you begin your new role. Of course, there is no way you could be that ready in your role that quickly. But no one ever said that being well received as a leader was a logical and rational process. You will be perceived through others' lenses and out of their needs, not your own. It is very important to know and understand this distinction before you start in your role.

Besides questions about job status and security, expect questions about the operational procedures and the current and future states of your business, organization, team, or school for which you are responsible. On day 1, others may also want to know how Problem XYZ will be solved. Right away, many will expect you somehow to define direction, solve standing issues, and know answers to just about everything.

You will begin to quickly appreciate the scope of the challenges and the complexity of the problems to be solved in a way you could never have done previously. You immediately own the role and the accountability. You have just been promoted, and the challenges and expectations will become real and very personal rapidly. We can remember situations in our careers when we looked in a mirror and rhetorically asked why and how we had ever managed to put ourselves in these circumstances.

As noted, it is very common for tempered emotions to quickly replace your previous feelings of excitement and pride. Many report what feels to them like a tug-of-war between their confidence and their concern about being successful. When things pile up quickly, as they often will, many newly promoted leaders often describe themselves as frenzied and periodically being nearly out of control. As we recall our own reactions in these situations as well as the many interviews and discussions we have had with newly promoted leaders, we think that this second caricature is quite representative:

After Six Months?
Weeks? Days?
Hours?

This wide range of feelings and reactions after accepting a new leadership role is so pervasive that you should expect it regardless of your role as a department head, team or plant leader, general manager, executive director, or school principal or superintendent. What is actually going on is one of the most important concepts discussed in this book. It is called the *newly promoted leader dilemma*, and it can be described in the following way:

The Just Promoted Leader Dilemma

Today's organizations have

- Very high expectations for results, probably higher than ever before
- Low levels of organizational patience and shorter time frames than ever before for achieving the results

For many years newly promoted managers and executives experienced a luxury that exists in very few organizations today. It was called the "honeymoon period," and it was common practice up until about the late 1980s or 1990s when so much changed in the work world. The honeymoon period frequently was as short as 2 to 3 months in some organizations and as long as 9 to 12 months in others. During this period the new managers could progressively learn the job, meet customers and staff, and build relationships. They would gradually diagnose what worked and what did not. The sense that new managers must "deliver results now," right from the start, was not as common then as it is today in many organizations. It was generally understood that during the latter half to two-thirds of whatever the honeymoon period was in an organization, new managers or executives would gain increasingly greater momentum in their roles and would somewhat gradually become highly productive and strong contributors.

Over the past decade we have asked several thousand participants in courses and seminars the following question: "How many of you work in an organization where a honeymoon period of two or three or more months is the common practice?" The responses to this question suggest that 10 percent or fewer organizations have any kind of significant honeymoon period of several months or more. Today's newly promoted leaders must become highly productive, and very rapidly! In most organizations there is no honeymoon period. There is little slack. There are high expectations and little, if any, patience for delivering results. These conditions create the "perils of promotion" that so many newly promoted leaders describe. Some leaders who thrive during this tenuous period are often, and prematurely, tagged with being "high risers" or "high flyers." Other leaders get off to a slower start. They may begin to experience performance and organizational problems during their early weeks and months in their role. This can be a function of an extended learning curve as well as other factors. In many of today's organizations, you just can't afford for that learning curve to be too long.

You should expect that the conditions that create the newly promoted leader dilemma will be in play in your organization. Be delighted if they are not. If this is the case, your organization would be the exception. Nevertheless, you will want to do everything you can to land smoothly on your feet and become very productive in as short a period of time as is possible. This book is designed to help you do just that.

Here is a list of transition challenges that you can anticipate. Most leaders face a variety of these challenges when they begin in their roles or very shortly thereafter. These challenges fuel the newly promoted leader dilemma.

Examples of the Challenges That Fuel the Newly Promoted Leader Dilemma

- Needing to rapidly turn around a business, team, or function
- Dealing with increased and unfamiliar responsibilities
- Overcoming a low or stagnant performance culture
- Acquiring needed knowledge and skills quickly
- Handling local, national, or global organizational structures that result in dual or multiple reporting relationships
- Needing to build networks of effective relationships with stakeholders
- Managing expectations of multiple stakeholders, some of whom may be halfway around the world in today's global business environment
- Managing initial impressions
- Needing to build early momentum and credibility by achieving short-term wins
- Needing to gain acceptance for longer-term strategies
- Making the right people "calls"
- Juggling organizational and out-of-work personal demands
- Anticipating 24/7 news reporting and social media—including the Internet, YouTube, Twitter, Facebook, and LinkedIn—that can make controversial issues that could affect you instantly available to potentially millions of people
- Economic conditions that require you to do more with decreasing headcount and staff support
- Shortages of experienced leaders who can share responsibility and who can develop a talent pipeline of currently less experienced leaders and professionals

Worksheet: Assessing Your Challenges

How many of the challenges listed above are you facing in your role? Place this number here: ____

List your top two to four challenges here:

The challenges we have just looked at can often create situations in which there are problems that, if unresolved, can derail newly promoted leaders. Let's take a look at these problems.

FREQUENTLY CITED PROBLEMS THAT DERAIL NEWLY PROMOTED LEADERS

- Confusion over one's "appointment charter"; that is, confusion over what is really expected of you
- Failure to identify stakeholders and build key partnerships
- Learning the role too slowly
- Failure to mesh with the existing culture or conversely to build the type of culture that is needed
- Unresolved differences with other key individuals in the organization
- Overuse of, or overreliance on, existing professional or managerial strengths
- Having to rely on previously untested skills or flaws
- Failure to deliver on performance expectations
- Failure to achieve the necessary integration between work and personal life

But wait. There is good news . . . very good news! You *can* take powerful steps to effectively deal with the newly promoted leader dilemma. Here are 12 practices that are at the heart of successful transitions for you and other newly promoted leaders.

How to Overcome the Newly Promoted Leader Dilemma: The 12 Success Practices for Getting Up to Speed More Quickly and Effectively Than Ever Before

In order to deal effectively with the newly promoted leader dilemma and achieve success in the first 12 months in your new leadership role, you will need to accomplish the following:

1. Confirm and deliver on your "must-do" priorities for your first 3, 6, 9, and 12 months.
2. Confirm the full scope of your responsibilities, available resources, levels of decision-making authority, ways in which your performance will be measured, and desired ways to communicate with your report-to leaders.
3. Begin to learn the essence of your role very quickly, preferably well before you actually begin in your position.
4. Determine who is "on the bus" and who is not.
5. Make excellent initial impressions, and convey your key leadership communication messages and strategies with conviction and enthusiasm.
6. Personally connect with your team and one-to-one with team members.
7. Build strong internal and external stakeholder partnerships.
8. Mesh with the existing culture, or decide to build the type of culture that you believe is necessary.
9. Decide what needs changing. Then execute, execute, execute!
10. Create and implement a robust leadership development and talent management plan.
11. Leverage your top strengths, but do not overuse them.
12. Manage the impact of your moving up on your family, health, and time.

Let's take a closer look at these success factors and preview how they will be addressed throughout the book.

In order to deal effectively with the newly promoted leader dilemma and achieve success in the first 12 months in your new leadership role, you will need to accomplish the following:

1. *Confirm and deliver on your must-do priorities for your first 3, 6, 9, and 12 months.* You will need to confirm your must-do deliverables with vital input from your report-to leader or leaders and also important stakeholders. Once

these priorities are confirmed, begin to set objectives related to these priorities with your team and organization. You can build positive momentum by achieving short-term wins. Then, through careful and inspiring work with your leadership team, develop longer-term business and organizational vision, strategies, and goals. Your must-do priorities are the goals and objectives "for which forgiveness will not be granted" no matter how many distractions arise or how busy you become.[2] These top priorities should be identified in the Just Promoted Leader Tool we call Confirming Your Appointment Charter. Another tool, Your 12-Month Road Map, will help you plan, by quarter, the milestones you must meet to achieve your priority goals. Both of these tools will be introduced in Chapter 2. You should anticipate that other priorities and distractions will pour over the transom throughout the year and challenge your focus, resolve, and execution skills.

2. *Confirm the full scope of your responsibilities, available resources, levels of decision-making authority, ways in which your performance will be measured, and desired ways to communicate with your report-to leaders.* These and other factors are vital to your first-year transition success. You should never assume or take for granted that there are explicit agreements with the leader or leaders to whom you report. Too often, these points are not discussed or they are left deliberately unclear. This is never a good situation. Frequently there is not full agreement on these and other factors when dual or multiple reporting relationships are involved. This can be further complicated when there are time zone and geographic differences involved between you, the individuals to whom you report, and/or other important stakeholders on whom you are dependent for your success.

Use the Confirming Your Appointment Charter tool as a way of engaging your boss or bosses in explicit discussions to clarify and confirm these points. This will help you to convert what sometimes is not discussed or is sometimes only implied or murky into clear and confirmed agreements about how you will operate and perform and what is expected of you.

3. *Begin to learn the essence of your role very quickly, preferably well before you actually begin in your position.* Learning your new leadership role too slowly can quickly become a problem for you in our "must have and deliver it now" work world. This is not logical or even reasonable. It simply is the way things are in many organizations. There are no honeymoons, and you will be

afforded little slack. You must learn what you have to very quickly and then learn continuously thereafter. We have been asked about the importance of what is called "learning agility." Learning agility is the ability to learn from your experiences, as well as in many other ways, and apply what you have learned to new, challenging, and often unmapped situations and challenges. Very frequently, leaders who are transitioning into new roles are faced with high-challenge responsibilities that lack clear maps or courses of action. For recently promoted leaders, well-lit paths to deal with their high-challenge roles are few and far between.

You will need to develop and act upon an accelerated learning plan. If at all possible, this should start before you even begin in your role and certainly no later than your actual start date. You and your organization will be greatly advantaged if you can develop a relationship with the incumbent and spend time being briefed and exchanging information, perceptions, and insights about the role and its many nuances. You can jump start your accelerated learning in many ways. Read as much relevant information as you can. Informally speak with people, and count on staff and resource professionals who may be available to you to provide information and support. Be sure to interview stakeholders who will have a role in either your success or failure. Your accelerated learning plan should address the knowledge, skills, and the organizational cultural elements specific to your new role and responsibilities. Importantly, you will also need to quickly learn the politics of how things really get done. The Just Promoted Leader Tool entitled Accelerating Your Job Learning, with its accompanying Accelerated Learning Plan, can help you organize your thinking and construct a course of action to rapidly address your knowledge, skills, and cultural learning needs. These tools will be presented in Chapter 2.

4. *Determine who is "on the bus" and who is not.* The old model of leadership transitions included gradually determining who would remain or be selected from outside to be on a leader's team. But today, because of modern management's very high expectations for results and its low patience in waiting to see results achieved, you will likely need to make your most important staffing decisions quickly and, frequently, more quickly than you might like. It is important that much of your leadership team be selected, whenever possible, before work begins to determine your longer-term business and organizational vision, strategies, and goals. This order is described very well in Jim

Collins's *Good to Great* research.[3] This Collins principle is referred to as "first who, then what." Chapter 4, "Selecting, Building, and Developing Your Work Team," provides helpful suggestions about how to choose and develop your leadership team.

The seventh Just Promoted Leader Tool, the Team Integrity and Capability Grid, should prove to be a very useful resource for you. It also will be introduced in Chapter 4. In order to determine who will be in your most important roles, you will need to decide the relative effectiveness, competence, trustworthiness, and leadership potential of your team members and other vital members of your organization. Making these determinations should be an ongoing process for you even after you have made the initial decisions as to who will be on your leadership team. You will need to exercise fine-tuned assessment, diagnostic, and organizational savvy skills to do this. You also will need to demonstrate a touch for managing difficult people. These assessments and your subsequent actions may also require courage when difficult people decisions need to be made.

One of the first careful choices you will want to make for your team will be to identify a very talented human resources leader who can partner with you in making tough leadership, people, and organizational decisions. Newly promoted leaders are often well served by selecting both their human resources and financial partners before selecting others.

5. *Make excellent initial impressions, and convey your key leadership communication messages and strategies with conviction and enthusiasm.* Perceptions of you as the team and organizational business leader will begin to form in seconds following your announcement and introduction. Positive initial impressions can be short-lived. But negative initial impressions tend to be long lasting, and they can be very difficult to change. Keep your lines of communication wide open. Be candid, upbeat, and appropriately forthcoming. Use *we* and *our* rather than *I* and *me* as your pronouns of choice. Listen as well as speak, and, as a general rule, try to listen more than you speak. Carefully, enthusiastically, and even inspirationally communicate your points of view, perspectives, and priorities. People observe their new leaders very carefully. Use multiple channels and methods to communicate. Stay visible, and make yourself accessible to those in your organization at a pace and in a way that is both reasonable and inviting. Chapter 2, "Entering the Organization," will address these points, and it contains many practical communication tips.

6. *Personally connect with your team and one-to-one with team members.* Your relationship with team members and the team as a whole begins with your very first interactions with them. Take time with individuals to begin building positive perceptions and chemistry. Show interest in them. Get to know what makes them tick and what lights their motivational fire. Suggestions in Chapters 2, 4, 5, and 8 can serve as valuable resources for you. Additionally, two Just Promoted Leader Tools are specifically designed to help you connect with your team. They are the New Leader and Team Assimilation Process (NLTAP) and Developing a Motivational Profile for Each Team Member tools. Both of these tools can help jump start your work with your team and build the foundation for trust as well as high individual and team engagement and performance. These tools are also introduced in Chapters 2 and 4, respectively.

7. *Build strong internal and external stakeholder partnerships.* Establish key working relationships with organizational superiors, peers, colleagues, and direct reports and, as appropriate, with boards, key customers, supply chain partners, government officials, and regulatory bodies. All of these stakeholders, and possibly others, can have an important impact on your success. You will want to decide who the most important stakeholders are for you. Then you will need to determine if you need to create, enhance, or repair each of your working relationships. One of the most important, if not the most important, of your stakeholders is your boss or bosses. These relationships are so important that all of Chapter 3, "Entering Your Boss's World," is dedicated to it. As a good rule of thumb, if you help your boss to be successful—even be a star—you will garner enormous support in return. Again, the Confirming Your Appointment Charter tool will be of great help to you because it will help you to communicate and work effectively with your boss.

The third Just Promoted Leader Tool, Building Stakeholder Partnerships, and its accompanying list of discussion questions for use in meetings with stakeholders, can prove to be especially useful for you in your stakeholder relationships. This tool is presented in Chapter 2.

8. *Mesh with the existing culture, or decide to build the type of culture that you believe is necessary.* Chapter 7, "Assessing Your Organization's Health," delves into this topic as well as other primary determinants of organizational health. Culture is extraordinarily powerful. It is so powerful that it is said that

culture eats strategy and best intentions for lunch.[4] Shaping and reinforcing desired culture is an area where all newly promoted leaders can and should have a positive impact with their teams and organizations.

9. *Decide what needs changing. Then execute, execute, execute!* Very few leaders move into new roles without having to lead small- to large-scale change. Expect that you will as well. Your diagnostic and problem-solving skills will be essential to your success. Part of the formula of success in moving up is determined by the quality of your problem-solving skills, the questions you ask, and the usefulness of the data or information you collect. You can be confounded by the questions you did not ask, the information you did not have, and the answers you did not pursue.

Successfully moving up is directly related to the body of information you have in order to use this information to identify, prevent, and solve problems. You will also need to determine how to sharpen day-to-day operations and institute methods of continuous improvement, where appropriate. You must be able to skillfully lead the "diagnose-decide-plan-engage-implement change cycle" in a highly effective manner. Many ideas and approaches are presented in Chapters 7 and 8 that can equip you for this difficult challenge.

10. *Create and implement a robust leadership development and talent management plan.* Your current leadership and talent capability will, to a very large extent, determine the short-term success of your business, function, or team. In turn, your organization's leadership and talent pipeline will have a tremendous impact on the future success of your organization. To be a top company or organization of any kind, leaders need to model their dedication to building strong and versatile leadership and talent pipelines. You will need to model the unrelenting focus on talent that you expect of others. When you lead in this way, effective leadership and talent development become a natural way of doing business. It will become a positive mindset and a way of life in your organization. You will want to make certain to seamlessly integrate your organization's or team's leadership and talent development plan as part of your broader business growth strategy and goals. Chapters 4 to 8 all contain ideas and tools that can help you with these important efforts.

11. *Leverage your top strengths, but do not overuse them.* Overused strengths can be some of the most powerful and insidious career derailing factors at any

point in your career and especially during your periods of leadership transition. The Just Promoted Leader Tool entitled Your Strengths and Overused Strengths Exercise will help you to understand and mitigate the overuse of your top strengths. This tool and exercise will be introduced in Chapter 4.

12. *Manage the impact of your moving up on your family, health, and time.* To achieve a new life integration, you will need to juggle the challenges of your new role and the systems effect of these challenges on your family and personal life. Success in navigating your leadership transition is synonymous with your personal definition of life integration between career, relationships, family, and other personal life values. There is no one correct equation or formula that fits for everyone. Many leaders fail to achieve the integration and formula for success they want.

Moving up will almost always disrupt the steadiness by which you work and live. The impetus that created the opportunity for your promotion can be abrupt or traumatic, such as a firing or forced transfer. Other transitions begin more gradually, such as with the desire for a promotion. In either case, the unrest caused by moving up can easily dominate your life until it is resolved. It can be a struggle to manage professional change and increased responsibility while maintaining equilibrium in your personal life. In the process, you can be energized and revitalized, and you can discover strengths and abilities you never knew you had. Being promoted can also be troublesome and stressful if you let it or if it runs out of control. If you manage it well, it can be the self-renewing proving grounds for subsequent success. Chapter 10 provides important principles and several Just Promoted Leader Tools that will help you to deal with the constant challenges of integrating your work with all other aspects of your life when you are promoted.

ADDITIONAL REASONS FOR FOCUSING ON EFFECTIVE TRANSITIONS FOR NEWLY PROMOTED LEADERS

Here are some of the most important reasons why you and your organization should pay great attention to systematically preparing leaders to successfully and smoothly enter the organization. The goal should be to have a successful onboarding every time a leader is promoted and moves into a new leadership role.

- We previously noted that available evidence has suggested that approximately 40 to 44 percent of newly promoted leaders demonstrate disappointing performance, are terminated, or voluntarily leave their role within 12 to 18 months of the time they start in their role.
- The underperformance, or worse yet, the failure of newly promoted leaders can be very expensive and very trying for the leader's team and others who are affected by the turmoil. If the role has to be filled from outside the organization, consider costs such as these:

  - Executive recruiter fees that are usually one-third of total compensation plus expenses
  - Candidate recruiting trips
  - Possible moving expenses and allowances
  - Possible signing bonus and start-up expenses

  Whether a candidate is selected from outside or inside the organization, start-up costs for replacing a disappointing or terminated leader can include these:

  - Learning curve for the new leader
  - Orientation and/or training costs including travel
  - Possible off-target results and general loss of focus
  - Low engagement of that leader's team and possibly others
  - Damaged relationships
  - Adverse customer impact
  - Lost opportunity costs
  - Extensive staff time

- Polling in courses we have conducted suggests that a larger-than-expected number of leaders may be changing roles and moving into new leadership responsibilities each year. Of just over 500 working managers and executives from approximately 100 organizations who have voluntarily participated in a seminar entitled Navigating Leadership Transitions, over 60 percent have indicated that they are either in a new role or they have experienced such major changes in responsibilities that it seems to them to be essentially a new role. The period we ask about is the previous 12 to 18 months.
- Each promotion and leadership transition that takes place has ripple effects that could directly or indirectly have an impact on a large

number of other employees. Depending on the scope of the position to which a leader is promoted, the numbers could be much greater. The domino effect every time someone is promoted or changes roles can be dramatic. It is not uncommon that 1 vacancy can set off a series of 6 or more openings as incumbents fill new roles and career movement occurs. In one organization a marketing executive who worked in the state of Maryland was selected for a general manager's role in Utah. Filling the role in Utah ultimately caused a very difficult to fill plant manager's role in Sweden to become open. Qualified internal candidates continued to post for available positions as they opened. A total of 12 positions across North America and Europe needed to be filled in this one case example. On one hand, it is healthy to have opportunities for career growth for well-qualified internal candidates. On the other hand, most organizations today have shortages of experienced leaders available to fill roles. Newly promoted leaders need to ensure that their organization has talent management processes that yield or can recruit talented candidates capable of assuming such roles.

- When leaders struggle following their promotion or appointment, those around them tend to struggle as well. There is a high likelihood that both performance levels and employee engagement levels of those struggling leaders' direct reports will be compromised.
- The 2009 Fortune-Hewitt Top Companies for Leaders research study identifies key leadership development processes that companies must rigorously and consistently implement to build core leadership strength and a robust leadership talent pipeline. One of those processes is the systematic onboarding of leaders as they enter new roles and expanded responsibilities. Of the more than 500 companies that submitted applications in this study, the North American results revealed that less than two-thirds had a formal onboarding process.[5]

OVERVIEW OF THE BOOK

We are surrounded by people promoted to more responsible, higher-paying jobs. Some seem to be on the way to the top so quickly that they do not stay in any one job long enough to be truly tested. Some seem to be promoted or moved into a new role just before the roof falls in. There are people who seem effortlessly to flow from one promotion and transition to the next, without much interruption and difficulty. They seem to know exactly what to do on a new job, and they do it successfully.

How do they do it? How can they move into a job, about which they may know very little, and perform as if they know exactly what they need to do? What do they know that you don't know? And how can you learn it? This book probes these questions and proposes practical solutions to very real challenges you will be or are now facing.

One of this book's primary goals is to help you achieve success at work, at home, and in your personal and professional lifestyle by setting your feet firmly under you during the first year following your promotion.

This book is divided into three parts:

The Process of Moving Up

Part I. Moving In: Establishing Yourself in Your New Role
Part II. Achieving an Impact on the Organization
Part III. Managing the Impact of Moving Up on Your Family and
    Personal Life

Dozens of tips and 13 Just Promoted Leader Tools with accompanying worksheets are included throughout the book.

Part I, "Moving In: Establishing Yourself in Your New Role," considers how to move into your new position. Chapter 2, "Entering the Organization," emphasizes making good initial impressions, developing key communication, influencing and political savvy strategies, building empowering relationships, and challenging the organization for high motivation and high performance. Additionally, analyzing and developing stakeholder relationships and accelerating your learning for your new role are included.

At the same time, there is no relationship more important than that with your boss, and Chapter 3, "Entering Your Boss's World," discusses making that relationship firm, clear, and mutually supportive.

Part II, "Achieving an Impact on the Organization," starts with how to select and build your team. Crafting vision and direction, the organizational diagnostic and change processes resulting in organizational renewal and improvement make up the bulk of Part II. Chapter 4 describes how to select, build, train, and develop work teams that will be responsible for high performance and achievement of the vision, strategies, and goals of the leader's team. With the help of your organization, you'll need to begin crafting your vision (Chapter 5), and understanding the diagnostic or assessment process as you analyze your organization (Chapter 6).

Chapter 7 introduces the *nine-target model*, which can be used as a diagnostic tool for assessing your organization's overall health. With a sense of ownership and responsibility for the organization's performance, health, and growth, the vision that results from your early efforts should involve many members of your function and will need to be implemented by them.

Chapter 8, "From Resistance to Renewal: Building Your Leadership Team's Commitment," describes how to build full commitment to that vision within the organization. The chapter emphasizes understanding, assessing, and managing your specific organizational politics, environment, and culture. The chapter introduces the tenth Just Promoted Leader Tool: Your Personal Political Inventory. Chapter 8 also examines the practical implications of group and organizational dynamics during your first year on the job. We examine forces resistant to change and principles of effective change, and we look at organizational change efforts that have succeeded and failed.

Chapter 9, "Settling into Your Renewing Organization," describes the period when the organization has absorbed change and is ready to seek equilibrium and enter a period of stability. This chapter discusses how to fine-tune your leadership role. This chapter introduces SOARING, which is a way to sharpen how you think about your work and personal life.

Part III covers "Managing the Impact of Moving Up on Your Family and Personal Life." Professional transitions inevitably result in personal transitions as well, and Chapter 10, "Creating Your New Life Integration," discusses how your transition to a new leadership role can affect your family, health, and time. It also discusses implications for dual-career marriages. To help you achieve the goal of a healthy work/life integration, this chapter includes activities dealing with your real and ideal self, your personal time, and your personal plan of action.

This book is about navigating your leadership transition. Such transitions involve professional and personal change. For leaders, both are essential. Success in one area supports success in the other. We start with the professional dimension, looking at how to begin your new leadership role and enter the organization.

Quick Reminders to Keep You on Track

This book is about what happens in the 12 months after you're promoted to a manager or leadership position.

In this chapter, there is useful information about the following:

- Great opportunities and hazardous duty: the two sides of being promoted
- The newly promoted leader dilemma
- Examples of the challenges that fuel the newly promoted leader dilemma
- Frequently cited problems that derail newly promoted leaders
- How to overcome the newly promoted leader dilemma: the 12 success practices needed for getting up to speed more quickly and effectively than ever before
- This is a period of professional and personal change unlike any other in your career. Your first year can, and likely will, be simultaneously vexing and energizing. You will certainly be challenged. You will need to draw on your professional, interpersonal, and personal abilities and resources.
- When you are promoted to your first or subsequent management positions, you are really dealing with two transitions simultaneously: (1) the organizational and management effects of moving up and (2) the personal effects of moving up such as those affecting you, possibly a spouse or partner, your family, and others with whom you are very close. Success in one major area of your life supports success in the others.
- A primary goal of *Just Promoted!* is to help you achieve success at work and at home during the first year after your appointment.
- There is a process for success during the 12 months after being promoted as a manager. This process corresponds with the organization of *Just Promoted!*

Part I. Moving In: Establishing Yourself in Your New Role
Part II. Achieving an Impact on the Organization
Part III. Managing the Impact of Moving Up on Your Family and
   Personal Life

Moving In: Establishing Yourself in Your New Role

ENTERING THE ORGANIZATION

You make a first impression only one time.
—Source unknown

I have climbed to the top of the greasy pole!
—Benjamin Disraeli

A major objective in establishing yourself in your new leadership assignment is to effectively enter the organization. You will need to accomplish the following:

- Meet all the people who work for you as well as new colleagues outside your function.
- Make good first impressions.
- Work well with your boss.
- Begin figuring out what you are supposed to do in this job and what your job really is.
- Be an advocate for your people.
- Build expectations and hope.
- Begin to increase or sustain the confidence of your people through your style and approach.

In this chapter, there is useful information about the following:

- The first meetings with your staff
- Establishing ground rules and communication with your boss about the transition process

- Learning your job
- Becoming an organizational advocate
- Raising expectations, hopes, and personal empowerment
- Empowering relationships using a self-concept approach to managing people

There are many ways that people become leaders. Some have planned to take on increased managerial and leadership roles for years, and the opportunity finally presents itself. For others, increased leadership opportunities arise suddenly and with no preparation or warning. There is usually a precipitating event that creates an open leadership position within the organization such as a promotion, resignation, termination, reorganization, or expansion of a business. Whatever the circumstances, a key opening needs to be filled.

Some people feel honored but decline the opportunity to move up into managerial and higher leadership positions. They are happy in their present job; they prefer to remain specialists in their chosen profession, such as research, law, finance, sales, or marketing. Bless these people; leaders need people who love doing the work they have trained themselves to do. Without a fair share of them, every leader would fail. But others compete feverishly for promotions, for the chance to show their ability to lead people and an organization. This is where we begin the process of moving up. You have just been promoted into your new leadership position, and you need to figure out how to begin and where to go from here.

Starting your job and entering the organization can be a treacherous time for a newly promoted leader. It's when the marbles are rolled out and the tap dancing begins. You will try to stay on a steady course, but it will not be easy. Whether in an old or a newly formed organization, you'll frequently run into expectations, resentments, and confusion. In almost all cases, change and management transitions intensify people's feelings. In this chapter we will look at six steps for effectively entering your new job and organization:

1. Personally connect with your new staff and meet with staff members one-on-one.
2. Confirm your must-do priorities for your first 3, 6, 9, and 12 months, and reconfirm the full scope of your responsibilities, available resources,

levels of decision-making authority, and ways in which your performance will be measured. You will also want to learn how to best communicate with your boss as well as negotiate his or her support.

3. Begin to actively learn the essence of your role very quickly. Learn your
   job and the organization's work from your predecessor, your boss, and
   organizational sources of information and power.
4. Become an organizational advocate.
5. Begin to empower your organization and your people to achieve their
   hopes, goals, and objectives for the organization.
6. Build strong internal and external stakeholder partnerships and
   relationships.

Manage these steps well, and you'll be off to a good start in your new job.

PERSONALLY CONNECT WITH YOUR NEW STAFF, AND MEET WITH STAFF MEMBERS ONE-ON-ONE

The First Meetings with Your Staff

Because rumors will develop quickly once you have been selected, the public
announcement of your selection should be made as quickly as possible. A
delayed announcement hurts the organization in two ways. First, those in the
running may continue expending energy in speculation and political maneu-
vering, affecting their own and others' productivity. Second, the people in the
department will be concerned with the impending change, their own futures,
what changes you will make—all of which affect productivity. Moreover, performance often decreases in departments with lame-duck leadership. People
may tend to let up; certainly they will be reluctant to make commitments that
may not be supported later. A timely announcement will help lessen negative
effects of the change.

You can predict many of the reactions to the announcement, so plan for
them. If the search was competitive, competitors' reactions will range from
disappointment to anger. If you were hired from the outside and are not
known, there will be many questions about you and your agenda. If you were
promoted from within, staff reactions will range from disbelief that you were
named (or someone else wasn't) to mild interest to genuine satisfaction that
you were the best choice. Be aware and sensitive to these reactions, but never
defend or feel that you must defend the decision to select you.

If there has been open competition for the job, your boss or a human resources professional should personally inform the internal candidates. Because they will not hold onto this information once they know, the meeting should take place as soon as possible before the announcement. If you have been moved in from another in-house function, simultaneously meet with colleagues in your old department to share the news of your new job. Your previous boss should always be the first to know. Let people know in person. If a replacement for you is known, help make the transition for that person easier; it is an act of goodwill for your former department.

In Chapter 1 we discussed the questions that your new staff will have as you start your new leadership role. They will be concerned about how their jobs will be impacted. They will want to know about changes you intend to make. Will their voice be heard as you think about changes in the business, department, or team? You can expect questions about operational procedures and how you intend to correct problem situations. Your staff may express these questions openly, or they may wonder about them silently. In either case, it is too early for you to be ready to answer these questions. It is important that you listen to your staff's concerns and let them know that you will address them in due time.

Plan on meeting with your new team, including support staff, as soon as possible. If at all possible, try to meet with your new staff within the hour of the announcement. A group meeting underscores your message that we are all part of one team in which each person individually and the organization as a whole are what counts. This meeting should be followed quickly with individual sessions, starting with key people, using the following guidelines:

- Keep the meeting short. Your overall tone and style will make as much of an impression as your specific message.
- Be positive. Project confidence, strength, and optimism.
- Be open, direct, and frank.
- It is a new beginning, for both you and your new staff. Be upbeat.

Briefly describe your background and qualifications. Be humble yet confident. Project the following:

- Convey the sentiment that you are honored and glad to be working with the business, department, team, or school and to have this new challenge.

■ Communicate that the department or team has strengths to build on; at the same time, every organization has challenges and problems, and everyone must strive for continuous improvement.

■ Affirm that the department or team's members are capable and committed. Be positive, and relay to them some of the complimentary things you have learned about them as a whole during the selection process.

■ Tell them, "We will solve our problems as a group. Our whole is greater than the sum of our parts." Stress that everyone is interdependent. Tell them that you expect to rely on them and trust them just as they can rely on and trust you.

■ Conclude by saying, "We will succeed, improve, and grow individually and as a team."

From this first meeting, concentrate on building relationships with your staff, developing your key communication messages, and ensuring personal access to each member of your work unit. Stress the people side of your role for these reasons:

■ You genuinely feel people are most important.
■ You need staff support to get the work done.
■ You need their assistance to meet the organization's challenges.
■ You need their assistance to plan and implement the future—that is, the organization's continual renewal.

During the first meeting, mention that within a few weeks you will be asking the staff to participate in a comprehensive analysis of the organization's mission, goals, policies, practices, and procedures. Indicate that you are undertaking this effort so the department or team can better control its own future direction and prerogatives. Tell the staff, "We want to confirm our strengths and identify what we can do to become stronger as a group. In other words, we want to adopt an organizational 'fitness program.'" Indicate that you will be meeting with the unit heads or management team members to map out the organizational analysis and that there will be a role in the process for as many people in the organization as possible.

People will want to know whether their jobs are secure. Assure them that no changes are imminent if, in fact, that is the case. If you know or think that staff reductions will occur, be careful not to indicate that all is well, or your credibility is at risk. Focus on what can be done. In these initial days you need to learn the organization, and the work needs to continue. You must stress that *we*, as an organization, need to assess how good we are and where we need to improve.

Finally, tell them, "I am here to listen and better understand where we are and how we need to grow. With the active help of everyone in the organization, we'll build a stronger, better organization."

Before adjourning, ask for questions, but keep your answers succinct and general. Don't get into the details of the organizational analysis. Indicate that over the next few weeks, you will meet and talk with everyone. Thank the staff for their warm welcome.

From I to *We* and *Our*

Your staff will have two fundamental concerns as you assume leadership: inclusion and control. By *inclusion*, we mean that employees will be wondering if they'll remain in their present jobs and maintain their primary work assignments. By *control*, we mean that they'll be hoping to have some say in what happens to them, and they'll be wondering how much input they will have in what happens to the department or work unit. Even at the first introductory meeting, you can address those concerns briefly. Although people may assume you will not announce any immediate changes, they need to be reassured that this is the case, at least in the short term.

A more important purpose of this meeting is to encourage the group to think collegially. Shift the group's perception away from you: "What is he going to do?" Focus on them: "What are *we* going to do?" Minimize the word *I* in your talk, and emphasize *we* and *our: our* effort, *our* department, *our* team, and *our* goals. Emphasize that "*our* department will only be as strong as *we* work to make it strong" and that "*we* will build on *our* individual, group, and organizational strengths." The sooner you can enlist your staff's support, the more success there will be for everyone.

The Unsuccessful Candidates

Meet individually with the job candidates within your function who were not selected. They can affect your future performance. Some will take the fact that they were not selected personally, and they will keenly feel disappointment, anger, and a sense of rejection or failure. Put yourself in their shoes. Acknowledge their feelings. At the same time, remember that they cannot let those feelings interfere with their responsibilities.

- Indicate that you will make every effort to use their expertise and experience. And mean it when you say it because many of them are your most experienced and competent people. If they weren't good, they would not have been considered for the job.
- Acknowledge that some may be thinking about their future and their alternatives, but that this must not interfere with their responsibilities. Assure them that their future in this organization is their choice, and that the organization needs their energy and skills (assuming that is how you feel).
- Emphasize that their individual success is a credit to the organization and the fact that they have grown in attaining skills and knowledge is attributable, in large part, to the work they have done in the department or team. Assure them that you want to help them continue to be successful in their jobs and in their future with the company. You intend to become an advocate for the organization's members.

Personally Connecting with People

On this first day, try to talk to as many people as possible. Begin with those who report to you directly. Stop and introduce yourself to everyone you can, including administrative assistants, line employees, and professional staff. When possible, go to their offices or work areas. In some cases, with virtual teams or global staff, this may not be possible. In those cases, try to contact them by phone and let them know when you will be able to plan a visit to their location. Going to meet your new staff members at their locations has a number of advantages:

- At first they may feel some natural distance, which may create reticence. You are not yet part of the group, and you are their new boss. Things are no longer quite the same, nor should you expect them to be. Going to their work location is a way to indicate that you want to work with them and that you seek their active cooperation.
- By visiting them in their work location, you show that you value them.
- They will be more comfortable in their own surroundings.

Visiting also establishes you as someone who will reach out and who wants to be accessible and "hands on," which is a good first impression to reinforce.

Because some of your new staff may be in global assignments, try to plan a visit to their locations as soon as it is feasible. Let them know when you will be able to make an in-person visit, and plan a number of meetings for each single location to make the trip as meaningful as possible. Use meal times as opportunities to spend extended time with the staff members and critical stakeholders.

Keep your office visits informal and low key. Get to know your staff by their first names. In pleasant conversation, find out how long they've been here, where they live, whether they have families. You'll find some commonalities to build on for the future. Let each person learn something about you as well: who comes from your area, went to one of the schools you attended, worked for a former company or boss, shares an interest, or has something else in common with you. You'll begin building bridges.

During your first week on the job, you will be winding down your initial entry activities, working hard to learn your job, and preparing to begin the organizational analysis.

By now you have met with as many people as you can, either individually or in groups. You have also met with the candidates who were not selected from your area. You have circulated throughout the department or team, made contact with everyone in your function, and identified some planned travel to the locations of other staff. During this same period, you may need to tie up some loose ends and continue strengthening new alliances. You need to do the following:

- Meet with your old department and their new leader. Help that person get an effective start in his or her new assignment.
- Meet or continue meeting with your predecessor to learn as much as you can about your new job.
- Meet with your boss.
- Continue meeting with each member of the department or team individually and with the department or team as a group.

One way to quickly and effectively engage with your new staff is to ask your human resources professional or organizational development (OD) consultant to conduct a New Leader and Team Assimilation Process (NLTAP), which is Just Promoted Leader Tool 1. Following is the NLTAP as we like to use it. The process was originally developed at GE, and it currently has many variations.

JUST PROMOTED LEADER TOOL 1
New Leader and Team Assimilation Process (NLTAP)

Overview

Objective To help the new leader (newly hired, appointed, or promoted) to rapidly develop a strong positive relationship with his or her team. The process promotes immediate open two-way communications between the leader and the team. The process is appropriate for highly or less experienced leaders.

Participants Usually the entire staff including the administrative assistant. May also include an extended staff where the larger team is key to success.

Where Typically conducted on site (in a conference room) or in a hotel meeting room.

When Normally conducted sometime between the first and fourth weeks after the leader has taken responsibility for the staff, work group, or department.

How long Approximately three to three and a half hours for the staff and four to five hours for the leader including the preparation and the debriefing meeting.

Facilitator A member of the human resources (HR) staff or an external OD facilitator.

Background of process The process was developed by a GE human resources team in the early 1970s. Since then, thousands of newly appointed managers and leaders from presidents to first-level supervisors have utilized the process.

Benefits Provides the leader with an opportunity to hear firsthand the initial questions, issues, and concerns that exist in people's minds. Also provides the leader with an opportunity to talk about himself and his business philosophy and to share his expectations for the organization. Many leaders have used the process again and again as they progress in the organization. Also, associates say the program makes them feel more appreciated and valued.

Process

Step 1 HR contacts the new leader to recommend and explain the assimilation process. It is essential that the process be voluntary. If the leader is forced to use it, the leader's reluctance will show in his conduct, which will defeat the purpose of the NLTAP.

Step 2 The new leader invites the staff by letter to attend an "assimilation meeting" and clarifies the objectives and/or reasons for having it.

Step 3 The new leader usually "kicks off" the assimilation, explaining the objectives and reasons for having the meeting. He introduces the facilitator and tells the group that he (the new leader) will leave the room for one to one and a half hours. Without the leader present, the group will feel more comfortable to speak freely.

Step 4 Once the leader leaves the room, the facilitator reiterates the group's objective. The facilitator then leads the staff through an icebreaker exercise designed to get the participants comfortable with sharing personal information and getting to know each other better. A sample exercise might be to ask each person to share with the group the answers to simple questions. (It would be ideal to put the questions on a flip chart so the participants can easily reflect on them.) The questions are these:

- Where is your hometown?
- What is your favorite nickname? Why is it your favorite? Or, What is your middle name? Why were you given this middle name?
- Where would you travel on vacation if you could go anywhere? Why would you go there?
- What leadership characteristics do you most admire in your ideal leader? Why?

Note the leadership characteristics on a flip chart for the group to view. Later review the leadership list with the leader.

Step 5 Following the icebreaker, the facilitator leads the group through eight standard questions. The facilitator raises the questions but does not indicate her feelings on any of them. She tries to get a sense of whether each comment is an individual one or whether the group overall agrees with the response. The facilitator guarantees confidentiality by not identifying who has made specific comments. The participants' responses are noted on a flip chart.

Step 6 The group is given a 30- to 45-minute break, and the leader returns to the room (alone with the facilitator) to review the staff questions and comments. The facilitator makes sure that the leader understands the points raised and coaches the leader, if appropriate, on possible responses to some of the more difficult questions, or at least recommends the thought processes the leader should work through in forming his responses to the questions. The key point is that the leader must feel that he needn't be an expert in all areas and that the group doesn't require, or expect, this. It is, however, quite important that the leader come across as a good, thoughtful listener. It is also very important that the leader not dominate the follow-up session. The most effective sessions are really dialogues, where the leader will make some comments, pause, seek additional data from the group, and then respond, so that it becomes an active exchange between the new leader and team, building the kind of relationship that will serve them well in the future.

Step 7 At the second session, the leader and team meet to review the notes that have been generated in the first session. The facilitator also participates, this time in both a facilitating and monitoring mode. In this role, the facilitator is trying to get a sense of the questions that were not asked but that are nevertheless on the minds of the group. The facilitator is also intervening to ensure that the leader is really addressing the questions raised by the group and that the questions and answers are clear to both the leader and the group.

Step 8 The leader closes the meeting by thanking the team for their help in the assimilation process, and he tells the group that the notes from the meeting will be distributed to the attendees. It is intended that the NLTAP information be used as a basis for building the agenda for a follow-up meeting and/or to establish a schedule for resolution of action items. Depending on the time of day, having a group lunch or going out to dinner together after the New Leader and Team Assimilation Process promotes continued team building (bonding).

Step 9 The leader and facilitator meet for a debriefing session on the process. This is an ideal time for the facilitator to provide feedback on what the leader did well in the session, comment on areas for improvement, and provide guidance for action planning to assist the leader and for team development.

Step 10 The leader writes a letter, which will be the cover page for
the meeting notes, in which he comments on the highlights of the
assimilation meeting and thanks the participants for their help. The
leader then distributes the letter and the meeting notes to the process
participants.

Conclusion

The New Leader and Team Assimilation Process is Stage I of your development and assimilation with the team. Stage II is periodic follow-up sessions
with you and your staff on the action items. As the leader, you want to solicit
feedback on your commitments and provide feedback to the staff on their
action items. Stage III is the New Leader and Team Assimilation Follow-
Up Process that is usually conducted six to nine months after the new leader's
promotion. A suite of additional resources for professionals who plan to
facilitate the New Leader and Team Assessment Process can be found at
www.mhprofessional.com/justpromoted.

Exiting Gracefully

Wrapping up unfinished business with your old responsibilities is an important part of the transition process. If you are an external candidate, your previous position can continue to be a source of friendships, connections,
information, and possible employees. If you are an internal candidate, members of your former department or team can extend your personal influence
within the organization. They can provide friendship, information, assistance,
recommendations, and referrals to help with staffing. If you have built strong,
credible, and positive relationships in your former function, it is likely that
they will communicate a positive "buzz" about you.

A very classy transition was managed by the outgoing vice president in an
operations area in a public utility. She met with her successor to share her perspective of what the staff had accomplished, each person's strengths and areas
for development, and the goals that had been previously set. She introduced
her successor and let the group know that he brought considerable experience
to his new role. She reviewed the past achievements of the team, praised her
successor's qualifications, and sketched out a bright future for the organization. She indicated that she would continue to cooperate with her successor
and help as needed.

Her successor, in turn, praised her accomplishments, thanked her for her warm welcome, and assured her of his need for her help and consultation in the future. The transition process was carried out with mutual respect and good humor. Both parties were sincere. The stage was set for the incumbent to step aside gracefully, her good name intact.

Once you're out, you're out. It is important to let the new leader take the reins and not interfere with his integration into his new assignment. This is true whether you are the president of the United States, the CEO of the organization, or a leader from another department. You do not help yourself, or your departing organization, by continual meddling—even if your friends within the organization encourage you to do so.

When you exit, consider taking the following steps:

- Help introduce your replacement to your former department if you know who it is. This ties your replacement's leadership to yours, emphasizes an orderly transition, and acknowledges your role in the transition. Even if you've been dismissed, exit with dignity. Even if you're angry, exit with grace.
- Offer your thanks to the entire department for their cooperation and assistance. Publicly thank people for special efforts, especially your administrative assistant and those who have helped your career. Give credit where credit is due.
- Ask for your former department's support in your new job. You may need to call them for recommendations, favors, and information.
- Privately talk to as many people from your former department or team as possible.
- Thank those who helped; make peace with those with whom you had differences. Provide former direct reports with developmental feedback where appropriate.
- Privately update your successor on your goals, performance plan, individual development plans, and other important information. Help him sustain improvements you made. Let him know what you are working on that needs finishing. Warn your successor about the icebergs and the glaciers.
- Clear out any personal items from your office or work area, including your desk, personal files, computer, cell phone, and PDA (unless you will continue to work with these). Contact your network and your old clients, and let them know of your new responsibilities and contact information.

First Impressions: A Personal Introduction to Your New Staff

First impressions powerfully affect attitudes your new staff and stakeholders will form toward you. People believe what they want to believe, not necessarily what is factual. Therefore, you want to make a personable, effective first impression.

Your influence and power base within the department or function may initially be fragile. You will need to build your organization's support quickly. To do this, on the continuum of work orientation to people orientation, concentrate your initial energies on the people side. As you move ahead, your people skills—interpersonal skills and emotional intelligence—will greatly complement your functional and technical skills. It is the style with which you do things and the impact you have on people that form early impressions. Remember that initial impressions are made very quickly, often in minutes. Positive impressions need to be sustained because they can be short-lived. In contrast, neutral or negative impressions can be long-lived. Here are six ways in which you can make a positive impression on your team and colleagues:

1. Quickly assess the style of the other person and match his style. Determine whether the person is results oriented (Give me the bottom line, not the details); detail oriented (Tell me all of the details so I understand how you reach conclusions); or socially oriented (Before you tell me about work, tell me about yourself and ask about me).
2. Be persuasive, and work on influencing others. Understand your own influencing style, and learn what influences your key stakeholders. If you are not sure how to influence a stakeholder, using reasoning is the best alternative. Reasoning as an influencing technique includes explaining why you are asking someone to do something or presenting evidence that supports your position.
3. Act like a high achiever. High achievers have upbeat and positive attitudes. They are confident and recognize the contributions of others.
4. Conduct or facilitate highly productive meetings. Be clear about your agenda and the result you want to achieve by having the meeting. Get meeting information and the agenda out early so participants can prepare. Understand your audience and how you will engage others. Communicate the high expectations you have of your team members' preparation and participation for the meetings they will participate in. Hold premeetings with important stakeholders to gain understanding of their positions on issues prior to the larger meetings, if possible.

5. Deliver presentations that match the audience's needs and interests. Prepare, prepare, prepare—giving yourself enough time to feel confident. Put yourself in your audience's place. What is it that they need or want to hear from you? Tell your story, and be clear on what messages or points you want to convey. Use PowerPoint or other visual aids *only* if they add to your message, and if you do use them, don't lean on them as a crutch.

6. Write clear and concise memos, e-mails, letters, and reports. Outline your main points for yourself prior to drafting your memo. Then begin to write. Be mindful of the tone you are trying to achieve. E-mails especially can be misinterpreted so avoid writing them too quickly or in a style that the receiver may perceive as negative or abusive. Before sending important or difficult e-mails, memos, or reports, go back and edit your work. Make sure that your message is conveyed with both the information and tone with which you want them to be received by the reader.

You can focus on these important relationships while your direct reports continue getting the day-to-day work done. Managing the work means, first and foremost, managing the people. This is where you should begin.

Confirm Your Must-Do Priorities, and Reconfirm Your Responsibilities

Establish ground rules and communication with your boss about the transition process. Throughout the preemployment interviews and the hiring process, you should provide a broad overview of your process for getting started in your job. Review the process with your boss again when you actually begin work. Make sure you both understand and agree to the process and the timetable. Mutually establish your ground rules, such as the following:

- Your boss should expect no significant changes for a specified period (usually one to three months) while you are fact-finding.
- Your boss should understand your change process. Explain thoroughly each step so your boss will support it and can handle inquiries or comments about the process. Good communication will stem your boss's impatience.

- Given an understanding of the process, your boss can more easily become a coach and consultant to you, advising you regarding the changes that may develop out of your data gathering and diagnostic efforts.
- Your boss should agree to meet regularly with you, to maintain strong lines of communication and information sharing. Questions or concerns should be aired immediately and not permitted to fester. Beware of a boss who is too quiet or nonevaluative. Whether or not your boss says anything, he or she is watching and thinking. Try to get your boss's views out in the open.
- You and your boss should agree on the type of reporting and decision making that will fit your boss's style. Agree on procedures for these.

Here is an example of how one newly promoted leader managed her transition in discussion with her boss. A telecommunications manager felt that she had received her promotion partly because she had worked closely with her new boss, which had convinced her new boss that she knew what was wrong and how to fix it. Nevertheless, the manager negotiated a transition period of at least three months, during which she was allowed to assess the organization's resources, personnel, structure, and work flow. Even though her boss was impatient for some changes, the manager held the boss to her promise and kept her informed step-by-step of the diagnostic process. As the new manager developed a better understanding of the organization, her boss changed some of her own prescriptions and agreed to let the new manager do it her way.

It is important that you and your boss confirm your must-do priorities for the first 3, 6, 9, and 12 months. In conversation with your boss, you will want to again confirm the scope of your responsibilities, available resources, levels of decision-making authority, and how your performance will be measured. It is best if this discussion occurs before the announcement of your new position, but sometimes it occurs right after you accept the position. The fourth Just Promoted Leader Tool, Confirming Your Appointment Charter, and the fifth Just Promoted Leader Tool, Your 12-Month Road Map, will be discussed more fully in Chapter 3 to help you plan for this discussion with your new boss.

BEGIN TO ACTIVELY LEARN YOUR NEW JOB

Even if you were the assistant, heir apparent, and right hand of your predecessor, and even if you think you know everything about the job, take time to learn what is needed. Learning your job means learning from your predecessor, department or team members, and colleagues both internal and external all the details you may have ignored up to now. Begin as soon as you can to start learning important information from the right people preferably before you begin in your new role. Remember that even if you have been in this function before, there will be new expectations and new challenges to face.

The following worksheet, Just Promoted Leader Tool 2, will help you plan your accelerated learning process.

JUST PROMOTED LEADER TOOL 2
Accelerating Your Job Learning

Directions

In order to facilitate the learning of key information and acquiring of essential skills for your new position, use the following questions to guide your thinking. Then follow the directions in your Accelerated Job Learning Plan.

Questions to Guide Your Learning

1. What is the *most critical information* and what are the *critical skills* you need to have to successfully fulfill your new leadership role?

   Information:

   Skills:

2. Which of this information and what skills are you currently missing?

Information:

Skills:

3. What are the best methods for acquiring this information and gaining these skills?

Information:

Skills:

4. Do you need additional strategies and/or approaches to accelerate your acquiring this information and learning these skills?   Yes ☐   No ☐

5. What are the written and unwritten rules, values, and guidelines—that is, the key elements of the culture—that you need to understand in order to be a success in this role and in this organization?

6. What are the best methods to learn these rules, values, and guidelines?

7. Do you need additional strategies and/or approaches to accelerate your learning of these rules, values, and guidelines?   Yes ☐   No ☐

8. Are there other questions that you feel are important to answer in order to quickly learn your new role? List them below:

Your Accelerated Job Learning Plan

Directions

1. List up to three accelerated learning objectives that will help you increase your effectiveness over your first 12 months in your new role.

   ▪

   ▪

   ▪

2. List learning approaches and/or alternatives that you can utilize to accelerate your learning. Use your human resources manager as a resource, as appropriate.

   ▪

   ▪

   ▪

3. Commit to a time frame for completing each of the learning objectives.

Accelerated Learning	Learning Approaches and/or Alternatives	Time Frame for Completion
Objective #1		
Objective #2		
Objective #3		

Learning from Your Predecessor and Key Staff

If you can, debrief your predecessor, preferably before he or she leaves. Even if the person's been fired and is angry, try to set up a meeting.

There is much information that only your predecessor has. You can shorten your learning curve, sometimes considerably, by tapping into this wonderful resource. More importantly, you can improve your odds in the organization's political jockeying. Your predecessor will describe the organization's competitors, enemies, and allies and can tell you how to deal with each and where the land mines are. There are many nuances about your new role that only your predecessor can know.

Sometimes the meeting is a courtesy session. A manager who had been abruptly moved from a staff position in human resources to a line job in manufacturing confessed, "I was scared to death. I talked with the person I was replacing for about three hours. That is, mostly he talked. I tried to take some notes, but I didn't understand much of what he said. I felt like a real dummy."

This is a meeting that may or may not help you much. You may be overwhelmed by the amount of information, the terms, the technology, and the politics. On the other hand, you may see why your predecessor is being moved; he or she may show a brilliant grasp of the job or a woeful absence of energy, commitment, and control of detail. You may be tempted to make this visit short, especially if your predecessor's tenure was not a success. You may feel you shouldn't have to ask these things because you are supposed to know these things—after all, that's why you were hired. You may feel embarrassed to ask the most elementary questions. This is a mistake. Strong people ask basic questions to get the information they need. They ask for help. Strong people even ask the questions when they think they know the answers.

You probably were not hired because you had the solutions immediately but because someone was confident that you could identify the opportunities and problems, analyze them, and implement the solutions. The solutions are not on your back alone. You should not position yourself as the answer person. Rather, you are a catalyst for problem solving that, at times, can involve the entire organization.

Ask your predecessor's view of the mission, history, objectives, personalities, problems, and concerns of the department. Probe. Ask in-depth questions. Learn more about the budget. Since few others in the department will understand where the money comes from, ask what the constraints are and how the funds are allocated. Ask what never got into the budget that should have. Ask basic questions, even those that may have obvious answers. You may be surprised by what you hear.

In many organizations, including the military, these debriefings are standard operating procedure. In many mature organizations, they are part of the expected management process in leadership transitions. It is expected that the outgoing leader will thoroughly brief his or her successor before leaving the current position. Today, with management changes occurring as frequently as every six months or that are ongoing in some cases, these debriefings play a critical role in maintaining the health of the organization.

In newer or less experienced businesses, such briefings are less common. Some businesses assume new managers will get the job done on their own. In more age-sensitive cultures, including many European and Asian countries, the outgoing manager or leader is more respected for his or her learning and wisdom and is treated with more deference and respect.

A checklist will help you focus the discussion. These topics can be used in your discussion with staff, which may give you even greater insights into the organization's health. The interview protocol is not very different from the one you will soon adopt to conduct the organizational fitness check, just a little more informal.

- *The organizational chart.* Ask about reporting relationships and "dotted-line relationships." Trace the work flow on the organizational chart. Does your predecessor think the organizational chart is functional and reflects the actual work flow? How should the organizational structure and work flow be changed?
- *The mission and goals of the organization.* What are the organization's mission and goals? What is your predecessor's assessment of how well the organization is reaching its goals? What does your predecessor feel are the strengths and weaknesses that affect how well the organization reaches its goals?
- *Your predecessor's evaluation of the organization.* What is your predecessor's assessment of the organization's capabilities, achievements, strengths, and weaknesses? What have been his or her greatest disappointments? Greatest achievements? What has brought the most satisfaction?
- *Your predecessor's judgment of the staff and team members.* What is your predecessor's assessment of department personnel? Who are the hard workers, high achievers, entrepreneurs, risk takers, and straight shooters? Where is the informal leadership? Who molds opinions? How does the grapevine work? Who pushes the limits, passes on stories, creates dissension? Who is temperamental? Who fudges time or information? Who would your predecessor like to get rid of? Who is in line for promotion? Who has earned it? Who expects it? Who can keep confidences? Who can be trusted? Who is reliable?
- *The most urgent needs.* What are the organization's most pressing needs to achieve its goals?
- *The budget.* What is in the budget? How much of it is discretionary? What can be moved around? How much are fixed costs? When an unexpected requirement develops, where is the money usually taken from?
- *The records.* What is in the files? Where are the personnel files? The confidential files?
- *Key management information.* How will your predecessor pass on key management information? What information is available to others, and which files are confidential?
- *Prioritization of your responsibilities.* What are the major job responsibilities? What did your predecessor spend his or her time on? What responsibilities are most important to the organization? Contrast

important responsibilities to how your predecessor actually spent time and energy.

- *The committees.* What are the major committees? Is there an executive committee? Who is its spokesperson? How are decisions delegated and made? How supportive and helpful is the executive team? Where is your likely competition?
- *The hidden problems.* Where are the land mines, the submerged icebergs both within and outside the department or team? What are sources of unseen problems and danger to the department and to your own career? Your predecessor should be able to tell you pitfalls to avoid, your boss's hot buttons, and organizational areas that can cause problems for you.
- *Critical stakeholders.* Who are the critical stakeholders with whom you need to build relationships? What are their chief concerns as it relates to your function? What is most important to each of them? What is the best way to get to know them and begin to build a relationship? Any hot buttons that it would be important for you to know about?
- *Horizontal work processes.* What are the work processes or work flows of which your function is a part? How are they working? What are the areas for improvement? Who are the strongest contributors to cross-functional teamwork? Who are the weak links in this regard?

It may not be a bad idea to set aside this information temporarily, using it only as a guide. You have gathered opinions and biases that may be different from your own, or from reality. You need to use this information carefully. Within days you will begin the formal organizational analysis. As this process progresses, review your predecessor's comments, and compare them with your own perceptions. In some cases, your hunches will be confirmed, and you may get some insights into situations you have observed. And certainly you will get a running start that will ensure a smoother transition for you.

Other Sources of Information

Another source of information is organizational documentation. As he met people and got to know them, one manager spent many hours in his office reviewing documents during his first weeks on the job. The following documents should be reviewed:

- *Departmental administrative or operations material, which should include the organizational chart, descriptions of work flow policies, department*

*forms, standard operating procedures, job descriptions and grades, person-
nel policies, performance standards, and the system for performance management.* You will learn how things are supposed to work, what policies
do not seem to be in place, and what seems out of date, illogical, or
wrong. You may discover, as one manager of a Fortune 500 company we
worked with found, that there are no policies, the work flow is ad hoc,
and there is no emphasis on quality and consistency.

- *Monthly or periodic departmental or team updates and divisional highlights.* These are usually good-news vehicles, but they may tell what's
  new and who is involved.
- *The corporate and department or team mission statement.* What is the
  department or team supposed to be doing? How does our mission fit
  into the corporate mission? When was it last updated and how?
- *Internal reports, including committee minutes and reports of task forces.*
  If task forces were formed or studies conducted to solve particular problems, read the report. Then ask whether any of the recommendations
  were implemented.

  One newly named manager, frustrated by what seemed to be the aim-
  lessness of one committee, asked to see the committee's mission statement
  and its minutes. Surprised to learn that the mission statement was meaningful (to review functional policies and policy decisions made by the
  leadership, and to assess leadership's performance), the manager suggested
  that the committee was not addressing its mission. Few on the committee
  knew its mandate, and some did not want to raise the potential issues and
  expend the effort that raising such issues would require. Committee minutes give an idea of issues people do not raise and may not be allowed to
  raise, and they may indicate how much people are willing to risk.

- *Consultants' proposals.* These generally describe problems serious
  enough to solicit proposals, as well as proposed solutions to those problems. However, often these proposals or the recommendations they
  generate are not implemented.
- *Performance reviews.* These records will provide information on who
  has performance problems, the nature of those problems, and steps
  managers have taken to correct the problems. Reviews are a good source
  to find hidden minefields.
- *Individual development plans.* These documents will provide information on the goals of individual team members and where they need or

want to further their abilities. They will also give you a good sense of how quickly individuals may move out of your function or whether you will have an opportunity to upgrade some capabilities in the near future.

The difference between learning your job and diagnosing your organization is important. Diagnosis encompasses data collection, analysis, making judgments and assessments, and making decisions; it implies organizational change. Learning your job may be a part of that, but resist the temptation to push toward organizational change prematurely. For now, take time to learn what your organization does before deciding what is wrong and what should be changed. One of the most common mistakes to avoid is coming in with your "playbook" because it worked somewhere else.

Other sources of information about your job may be the company's annual reports or, if its stock is publicly traded, its annual reports to shareholders and its 10-K reports that it files with the Securities and Exchange Commission (SEC). While these reports probably will not address your department's mission, they will describe the company's strategic direction, lines of business, branches or subsidiaries, successes and failures, and the philosophies and values of officers and board members. An important consideration is the prospective role your department is to play in the coming years. For example, if you are in a research department and the company depends on a steady flow of new products, it would be chilling to find out that the board of directors has decided to downsize all departments, including research.

Other similar sources of information include industry journals, trade publications, industry and trade organizations, and meetings of peers from other companies. For example, the Drug Information Association holds an annual conference, and the Pharmaceutical Research and Manufacturers Association (PhRMA) provides updates on the latest research being conducted in pharmaceutical and biotech companies. Every major industry sector and most business functions (for example, finance, human resources, project management) have professional organizations or councils such as those sponsored by the Conference Board that can provide the latest information about issues in the field and what other companies are doing in these areas. Over the past several years, many professional meetings have dealt with emerging technology and the environment. The Internet, reputable social networks, and professional journals and conference proceedings in a particular field are replete with information that a leader can turn into plans and decisions.

Another source of information about your job is your predecessor's administrative assistant. He or she will know the whereabouts of vast stores of information—files, reports, and procedures—and will offer a ground-level view of how the work gets done, and how well. That administrative assistant probably has access to more confidential information than anyone else in the organization. Consider hiring this individual for yourself, if feasible.

As you mine these sources of information about your job, don't tire of asking the same questions over and over. Even if you think you already know the answers, ask the questions anyway. Knowing the right questions to ask and hearing the range of responses will help you gather valuable information about your job in an efficient manner.

Become an Organizational Advocate

You must become an advocate for your organization's people, resources, and mission. Working with your boss, you have to fight for what your new organization needs to do the job.

Being an advocate also means communicating your enthusiasm and optimism to your organization. Being positive about the organization raises the morale, energy, and confidence of the entire group. High performance is often a self-fulfilling prophecy. You tend to get what you expect. If you expect a lot, you often get a lot.

An Example of Advocacy

A physician leader who was vice president of a clinical research and development department was handed a big task from the senior management team of a global pharmaceutical company. The company had decided to opt for an early Federal Drug Administration (FDA) review of a drug that they were developing. The company wanted an early review because if the FDA were to approve the drug, it would mean millions of dollars of revenue for the company at a time when it was experiencing a revenue shortfall. Under normal circumstances, preparation for an FDA review can take up to a year.

The decision to ask for an early review meant that the preparation had to be completed within a four-month period. And in addition to the FDA approval, the senior management wanted the review prepared for European approval as well. Knowing the inherent difficulties and risks involved in such a short time period, the vice president selected the very best cross-functional team members in the company with the help of her critical stakeholders. She laid out a basic timeline and project plan and then challenged her team to figure out with her how they would accomplish this mammoth task together. She saw her role as removing obstacles from their path, getting them the resources they needed, giving them focus and direction when needed, and challenging them to think of new ways to accelerate their preparation for the FDA review.

The team responded by fully committing their time and energy to the project. No one complained about working long hours or the difficulty in achieving the task. Everyone's focus was on the preparation for achieving the FDA approval needed and submission to the European drug regulatory body for early approval. The physician leader got them the people and other resources they needed, ensured that they weren't distracted by other projects, and made sure that senior management knew how effectively they were working to meet their goal. She openly praised them for the work they were doing and congratulated them on their successes.

Organizational advocacy means promoting your organization with insiders and outsiders alike. Fight to see that your people are awarded training slots, conference attendance, and memberships on important committees and task forces, and make sure that they get promotions. You will get as you give. If you are generous in your support for your people, they in turn will be generous in their time and energy. Their successes will reflect positively on your grasp of one of a leader's most important tasks: the ability to identify, nurture, and promote talent.

Similarly, if you are generous in your praise for people in your organization, they in turn will be loyal and generous in their praise for you. Hand out credit freely. Mention names of people who contributed to special accomplishments; give credit for ideas and suggestions, even if the help was only incidental to something you did. Above all, do not take credit for what your subordinates did. Actually, this is an example of a positive influencing technique called *reciprocation*. When you do something good or helpful for another person, that person is most likely to reciprocate and do something nice or helpful for you.

One manager talked as though he was at the vortex of every decision, solution, or accomplishment in his department. In describing department activities, he spoke as if they were his ideas or as if he had been highly instrumental in planning and achieving them even when he had been only peripherally associated with an activity or had been only the coordinator. Asked to coordinate and facilitate communications between four different corporate subcommittees but given a decision-making or leadership role on none of them, he nonetheless talked about the subcommittees as if he were directing all four of them and all four were reporting to him, much to the chagrin of the committee chairs. He name dropped shamelessly and had a way of dramatizing conversations with big names as if they were asking him for advice:

"Yesterday, Gabe called me to his office, and he said to me, 'Jim, things aren't going very well over there, are they?' 'No,' I agreed, 'they're not.' 'Well, Jim,' Gabe said, 'what would you do to fix it?'"

Notice that the dramatizations are inevitably on an insider, first-name basis. Eventually, this leader's people and coworkers shared less and less information with him and increasingly distrusted him because they felt he would either intrude where he was not wanted or would take credit for what was not his. An organizational advocate supports when support is needed, stays out of where he or she is not needed, and lets those who earned the success get the credit.

Finally, an organization advocate supports the organization's goals and mission in a way that people become committed to the organization's success. A street sweeper at Disneyworld was asked about the tedium of the job. He replied that he was an entertainer, not a street sweeper. An advocate promotes the mission, the people, and the vision of his or her organization.

EMPOWER YOUR ORGANIZATION: RAISING EXPECTATIONS AND HOPES

There is no lever more forceful in your transition process than the notion that all members of an organization are personally empowered within their scope of responsibility. To feel empowered is to feel a sense of control, a sense that you have the power to affect the work and the organization. Rather than feeling helpless and on the dependent end of a parent-child relationship, empowerment gives employees a sense that they can exert control. By personal empowerment, leaders engender these feelings:

- People are part of the management, and they can improve the organization.
- Good ideas will be implemented.

- Suggestions will be appreciated and rewarded, even if not accepted.
- People can be trusted with responsibility.
- People are respected for their ideas and judgment.

Personal empowerment assumes that each employee has the ability and the will to do the job as well as he or she knows how. When the manager removes barriers to effective performance and creates a supportive climate, most employees will improve their performance, and some will achieve new levels of results.

The goal of personal empowerment is a sense of commitment and alignment, a feeling that members of the organization have an investment in, and can affect, the success of the organization. This sense of "psychological ownership" engenders feelings of responsibility, concern, and interest among the employees. We invest energy, commitment, and concern in things for which we feel ownership, in our children, spouses, homes, careers, jobs, and ideas.

When employees feel that the organization is not theirs, that it is not a part of them, they feel only minimum responsibility and often do the job only as it is given to them. The problems and difficulties are someone else's—whoever owns the organization therefore owns the responsibility. If employees think the organization is yours (as the leader), they will believe that the problems are yours, challenges are yours, failures are yours, and successes are yours. Their actions will say "You folks had better do something about this."

Some leaders want to be the people who get the glory, have the power, take the responsibility, have all the answers, and know all the details. A mayor of a large U.S. city was a leader who did very little work to empower his staff and rarely deliberated with his aides or consulted with other politicians, city council members, or ward leaders. When asked questions, he rarely deferred answers to the people on the job. He personally cut every ribbon and made every important public appearance and every important announcement. He gained a reputation for shooting from the hip (and being wrong and often contradictory). He was seen as aloof and isolated from both those who worked for him and those who supported him. He increasingly viewed the job as his job, his city, and his responsibilities, and he saw the city's problems as his problems.

As his top people sensed the erosion of their authority, their sense of ownership eroded. Some left the administration, others marked time. Responsibility for making things happen increasingly fell to the mayor, and he became personally less effective as his organization got weaker. He ended up with all the problems on his desk, without the organization to take them on and manage them effectively.

Empowerment must be genuine. To tell people they have power and responsibility and then not empower them with responsibility lowers morale, lowers your leadership credibility, and creates hostility and opposition.

A common form of false empowerment is found in many public schools. Principals and teachers endlessly exhort students to take care of the school by saying "It's your school." But that is not the truth in a place where students sit silently in rows, listening and doing only what they're told to do. They follow the principal's rules, teachers' rules, custodians' rules, coaches' rules, lunchroom rules, attendance rules, and hallway aides' rules. Go up the up staircases, down the down staircases, and one way in the one-way hallways. Take notes, finish the assignments, read these books, exit when you're told, do what you're told, and succeed and fail by someone else's standards. At no time in our lives will we be so strongly a part of an institution in which we are so powerless—unless we go to prison.

Nor do schools belong to parents, as can be verified by any parent who has ever complained about a rule or a teacher, or made a suggestion to improve the school. Parents who are active are often snowed by public relations–minded administrators who relegate parent participation to deciding what to buy with the parent-teacher organization (PTO) treasury. Parents who want to get actively involved are asked to be teachers' aides or classroom parents. Meanwhile administrators retain any meaningful decision making and, when necessary, share it with the teachers' union. Then they complain that neither parents nor students care about the school. Why should they? They know the school is not truly theirs, that they are visitors in someone else's institution. We are now seeing the development of a number of charter schools where these dynamics are being overcome and reversed. The learning and engagement of the students are palpable.

The advantage that empowerment has was never as apparent as it was in the bailout of the Big Three Automakers in 2009. The battles between the United Automobile Workers (UAW) and the auto industry have been legendary. Historically, management gave the orders and labor followed the orders. Labor felt that if management wanted the responsibility and power, it could have all the problems too. With labor uninvolved in management and productivity, quality fell. As management's control tightened, unions carved out work rules and job classifications to limit management's power. And as the unions won work rules, both management and union increasingly went by the book.

With the advent of the Japanese entering the U.S. car market and the consumers' desire for higher-mileage, lower-maintenance vehicles, the auto industry had serious competition. By the late 1970s, Ford knew it was in trouble. Ford Motor Company reacted by undertaking three broad responses to the crisis. First, with a product engineer at the helm, they determined to produce autos designed according to customer preferences. Second, Ford adopted more efficient manufacturing procedures, such as just-in-time inventory control. Third, in adopting their Quality Is Job 1 campaign, Ford instituted Quality Circles to solicit employees' suggestions and foster union-management cooperation.

Managers were trained to listen to and work with line workers. Through more active participation in the decision-making process, labor felt greater responsibility for the quality of the product and the company's productivity. Quality improved, and worker productivity increased for the first time in many years. By 1986, Ford's profits had outstripped General Motors' for the first time in 50 years, and in 1987 and 1988, only Ford, among the four American automakers, had increased sales over the previous year. Through 1991, only Ford was maintaining market share, while GM and Chrysler had lost market share to the Japanese.

Ford had improved its products, but GM thought they had too. No American company committed itself to automation, robots, and technology the way GM did. But Ford was preeminently committed to empowering employees. They brought employee input into the manufacturing process, depended on their input for improving the product, and shared responsibility and credit for the product. In 2001, Henry Clay Ford was named CEO of Ford, ousting Jacque Nassar who had angered employees and the Firestone Company after the firestorm caused by Firestone tire problems. This action put a leader at the helm who had a reputation for being pro-employee, even pro-union, and who had said that improving relationships with the UAW union as well as other employees and constituency groups would be a key to his job going forward.[1]

When the recession hit in 2007 to 2010, Ford was the only automaker that refused bailout money. The company had developed a restructuring plan that would make certain changes necessary, with the support of their unions, that would enable it to compete with its Japanese competitors on cost and quality. Ford and leaders of the UAW announced an agreement on February 23, 2009, under which the company could substitute its stock for as much as half of its payments into a retiree health-care trust. "The modifications will protect jobs for UAW members by ensuring the long-term viability of the company," the union's president, Ron Gettelfinger, said.[2] On March 9, the UAW announced that its Ford members had accepted the agreement, which also required court approval. In large part because of the company's history of working with the union leadership and listening to employees, Ford has fared better than its domestic competitors. Jobs have still been lost, but Ford is still in business and the company will need to continue to empower its employees to survive for the long term. As we saw in the example of public schools, paying lip service to empowerment without adequate follow-through demoralizes the organization. Real empowerment can make dramatic improvements in productivity, quality, and employee engagement. During your first months on the job, you will have great opportunities to help your people be a real part of the action.

Empowering Relationships: A Self-Concept Approach to Managing People

A manager's ability to empower is an important element in facilitating successful employee job performance. The manager's or leader's attentiveness, expectations, encouragement, attitudes, and evaluations are primary forces in influencing an employee's productivity and engagement.

Think about the following example: "After working at an entry-level position for two years, I wanted to challenge myself. I wanted to go back to school while looking for a higher-level job at the company where I worked. So I went to my boss to discuss it. My fear was that he would discourage me because I had worked at only an entry-level position. But he surprised me and said he was hoping that I would decide to do this. What a relief and a great feeling." An individual's self-concept and feeling of personal power can be influenced by his or her boss's support.

Feelings of personal power are linked to how one approaches the job and to actual success at work. What and how we think about who we are, and how we see ourselves in the eyes of others, often triggers a self-fulfilling prophecy. If we see ourselves as being effective, responsible, creative, and productive on the job, we generally will be. The high-achieving individual almost always feels his or her supervisor's support and encouragement.

Whether or not we perceive ourselves as high or low performers often depends on how we interpret reactions from important people in our work lives. Key to these perceptions are the behaviors and expectancies of our boss. These messages can be verbal or nonverbal, overt or subtle, strong or weak, supportive or destructive, but they are powerful. People will begin to sense how you feel about them in the first minute of your first meeting with them. Their emotional barometers will be fine-tuned, looking for clues about how you perceive them. They will be carefully assessing themselves through your communication with them.

Communication as an Empowering Experience

The process of empowering people to be productive depends on clear communication. Unclear communication can lead to an employee's feeling apathetic, angry, or depressed. But clear communication can result in a subordinate's feeling motivated to succeed. An empowering interaction between boss and employee can be potent. You can set up positive self-fulfilling prophecies for those who work for you that will strongly affect job performance.

In a moment of reflection, a sales representative said, "My sales manager saw things in me that I didn't even see in myself. She kept challenging me with a variety of tasks and projects and truly expected that I would handle them well. She provided me with support when I needed it, and at other times left me alone to work. She seemed not at all surprised when I successfully met the challenges. Funny, it reminded me of when I was a kid and a neighbor asked if he could pay me to work on his lawn because I was doing such a good job on mine. I did an even better job on his."

How an Empowering Leader Views Others

A boss's style tends to be perceived as either personally empowering or personally diminishing. The impact that the empowering leader's behavior has on employees is great whether it is verbal or nonverbal, intended or not intended. People need to feel *able, valuable,* and *responsible,* and when they feel that way, it can have dramatic implications in the way they approach and perform their work. The opposite is also true. The leader may not be aware of the negative impact of skewed glances or "funny" putdowns, but nonetheless they have a very real effect. The empowering leader goes out of the way to challenge, coach, support, and reward.

There are psychological reasons for using empowering approaches and carefully timing your initial interactions with people. Two basic needs of people are to feel worthwhile and to feel respected. People who work for empowering leaders typically describe themselves as feeling more *able, valuable,* and *responsible*. They feel that way because they are treated that way. Creating the right conditions and empowering others to succeed will act as strong motivators for 9 out of 10 workers.

Empowering leaders have flexible styles. They adapt their approach to people's needs and to the situation. The empowering leader creates the best possible conditions for performance and career development. The message sounds like this: "I believe in you, your judgment, capabilities, and your potential. I expect you to be successful. I am here to aid you, to act as a catalyst and coach for your success. My job is to create the conditions for your success; your job is to get it done. We will work on it together."

The psychological dynamics of this approach are both predictable and potent. It creates the Pygmalion effect, the self-fulfilling prophecy of success. Empowering leadership touches the core of our humanity, our self-concept. Nothing affects our behavior, our performance, and the achievement of our potential more than this vision of who we are.

To appreciate the potency of empowering leadership, you must understand the following principle: how we see ourselves on the job depends on how we interpret messages (verbal and nonverbal) from key individuals in our professional environment. One of these key people is our leader or manager. This is especially true as newly promoted leaders assume their responsibilities. In new situations, people are often wary and inquisitive. Most want to look for opportunity, and they hope for a bright future. During your first few months, your empowering style can have an early and positive effect on an entire organization through your attitude, direct discussion, and behaviors.

Examples of Empowering and Diminishing Behaviors

There is a wide range of leadership behaviors that empower or diminish people and their performance.

Empowering	Diminishing
Shows approval	Resorts to name calling
Shows concern and empathy	Uses putdown statements
Shows interest	Embarrasses people
Facilitates learning	Has a sink-or-swim attitude
Reinforces	Blames; tends to look for the negative first

Respects	Gossips about shortcomings
Communicates and listens	Tells; directs
Sees the small and big picture	Picks on details
Trusts; tends to see the good as well as bad	Creates dependent relationships; primarily sees mistakes
Smiles and invites	Is noncommittal; frowns and rejects
Is seen as supportive	Is seen as critical
Is assertive	Is aggressive
Creates cooperative and independent relationships	Creates competition and dependency
In conflict situations is balanced; sees others' viewpoints and sees mutual solutions	Focuses on problems, not solutions
Usually uses an I win/you win style	In conflict looks for I win/you lose solutions

Creating the Conditions for Optimal Performance

Think of yourself as a catalyst striving for the best "chemistry" between you, your employees, and your work environment. Just as a farmer tends the soil, the empowering leader nurtures his or her people. There are six critical actions that will help you build a positive self-fulfilling prophecy resulting in high performance:

1. Challenge and "stretch" people.
2. Give people choice in how to get the job done.
3. Show respect for others.
4. Relate to people in a mutually supportive way.
5. Practice self-monitoring.
6. Build on successful experiences.

Challenge People

We know that people tend to perform best when they need to "stretch" in their jobs. This usually means that people should be pushed (or preferably push themselves) to work just beyond their own view of what is comfortable. "Just out of reach, but not out of sight," is an excellent rule of thumb. Leaders and employees should agree to performance and achievement standards that provide stretch and that enhance high-level performance. Here again, the self-ful-filling prophecy comes into play. People with low expectations usually work at that level. High expectations tend to result in high performance. Help your people set goals that will help them stretch.

Give People a Choice in How to Get the Job Done

We tend to perform best when we are allowed to develop our own best way to meet established standards and expectations. We are energized when we bring our own knowledge, creativity, and resources to the solution of a problem.

Last year we had a problem with a part for a light fixture that we had bought from one of the large retail chain stores. Some companies empower their customer service representatives to satisfy a customer's complaint however they think best. The customer service representative checked our records and saw that we had been charged for a part that we had never received. She credited our account and offered us a small gift card for our inconvenience. She never had to ask her supervisor for permission, and she quickly and effectively resolved our complaint making us feel like valued customers in just one call. She was empowered by the company to do what *she* felt was needed to satisfy the customer and resolve any complaints. Companies that go in the opposite direction, giving responsibility without control, engender resentment and defeat.

Show Respect for Others

People with healthy self-concepts generally feel that they are respected by their peers and managers alike. Agreement or disagreement—even conflict—especially with new bosses, subsides when people feel that their opinions and ideas are respected. Organizations need exchange of ideas. Better ideas are often forged from the white heat of disagreement. When we feel a foundation of mutual respect and support, we perform more confidently and use all our resources.

Relate to People in a Mutually Supportive Way

Empathy, the ability to relate to another's feelings and perceptions, is essential to empowerment. Empathy is one of the fundamental emotional intelligence skills. For years, psychologists have shown that the ability to "put ourselves in the shoes of the other" so as to understand another person's frame of reference is a critical factor in building trusting relationships helping that person achieve his or her potential. Leaders need to understand and respect the perspective of their employees, and employees need to understand and respect the perspective of the leader. There is no better time to begin working on your relationships than your first day and throughout your first year. Mutual respect is based on mutual understanding of needs and demands.

Practice Self-Monitoring

Employees need feedback on how well they are doing, and leaders and managers need information on what employees are doing. Monitoring and feedback are essential in helping employees keep track of how well they are meeting the challenge. Enabling employees to choose how to get the work done requires self-monitoring and personal responsibility for quality and output. Periodic checks on progress, process, and quality, as well as coaching with reassessment and adjustment of work goals, help employees achieve their quality and quantity goals. Many managers also encourage peer monitoring, usually in team meetings where team members discuss goals and achievements and their contribution to the team's accomplishments. This approach is popular in self-directed, peer-led teams.

Build on Successful Experiences

Success begets success! People who use their abilities in challenging situations are more consistently successful. They learn to use their capabilities, develop new skills and abilities, and learn what is required for success. Empowering leaders offer challenges that build on their people's successes and increase the chances for top performance under trying circumstances.

Empowering leaders help their people to be successful. They set up an environment that encourages a positive self-concept and a feeling that people are fulfilling constructive and valuable goals.

We have identified six things leaders can do to help ensure high employee performance. As a newly appointed leader, you have an excellent opportunity to affect your people in ways that can truly make a difference on the job. The process of "buying in" versus "dropping out" begins in the first days following your appointment. Employees often make the decision to be part of the solution rather than part of the problem within weeks, certainly within a few months, of your arrival. With strong engagement comes the use of discretionary effort and time. Employees who feel empowered become positive and creatively committed to the organization's success.

BUILD STRONG INTERNAL AND EXTERNAL STAKEHOLDER RELATIONSHIPS

Throughout this book we emphasize the importance of building and sustaining critical stakeholder relationships throughout the organization. As much as any other single factor, trusting, empowering interpersonal behaviors determine success and failure. Be conscious of establishing solid relationships at all levels in the organization. Work at building trust and rapport with those who are under your leadership; with your boss and others at his or her level; and, importantly, with your peers and colleagues.

Make sure you begin spending meaningful time with your peers during your first two or three days. Think about others in the organization. Any administrative assistant, for example, can help or hurt you depending on how he or she has been treated. Genuine concern and consideration for others, even small things like saying please and thank you, go a long way toward building strong relationships. Extend yourself and others will reciprocate and will tend to do the same. Ask yourself the following:

- What can I do to build stronger relationships at all levels?
- Do I go out of my way for others?
- Do I ask for what I want, or do I demand things from others?
- What can I do to help people trust me?
- Am I straight with people? Do I minimize conflicts?
- Do I listen well to needs and feelings?
- Do I show warmth and concern and extend myself to others?
- Do I make people come to me, or do I reach out to them?

A stakeholder is any individual who has an investment in your success or failure. Clearly your new boss is a stakeholder as are your direct reports because their success depends on your success. In addition, peers may be critical stakeholders as well. Your department or team's work may interface or directly impact other functions. In addition to internal staff, some stakeholder relationships are external to your organization. Key clients, vendors, consultants, key opinion leaders, and others may all be critical stakeholders. The third Just Promoted Leader Tool, Building Stakeholder Partnerships, will help you identify your critical stakeholders and the steps necessary for building strong relationships with them.

Building Stakeholder Partnerships

Your List of Stakeholders

Stakeholder	Stake in Your Success	Current Relationship	Desired Relationship

Action Steps Needed

1.

2.

3.

4.

Discussion Questions for Meetings with Stakeholders

Here are some questions that you can use during meetings with your new stakeholders that will help you build your relationship with them:

1. What do you see as your most critical business goals and issues over the next one to two years?
2. Are there any organizational impediments to your achieving the results you intend?
3. How can I (or my function) help you achieve your goals?
4. In what ways have our departments (or functions) cooperated successfully in the past? Should we continue these behaviors?
5. In what ways have our departments (or functions) worked to each other's disadvantage in the past? What can we do differently that would be more effective?
6. What service gaps or concerns have you experienced from our department (or function)? How can we better support your business?

7. I'd like to talk to you about my goals in this new position. The two or three major accomplishments I need to achieve this year are:

_____.

8. What thoughts or concerns do you have about these goals? How do they impact you and your people?
9. What are the political forces I should understand as my unit tries to accomplish these goals? Are there any people in the organization who might be openly or less openly against our achieving them?
10. I see the following people as key to the success of these goals:

_____

_____

11. Do you have any advice about approaching these people for their support? Are there any other people I should be talking to (either in your department or elsewhere)?
12. In general, what are your expectations of _____ [our department] for the future?
13. How can we stay linked in terms of your needs to meet your business plan? (Probe for ways to assure communication, coordination, and collaboration.)
14. Could I attend one of your staff meetings sometime soon to learn more about your business? Would you like to attend one of my staff meetings?
15. What other advice do you have for me in working in this organizational culture? What are some of the unwritten rules?

Early Resentment: Piranhas and Icebergs

Not all relationships will be positive ones. We have already mentioned that candidates who were not selected may be resentful and ready to criticize. Don't underestimate their resentment. One newly named hotel manager had been promoted from her previous position as the director of food service, and it was a surprising and substantial promotion. More than a few staff members felt that she was unqualified; some suggested it had been an affirmative action promotion. While some opponents resigned within her first month on the job, others who stayed were more passive-aggressive, withholding information, not communicating, offering lukewarm support for management decisions, and passing on critical comments as if they were informational.

Some employees will resent an insider's promotion. They are more familiar with an insider's strengths and weaknesses, and they may not feel that he or she was the strongest candidate. Some will welcome an outsider's fresh perspective. If business is bad, your chances of a warm welcome are better, no matter where you come from. In one company, an experienced sales director's energy and direction was greeted with relief, even by the piranhas.

Piranhas are those who would rather attack and criticize than support and fit into the new organization. Their behavior may be overt or subtle. There will be histories you probably won't know—for example, that a veteran was bypassed by your predecessor and is still resentful, or that another's conflict with a former leader makes him a suspicious subordinate. The management team may not work well together because of jealousy or disagreements. Administrative assistants, employees, or other managers may have morale problems.

You may be associated with a disliked senior leader. Your promotion may have been the outcome of a power struggle, and your promotion has already alienated a power block. Managers or other leaders associated with a losing candidate may be uncooperative.

Happily, most situations are mixed. Some people will be pleased, others disappointed, but most will give you the benefit of the doubt. There are usually only a few certified piranhas in any organization.

Along with piranhas, watch out for submerged icebergs, which may be more numerous and can appear unexpectedly. They evolve from the politics, morale, jealousies, inefficiencies, and problems of an organization. Many will be political.

The new hotel manager could not have known that the often inept director of sales had once been the administrative assistant to the corporate financial vice president, or that the director of housekeeping was another corporate officer's mother. Nor could she have known that the hotel's advertising director was a make-work assignment for a favored but basically inept corporate manager. She could not have known that the parent corporation, which was not in the hotel business, viewed the hotel as a dumping ground for people the company wanted to get rid of but didn't have the heart to fire.

New leaders are frequently blindsided by networks they didn't know existed. Something you say about someone, some department, or some issue gets passed on to people you didn't necessarily intend to hear it. Offhand and often innocent remarks may come back to haunt you. The successful leader learns not to talk critically about people and personalities, not to comment on issues of no direct concern to him or her, and to describe decisions and issues in objective, problem-solving terms ("the program did not achieve its objective") rather than in the subjective vocabulary of personalities and people ("Robert failed").

An organization's economics contains its own icebergs. Until you see your budget, know how it was spent, and know how it was managed and what you have to work with, you won't fully appreciate your position. Where do the sales come from? Who are the buyers? Who are the clients? Who uses what your department does? What is the market? What do they buy from you? How are financial decisions made? Whose approval do you need at what points?

Quick Reminders to Keep You on Track

- As you assume your new position and begin to meet people, you make a first impression only one time! Reach out, be personable, and make contact with everyone in your new function as only you can.
- As you begin your new management job, you'll frequently run into a wide range of expectations, including hope, resentment, confusion, and concern.
- There are six major steps to keep in mind as you enter your new management job and organization:

  1. Make a good first impression during your first meetings with your new staff. Immediately begin to connect with people on a personal level and build support.
     - Expect a wide variety of feelings regarding your appointment, ranging from optimism and relief to concern, disappointment, resentment, and confusion.
     - Initially, you will likely have a fragile base of influence and power that will need to be strengthened through credible work and positive relationships.
     - Hold an initial brief but very upbeat meeting with your new organization.
     - Spend a lot of one-on-one time with people.

- Begin to seed the idea that you will be asking people to help in an "organizational health check" program.
- Try to develop an inclusionary management style.
- Be careful of your vocabulary—emphasize *we*'s and *our*'s in your language.
- Meet individually with the unsuccessful candidates for your position if they are in your new function, and extend an invitation to fully utilize their skills and experience.
- You should plan to exit your previous position effectively. If possible, help with the transition of your replacement. This may go on simultaneously with your transition into your new job.

2. Establish ground rules and communication with your boss about the transition process.
   - Make sure you both understand and agree to the process and the timetable.
   - Mutually establish these ground rules.
3. You need to accelerate your job learning.
   - Use your predecessor and key staff as major sources of information. Review documents, files, organization charts, and many other available sources of information.
   - Ask many people a wide variety of questions. Do perception checks.
4. Become an organizational advocate. Actively promote your organization, its people, and its resources with insiders and outsiders alike.
5. Accept the challenge of raising expectations, hopes, and personal empowerment of your people.
6. Build empowering relationships. Utilize a self-concept approach to managing people. Certain specific communication patterns and behaviors create the conditions for optimal employee performance. These build and strengthen employees' confidence and self-concept on the job.

ENTERING YOUR BOSS'S WORLD

With assertiveness training, he confronted his boss in a manner far from benign and became the most assertive claimant on the unemployment line.

—Source unknown

An important aspect of establishing yourself is working effectively with your new boss. You will need to accomplish the following:

- Clearly understand why you were hired.
- Conduct a perception check with your boss as you both make sure you agree on what your job is and what is expected of you.
- Act in the best interests of your boss and help him or her be successful.
- Understand the demands and expectations that others have of your boss.

In this chapter, there is useful information about the following:

- Why were you hired?
- Clarifying your role and what is expected of you: a perception check with your boss
- Contracting with your boss: Confirming Your Appointment Charter and Your 12-Month Road Map
- Helping your boss be a star
- Understanding your boss's responsibilities and preferences

In Chapter 2 we briefly examined the importance of establishing ground rules and clear communication with your boss regarding your transition strategy. This chapter pursues that relationship in greater detail.

WHY WERE YOU HIRED?

In the heady moments surrounding your promotion, you'll feel proud of what you've achieved. It was the result of your hard work, ability, and commitment. You have a right to feel great satisfaction. But before you get too carried away, stop to think about the primary reason why you are where you are: your boss's need to have someone to count on for a major area of responsibility. When you succeed, your boss succeeds. Your selection and ability to perform is a direct reflection on your boss.

That you were hired to help someone else perform better means that you do not have a free hand to do and say as you wish. Rather, your decisions must fit into your boss's plans, goals, and style. You were hired to help your boss meet his or her goals.

William was hired to direct the mass transit authority in a large U.S. city. He pursued the job aggressively. He and his wife had attended school in that city and had personal ties to the region. He had been the successful managing director of the mass transit authority in another large city, he was well qualified and experienced, and he seemed to be the ideal candidate for the job.

But within a week on the job, he was embroiled in controversy. Within a month, the head of the transit authority was asking for William's resignation. The suburban representatives on the transit authority had voted "no confidence." The Democratic city mayor and governor urged him to stay, and the Republican suburban head of the transit authority urged him to resign. What had happened? Certainly, party politics had played a role, but the political pressures developed primarily after the situation had deteriorated. The opposing political factions on the transit authority board—Democratic and largely urban, Republican and largely suburban—were quick to take sides and seize the political advantage. But what events had triggered the crisis?

During his first day on the job, William announced on television that fares were too high, and he would like to reduce them. Within a week he had completely reversed himself, saying that the finances were in terrible shape (which the transit authority's chairman had been telling the public all along) and that he may have to seek a fare hike. That same week, he publicly disagreed with the chairman about resources, making a statement that led to the chairman's first and then rapid subsequent public criticisms. In turn, William responded in public. The ensuing discourse, including the conditions and price tag for a proposed contract buyout, were conducted for others to hear, usually reported by an enchanted media.

Of course, a number of mistakes were made. First, William was too public before he had taken time to assess the situation. In his premature diagnosis of the problems and choice of solutions, he caught himself in contradictions.

Second, as we will see in a later chapter, William acted before he had formed a leadership team that supported him. Essentially, when he made his statements, he was speaking for himself, not for his leadership team. He had formed no management consensus. He had no support, no one to help him shape and defend his statements within his organization, with the board, and with the public.

Third (and more to the point of this chapter), William violated a cardinal rule of transitions: *He did not understand the reasons for which he was hired.* From his boss's point of view, several applicants could have done a good technical job. William was hired because his boss, the chairman of the transit authority's board, felt that William would do a good job for *him*. In doing a good job, William would make the transit authority successful and make his boss appear more professional, capable, and effective. William did not adequately appreciate that doing a good job was linked to the mutual self-interest of both William and his boss, and that both wanted to be effective.

If you have any doubt about the importance of safeguarding mutual self-interests, it should be put to rest when you consider what happens when it is destroyed. When it appeared that William was not serving his boss's self-interests, the situation deteriorated rapidly. Each side lost confidence in the other, and both suffered. The public increasingly perceived that the transit authority was not being well led and was riddled with politics. Similarly, the transit authority's reputation for being well managed suffered. William seemed ineffective. Democratic politicians called for the chairman's resignation; the area's major newspaper editorialized about the politicizing of the transit authority's management; one editorial called the transit authority "the laughing stock of the nation." The Chamber of Commerce publicly said that the transit authority's ability to manage itself was in question. How different would these perceptions have been had the rift not occurred, had William abided by a primary law of successful transition and served his boss's self-interest while determining how to perform well in his job?

CLARIFYING YOUR ROLE AND WHAT IS EXPECTED OF YOU: A PERCEPTION CHECK WITH YOUR BOSS

Given the differing sets of expectations for you, things can become very confusing. Your own expectations can be both your greatest source of strength and your greatest problem. If you conducted careful, two-way discussions with your boss before you were hired, you will understand his or her expectations.

Ted felt he had a clear reading of his mission. His boss, who was the director of learning and development (L&D), wanted new programs, "the ones written about in the L&D journals," including some internal consulting, organizational diagnosis, and executive team building. That's what Ted thought he had been told, and soon after he was hired he was well on his way. He conducted needs assessments with first-line supervisors and midlevel managers, and he organized problem-solving teams. He instituted midlevel and upper-level management development programs, planned and facilitated a retreat for top management, and developed a succession plan. He was confidently moving quickly ahead with what he had been told to do, and he thought that he was regularly staying in touch with and tuned into his boss. He was fired after about six months by a boss who felt that Ted had been too pushy, had disrupted the organization, and had upset the people he was supposed to help.

In getting the programs started, Ted had become more aggressive and prominent than his boss had anticipated. Ted was becoming a star. Even worse, he took credit for others' accomplishments. He acted as the spokesperson and leader for his programs. He gave little of the limelight or spokesperson roles to his boss, and his boss got little of the credit for the new programs. In brief, Ted had not met an important part of his boss's expectations: that his boss's standing would be enhanced by Ted's activities. Rather, Ted was building his own reputation and role, and little of the activity was benefiting his boss. In making himself look good, Ted had failed to make his boss look good and, in fact, his boss viewed Ted as a threat.

Another common difficulty is a boss who hires you to implement his or her solutions rather than solve a problem. You cannot be sure the solution addresses the problem, or even that there is a problem.

Sally, an internal consultant, was asked to plan a one-day problem-solving conference in which the department would come together for the day to identify solutions for some organizational problems. Her boss had decided that a workshop was the best way to identify the organization's problems and identify solutions. Sally spent three days interviewing people, identifying the critical problems, and planning the workshop. But in the one-day workshop, the group of 35 did not get beyond defining the problems or identifying possible solutions. Her boss, disappointed with the group's progress, blamed her. In retrospect, Sally doubted all along that the goal could be accomplished in one day, and she wished she had used better approaches. She should have rethought the solution to the problem instead of accepting her boss's solution at face value.

Diane is the marketing director for a financial organization in a large city. Her manager contracted with an advertising firm to design the annual promotional campaign. The agency designed a $685,000 program that included image ads in a local business magazine, the local mass audience magazine, the daily newspaper, and some mailings. Fortunately, the large budget gave both Diane and her boss pause to reanalyze the problem. When they did, they came up with a different solution, including more direct sales, a larger sales force, and more face-to-face contact with qualified customers. The ad campaign was scrapped, and the new program worked for about one-fourth of the cost. Diane was lucky—the shock of the large budget gave her and her boss cause to refocus on the problem. But even while changing direction, Diane was careful not to outdistance her boss or to make her boss's original decision seem like a bad one.

Pay attention to your boss's expectations about the role you will play and what you will accomplish. But you should not assume that you have his or her mandate to do what you're doing. Nor should you assume that what you are handed is exactly what you have to do without discussion and negotiation.

Another of your boss's expectations regards the pace of your work. You may feel lots of pressure to make something happen, to be decisive. As part of your hiring discussions, you should have agreed on how your transition will progress, with a rough timeline. In the continuing discussions, you need to remind your boss of those agreements and to keep your commitment about regularly discussing your progress. Reiterate that the first major part of the transition may take up to six months, that your boss should not expect to see changes of any consequence for at least one to three months, and that your completed diagnosis is going to precede any big decisions. Even though you negotiated those conditions with your boss when you were hired, you need continually to provide updates on that plan, with reminders that you are sticking to it.

Review what stage of the plan you are at. Review your progress and the steps you have taken, and indicate your next steps. Be sure your boss is fully briefed and has the chance to voice and work through any reservations or concerns about your progress. Don't assume that just because your boss has not said anything, he or she is not interested or worried. Keep your boss informed and up to date. Your boss's silence is often an expression of concern. Suffered quietly, this can explode on you with surprising force. Be aware that your boss is under pressure, just as you are. Your boss's leader, and other influential stakeholders, expect that when your boss hired you, he or she hired the right person.

Other sources of expectations can also make you doubt yourself. Those who work for you will have their own expectations that you will be decisive, "hands on" or "hands off," innovative, experimental, cautious, or participatory. Some will feel that they know what the organization needs, and in both subtle and direct ways they will make these needs known to you. You'll feel the pressure.

You may feel expectations from many other stakeholders, including upper management, your peers in other departments, the department's informal leadership, customers, consultants and contractors with whom you have contracts, friends, and even your spouse. All their expectations will affect how you approach the job and the pace of the transition. If your spouse is anxious about your success, you could begin to resent the trip home to face the same inquiries, the same disappointment, the same impatient (or exasperated) tone of voice, and the same advice about being more decisive. You may have the same feelings from friends. You will feel people's expectations and pressure from many directions at once.

That is why you need a transitional plan. When you are secure in the knowledge that you are on schedule, moving ahead, and the goal is in sight, you will be able to parry the pressures by placing expectations in context. You will feel more secure knowing that at the appropriate time, expectations, including your own, will be met.

CONTRACTING WITH YOUR BOSS: CONFIRMING YOUR APPOINTMENT CHARTER AND YOUR 12-MONTH ROAD MAP

Having a clear and specific agreement with your boss governing your transition is very important; in fact, it is vital to your success. We refer to this contracting process as Confirming Your Appointment Charter, and it is Just Promoted Leader Tool 4. During this process, you will confirm the top several objectives that you must complete over the next 12 months as well as numerous other elements critical to your performance and the agreements you make with your boss or bosses. (In Chapter 1, we described these objectives as so important that "forgiveness will not be granted" if you are not successful in completing or delivering on them.) Even if it is not a written, signed agreement between you and your boss, Your Appointment Charter is a clear understanding of the terms of your transition into the job.

Your 12-Month Road Map is Just Promoted Leader Tool 5. This tool will help you to plan and monitor your progress in 3-month increments to help you stay on track in meeting the benchmarks in Your Appointment Charter. The explicit contract or agreement between you and your boss should support an evolving transition process.

Many leaders report to two or more bosses. These dual or multiple reporting relationships are common in today's complex organizations. For example, in matrix organizations, a leader could easily have business or product line reporting structures as well as geographic reporting structures. We know of many leaders who work in multiple reporting relationships. The largest number of reporting relationships that we have come across is seven.

It is vitally important that your expectations and working agreements be agreed to by each person to whom you report. While it should be the case that those to whom you report have all consulted with each other and are all following the same plan, this is often not the case. Remember that it takes many factors and many stakeholders for you to be successful and as few as *one* factor or dissatisfied boss or stakeholder to fail. It may be necessary for you to have one-on-one meetings with each of your bosses and key stakeholders to ensure alignment in relation to your performance expectations. You might also need to circle back and convene some or all of these individuals to ensure that everyone agrees on what you need to deliver, in what time frames, and with what resources and decision-making authority. Not to do so is to operate at your own peril.

The following points are examples of those you might cover with your boss or bosses when confirming Your Appointment Charter. Specifically, the example below refers to the steps in the diagnostic and change processes during the initial steps in your transition:

- That you will describe each step in the process and the milestones to your boss, preferably in writing, and that you and your boss will agree on the schedule and the milestones.
- That you will update your boss regularly on where you are in the process, including what you have accomplished, what you have learned, and what your next steps will be.
- That before the next steps are taken, you will review the process with your boss and listen to and, whenever possible, implement his or her advice. Advice you do not implement you will discuss with your boss candidly.
- That communications between you and your boss, especially disagreements, will remain private and privileged, between the two of you.
- That your boss will not pressure you to make premature changes to the transition plan, and that he or she will allow you to stay on the schedule you negotiated together.

Decide how success will be defined, first in terms of process and then in terms of measurable results. Early success should be defined by how well you conceive, organize, and manage the transition process, and it should include at least the following:

- The effectiveness with which you develop a leadership and management team to make policy decisions and help manage the diagnosis
- The success with which your leadership team identifies and confronts the organization's problems
- The effectiveness with which you schedule the organizational diagnosis, keep it on schedule, and troubleshoot
- The effectiveness with which you build and maintain your organization's support for the diagnosis and the effectiveness with which you communicate the process so it is understandable to the organization, including parts outside your immediate functional area

- The success with which you delegate and manage the problem-solving process, implement changes, and maintain the things that do not need fixing
- The effectiveness with which you communicate the process and your decisions with your bosses and the effectiveness with which you communicate decisions to your peers in functions and teams affected by any changes

The bottom line is the effect of the decisions you make and implement on organizational productivity and effectiveness—in short, the real results. The bottom line depends on your specific situation and may include goals such as increased profitability, product launches, targeted increases in sales, improvements in six sigma quality measures, higher engagement scores among those asked to participate in decisions, better work flow as bottlenecks and inefficiencies are eliminated, and/or better quality or service as suggestions are implemented. It may be a change in the financial picture, a measure of productivity, a measure of staff morale or stability, or a change in the way work gets done.

Define the bottom line with your boss or bosses. How will he or she measure your success, and do you all agree on these metrics? Put it in writing, or at least talk through your agreements in explicit terms if this is your boss's style. Make sure you know and have both agreed on these goals as well as the expectations of how you are going to work together.

You should tailor the use of Your Appointment Charter to the communication style of your boss or bosses. The most common approach would be for you and your boss to fill out the information separately and then discuss it together. Just as effective would be the two of you using Your Appointment Charter as the focus of a discussion without having written the charter separately ahead of time. Either together or sequentially, these same kinds of discussions should occur with others with whom you have a reporting relationship. These discussions serve as a great way for you to receive excellent coaching that you might not otherwise receive as you move into your role. You may modify the elements of Your Appointment Charter in any way that fits your situation. The fourth Just Promoted Leader Tool that follows is based on a template that has been used in one successful organization.

Confirming Your Appointment Charter

Directions
The confirmation of Your Appointment Charter is designed to make explicit those factors that are often implicit or poorly understood during the difficult transition period of assuming new leadership responsibility. List the explicit agreements that you should make with your immediate managers. Use the following factors that constitute Your Appointment Charter. It may be necessary to include agreements with other leaders or key stakeholders. This is especially important if you are accountable to more than one person and/or team.

Name:

Name of immediate managers or leaders with whom this appointment charter has been or should be negotiated (include more than one individual if there are dual or multiple reporting relationships):

Names of other managers or leaders or key stakeholders who are involved in confirming this appointment charter (*optional*):

New title:

Scope of responsibilities:

Limits of decision-making authority:

Reporting relationships:
   Up:

   Down (who reports to you):

   Across (that is, roles that you have on teams):

Plans for orientation and integration into this organization, including ways that the announcement will be made:

Time commitments for this role (expected length of time in this role, if appropriate):

Timing and key elements of transition into this role (for example, start and expectations for early actions and/or accomplishments during transition):

Specific ways the managers or leaders to whom you report would like to be supported with their accountabilities:

Ways in which progress and performance will be monitored and ways of updating those to whom you report and others (this may require you to "flex" your communication style in order to best meet your reports' communication needs and styles):

Ways to give and receive feedback with those to whom you report and others (as appropriate):

Agreement on developmental needs and/or plans pertaining to this new role:

Other agreements:

List the two to three most important performance goals you must achieve within one year. These goals should reflect the most significant contributions you plan to make to the business or function of which you are a part. Identify criteria by which these goals will be measured whenever possible.

_____

Once your new charter is confirmed, establish a schedule of events so both you and your boss will know the sequence of events and timeline for making your transition. You will lessen the pressure you feel to make something happen immediately if you plan the process in writing.

We suggest using the fifth Just Promoted Leader Tool, Your 12-Month Road Map, as a way of capturing your must-do goals and planning for them.

JUST PROMOTED LEADER TOOL 5
Your 12-Month Road Map

Directions
Use the form below to assist you in planning how you will successfully accomplish the two to three most important performance goals that you have to meet in the first year in your new role.

List the 2 to 3 Most Important Goals That You Must Achieve in 1 Year, Including the Criteria by Which Each Will Be Measured	Expected Progress within 3 Months	Expected Progress within 6 Months	Expected Progress within 9 Months
1.			
2.			
3.			

HELPING YOUR BOSS BE A STAR: A SMART AND POLITICALLY SAVVY STRATEGY

To discuss why you were hired is to discuss how to help your boss be a star. There is little difference between the two. One of the primary goals of your promotion or appointment is to make sure your boss looks good. Forget or disregard this principle at your own peril. When William, head of the transit authority, inadvertently made his boss look bad, he diminished his own, his boss's, and ultimately his agency's real and perceived effectiveness. The result was that it cost him his job.

Lu, on the other hand, was much more careful. She carefully negotiated with Marsha (her boss) the scope of her authority and the scope of decision making she would have. Even though she had negotiated the power to make key decisions, she discussed each decision with Marsha before it was implemented. When Marsha seemed ambivalent, Lu backed off making the decision until they had discussed it more and Marsha seemed more positive. They began to work as a team: Lu would discuss organizational problems and needed changes with Marsha, and Marsha would delegate to Lu many of the decisions agreed on. Thus, the first rule Lu followed was to discuss organizational issues with her boss and to agree on the decisions. The second was to follow through on those decisions her boss supported and to back off or continue to "sell" where Marsha seemed unsure or ambivalent.

The third rule Lu followed was to keep disagreements with her boss private. As far as the rest of the organization was concerned, Lu and Marsha understood each other and were a perfectly synchronized team. This made the organization's top management seem well oiled and well organized, and it enhanced the organization's leadership reputation.

The least-known element of their partnership was that Lu made sure that Marsha was the star. Even though Lu had written most of the business plan, Marsha presented it to the board of directors. When sales dramatically increased, Lu deflected much of the credit to Marsha, even though Marsha and the management team attributed much of the credit for the sales increases to Lu's marketing efforts. When a national magazine contacted Lu for a feature about women leaders, she suggested they do the piece on Marsha instead. This was smart and politically very savvy.

In the process, Marsha appreciated Lu's essential contribution toward her success. Within the executive team, Marsha publicly credited Lu for helping with the company's turnaround and promoted her to group head. But as far as the board of directors and the outside world was concerned, Marsha was and is the star. Lu's loyalty enhanced both her own and her boss's careers.

Understanding Your Boss's Responsibilities and Preferences

Your boss can't always give you what you want. Monies you need may be committed for other purposes; people you don't want may be politically connected; capital improvements you want to make may be slated for other departments. The needed purchasing program cannot be acquired in the next fiscal year, and you have to wait your turn.

Nonetheless, you can help your boss help you. As you help make your boss a star, he or she should also help you succeed. But your boss's attention will be pulled in many directions. Thus, for your boss to help you, you may have to ask.

First, be part of and high in your boss's very busy "mental inbox." Have a set time every week when you meet. Choose a time that's relatively unpressured, like early morning for coffee, Friday afternoon, or maybe even after five o'clock, when much of the workforce has gone home and you both are beginning to unwind. Your boss may be more relaxed and in a frame of mind to listen and think with you. It is critical that you get your boss's dedicated time.

Many a transition has gone sour because, in the absence of regular communication, the new manager thought he had a mandate, thought he was doing what he had been hired to do, and thought his boss was pleased with what was happening.

Nancy is an independent, self-reliant person. She was a field representative for the home office, a job that afforded her a great deal of personal independence and authority. She liked making her own decisions, doing things her own way. When she represented the company in the field, she was generally the final authority. Even though her independence could make her difficult to work with, she was quite effective. The field force generally felt that she made things better for them.

However, Nancy's effectiveness in-house was tempered by her difficulty in being a team player. She felt that she was competent and should be allowed to do her job as she felt best, and she resented her boss's oversight. Accordingly, she often made decisions without checking them out; she distributed reports, directions, and analyses that her boss had not reviewed. She made commitments her boss had not approved; and at one point she used her boss's initials on a proposal that they had discussed in concept but that he had not approved. Her boss saw the reports after they had already been sent out and bound.

At heart, Nancy may have felt that she was more competent than her boss. Certainly her expressed need was "Hire me to do the job and I'll do it," which was a style different from her boss's. He had worked hard to develop the product line and the clients, and he was very fastidious about what was done with clients. He expected to review materials before they were sent to clients, and he expected to be told of client decisions before the fact. In defending her need for authority, Nancy avoided interactions with her boss because she felt they might lead to control, but her short-term strategy would defeat her in the long run. The promotion to department head went to someone who was less experienced and younger but was someone the boss felt would work better with the clients and keep him better informed.

Nancy did not adequately discern the limits of her authority. She did not appreciate that her boss felt proprietary about the work in the department and that Nancy's decisions and performance directly affected her boss—the amount of business, the clients he had developed, and the product lines he had developed. She did not adequately appreciate that authority is delegated by one's superior and that her performance directly affected her boss's performance.

You need to work *through* your boss. Meet regularly. Keep the meetings brief and to the point. Make sure you come prepared, with an agenda. List the milestones achieved, things you are working on, pending decisions and choices, and problems and recommendations. Solicit your boss's feedback and advice, and really listen. Don't agree and then not follow through. Involve your boss, especially in the parts of your job that will make him or her shine or would otherwise be areas of vulnerability.

Determine to build your career, in part, through your excellent performance and also through your collaboration and support and teamwork with your boss and other key stakeholders. When appropriate, ask to be included at lunch with his or her peers or with influential others. Ask your boss to nominate you for corporate committees or for special assignments and task forces where you can gain some corporate visibility.

Joe had built an excellent relationship with his boss. In turn, Joe's reputation in the company grew through the good efforts of his boss, Mattie. Mattie had him appointed to important corporate committees, important accounts, important products, and significant new product development efforts. Mattie always felt she could rely on Joe to represent her interests, to keep her informed, to follow her counsel. But as Joe matured, developed his own network and his own corporate constituency, he became less and less part of Mattie's inbox and depended less on Mattie for help and direction. When Joe finally took an independent stand on an important policy issue that was directly contradictory to Mattie's, the relationship was damaged, and Mattie's support receded. Joe now had to be strong enough to stand on his own, as Mattie's peer, or to seek a new employer. He was no longer a part of Mattie's world, and that part of his career had ended. Within a few months Joe had joined a competitor. As long as you are dependent on your boss, you must stay close to his or her thinking. When you show independence, you had better be prepared to stand on your own.

In this chapter, we stressed the importance of working well with your boss and helping your boss to be a success. Pay attention to these points throughout your first year, especially in the first few months after you begin your new position. It is then that you have the opportunity to start off smoothly and build the impression of your value to your boss and organization. In Chapter 4 we turn our attention to one of the first elements necessary for having an impact on the organization: selecting, building, and developing your team.

Quick Reminders to Keep You on Track

- Most likely, the primary reason you were promoted was your boss's need to have someone to count on for a major area of responsibility. When you succeed, your boss succeeds.
- You won't be completely free to do as you wish; your decisions must fit into your boss's plans, goals, and style.
- Take time to assess each situation and evaluate your choice of solutions. A premature assessment or diagnosis of your situation may cause you to contradict yourself later, or it may result in embarrassment to you and your boss.
- Recall the example of William, the newly appointed director of a large mass transit authority. Your self-interest is linked to your boss's self-interest. Remember the reason you were hired.
- In your discussions with your boss before you were hired, you should have clarified your role and your boss's expectations of you. Understanding your role is critical to your success.
- It is important to contract with your boss or bosses. In doing so, two Just Promoted Leader Tools are especially helpful: Confirming Your Appointment Charter and Your 12-Month Road Map.
- Even though you think you understand your boss's expectations in general, don't assume that you have his or her mandate to take a particular action.
- Remember that you and your boss agreed about the pace of your work during your transition period. Provide your boss with updates on your progress as a reminder that you are achieving your mutually agreed upon goals.
- Make sure you have defined the "bottom line" with your boss. What is his or her measure of success?
- As we saw in one example, Lu helped Marsha be a star by discussing organizational issues with her and agreeing on decisions, by following through on the decisions that her boss supported and "reselling" those

that her boss still doubted, and by keeping disagreements with her boss private.

■ You can help your boss help you by being a part of your boss's mental inbox, meeting regularly, and soliciting your boss's feedback and paying attention to it.

■ Always remember why you were hired.

PART II

Achieving an Impact on the Organization

SELECTING, BUILDING, AND DEVELOPING YOUR WORK TEAM

Even the best strategies can have a short half-life. If you are going to bet on anything, bet on the best people.

—Larry Bossidy

I'm not looking for the best players. I'm looking for the right players.

—Herb Brooks, coach of the U.S. Ice Hockey Team that won the Olympic Gold Medal in 1980

Some of the most important decisions that you will make during your first year will be in selecting your leadership team. You then need to decide how to build teamwork, making sure your team and organization are effectively trained and developed. You will need to accomplish the following:

- Skillfully use a selection process and make good choices in establishing your work team.
- Make careful, sensitive, and sometimes difficult decisions about people in order to continuously raise the bar on your leadership and professional talent.
- Decide if certain people must be redeployed or terminated.
- Implement a strong team-building process.
- Train, coach, and develop your people.

In this chapter, there is useful information about the following:

- A conceptual model for selecting your leadership team
- Deciding whether to keep everyone

- Using the Team Integrity and Capability Grid to help you assess your team
- Using the Motivational Profile to understand and work well with your team members
- Building a strong work team and strong teamwork
- Training and developing your work team
- Leveraging your strengths while not overusing them

Some of your most important responsibilities during the 12 months following your appointment include selecting your leadership staff, molding this group into a productive and confident management force, and ensuring the best possible training and development for your people. This is a process that begins in the first days after your appointment and continues thereafter. Accomplishing this is sometimes easy—if the organization already has good people, good direction, and good results. Unfortunately, when moving up to your new leadership role, the situation is usually neither that simple nor that clear. The following scenarios illustrate this point.

FOUR TEAM-BUILDING SCENARIOS

Scenario A

Claudia has been named general counsel for a large financial services corporation. The opening resulted from the retirement of a highly respected veteran, who announced his retirement 12 months in advance of the effective date. With some reservation, the incumbent weakly recommended two of the three associate general counsels as his successors. The CEO decided to go to the outside. Claudia was selected from a major competitor, where she was second in command of the law department. She is bright, experienced, and highly qualified. As Claudia assumes her new responsibility, she has little information about the commitment and competence of the staff she has inherited.

- What should Claudia be thinking about?
- What type of plan should she develop in regard to her staff?
- What, how, and when should she communicate with her department?

Scenario B

Phyllis has been appointed dean of a college, one of five deans at a large, private university. Selected from within, she was just about everyone's obvious choice—she had an excellent intellectual and research record, was a fine administrator, and was well liked and respected. Her peers considered her a "safe choice." Phyllis's major dilemma is that she is not confident that the existing department heads can lead the college in achieving her vision for it. She has been a long-time friend and a close colleague of the tenured staff, which now reports to her. While professional and social ties are close, she realizes that about half the tenured faculty has become stagnant and overly comfortable. She faces many of the predictable problems of those selected to move up from among their professional peers. In a rather conservative and traditional environment, Phyllis has a different vision for the college than those with whom she has worked for many years.

- How would you handle this situation if you were Phyllis?
- What are some of her alternatives and likely consequences of these potential choices?
- What time frame would you establish for progress in achieving her vision?

Scenario C

Ron is a true entrepreneur. At 32, he is well-to-do, confident, and experienced, and he is about to start his own company. He has identified a niche in the communications industry and is preparing to exploit it commercially. Ron's strengths are accounting and marketing. He needs help in new product development, sales, and in day-to-day operations. His plan is to form a new company within 12 months. Financial backing exists; he has many contacts in the financial and marketing community. Ron is unsure how to proceed in selecting his top management team.

- What should Ron be thinking about?
- What type of expertise should he be seeking? What criteria should he establish for making his selections?
- What type of help is available to him in making these important choices?

Scenario D

Len has just been appointed CEO of a medium-sized health-care company. The company's sales and profits have waned over a five-year period. There are six major competitors, with several others gaining market share. Len's predecessor retired, but the rumor is that he was forced out.

Len was appointed from within the corporation. He had two other serious internal challengers for the position, both of whom are experienced and possess valuable skills and experience. The three have worked in a wide variety of management positions in the company. They have been with the company for periods ranging from 15 (Len) to 22 years. The competition for the top spot was spirited; each of the three felt uniquely qualified. As Len took over the CEO position, he was not sure how many scars remained, and he was not sure how the residual politics resulting from his selection would play out.

- How should Len proceed in selecting and building his management team?
- What factors should be most important? Least important?
- What time frame should he give himself?
- How can he best learn from the experiences of others?

A CONCEPTUAL MODEL FOR SELECTING YOUR LEADERSHIP TEAM

One of the clear findings of the *Good to Great* research conducted by Jim Collins and his research team relates specifically to selecting who will and will not be chosen to be on a leadership or executive team. Specifically, Collins strongly recommends that the team, or as much of the team as possible, be selected before beginning to determine the organization's strategy. In this way, you have your best people working on the strategy and plan that envision the future of the business or organization. Collins refers to this principle as "first who, then what."[1]

The approach you use to select and establish your leadership team will be based on a number of factors:

- Your organization's mission and the ultimate vision you hope to achieve. You need people who have the skills and attitudes to carry out the mission and your vision.
- The presence of people who have the ability to help you determine your organization's vision and key strategies.
- The work. Are the managers and leaders knowledgeable about the present and future work of the organization?

- The leadership talent that presently exists. Does the leadership group get the present job done effectively? How effectively will they create future strategy and achieve desired results? Is there talent you can trust? Can you rely on them, especially in unanticipated and stressful situations?
- How well the present leaders work together. Is this a group in which each individual has his or her own agenda or is it a team with synergy? Do the individuals have the potential for working cooperatively and creatively as your team?
- The talent outside your organization that could fill gaps or strengthen your team. Who is available to bring new perspective, knowledge, skills, and experiences to strengthen your leadership team? What would it cost to bring one or more new members into your team?
- The extent to which staff members will align themselves with you as you assume leadership of the team and organization. Do they want to be on your team?
- Your prediction of which leaders, managers, and staff members will choose to leave on their own during the next year. Anticipate some inevitable fallout whenever there is a formal shift of power. Whom might you need to replace in the short term? Remember, you may also need or choose to force some personnel changes.
- The organization's ability to attract talent based on its prestige, compensation, or opportunity. Will you need to take exceptional action to attract the talent that's needed? You may need to structure a job to be especially appealing or custom design a compensation package—with signing bonuses, benefits, or relocation arrangements—to get the talent you need.
- In some situations you many wish to offer a retention bonus to one or more very valuable leaders or subject matter experts.

Once these points have been considered, you can assess the organization's needs and begin to determine whether to retain or select new individuals for your management team. In this chapter you will be introduced to four Just Promoted Leader Tools. These include Tool 6, Selection Model for Determining What the Individual Brings to the Leadership Position; Tool 7, Team Integrity and Capability Grid; Tool 8, Developing a Motivational Profile for Each Team Member; and Tool 9, Strengths and Overused Strengths Exercise.

In assessing and selecting talent, first define the job and then determine whether the candidate measures up.

Defining the Role

Defining the job requires identifying four job elements:

1. Tasks performed on the job, including functional-technical tasks, and leadership abilities needed to do the role
2. Elements of emotional intelligence such as high levels of self-awareness, empathy, and teamwork needed to be effective
3. Expected performance level
4. Performance conditions

Tasks Performed in the Role

First review the functional-technical and leadership tasks performed on the job under review. Reviewing these tasks will give you a sense of the type of training, background, and experience a good candidate will need. In general, a position will have between 6 and 12 primary tasks, including leadership and management tasks and functional-technical and professional tasks.

Directly related to the tasks performed on the job are competencies needed to complete the tasks. Competencies are the skills, abilities, or talents required to perform the job tasks successfully. In what areas must the candidate demonstrate competence in the functional-technical and professional skills needed to do the work? What are the necessary leadership and management abilities?

There are often one to two *mission-critical competencies* for a position. These are essential competencies that any incumbent or candidate for a role must have from the first day in the position. An all-too-common mistake is to select someone who currently lacks capability in one or more mission-critical competencies. Usually, the rationale is that the person has most of what you are looking for and can develop the rest. This is almost always a very bad selection mistake. The reason a particular competency is mission critical is because it is vital to the role and will undoubtedly be extremely hard for someone to develop in the amount of time necessary for it to be consistently deployed in the role. In this regard, do not let hope and optimism overcome good common and business sense.

Examples of functional-technical competencies include these:

- Ability to perform a highly specialized task
- Ability to follow government regulations
- Ability to operate a particular piece of equipment or device for a specific outcome

- Ability to analyze and evaluate technical or scientific material of a particular field
- Ability to describe, analyze, and improve the work processes or procedures
- Ability to perform a particular financial or IT application

Examples of leadership and/or management competencies include these:

- Ability to set business and organizational vision, strategies, and goals
- Ability to create an operational plan to achieve goals
- Ability to implement an operational plan to achieve goals
- Ability to negotiate
- Ability to engage diverse staff members
- Ability to make an effective management presentation

Elements of Emotional Intelligence

Emotional intelligence competencies include selected *soft skills*: the self-awareness, values, and attitudes and orientation for positive outcomes needed for effective performance. You will need to determine which of these will be needed for the roles you must fill. Examples of the soft skills you may require include the following:

- Emotional self-awareness
- Empathy
- Emotional expression
- Interpersonal effectiveness
- Healthy trust practices such as tending to trust people until there is a specific reason not to
- Intuition
- Intentionality as it is related to initiative

Does the job require a self-starter who likes working on his or her own, or someone who prefers collaboration, teamwork, and communication?

Motivation

- Does the job require a highly motivated professional, or can the job be adequately performed by a less directed employee?
- What are the requirements for teamwork, cooperativeness, and the ability to work with others?

- Do you require a close working relationship for this position, or do you prefer to delegate at arm's length?
- How closely will you need someone to align himself or herself with the values and culture of the organization? Does the position require someone who will fit in closely, or can it (and you) tolerate independence from the organization's values and culture?
- What are the requirements in terms of working with diverse groups of employees? Across time zones? Nationalities?

Expected Performance Level

For each role requirement, analyze the level of competence required for the position you are assessing. Levels may range from awareness to partial performance to full and mature performance.

Describe the level of performance in concrete terms. For example, an accountant will require detailed, extensive knowledge of financial management systems, with many financial subskills. An operations manager may require only a general knowledge of financial systems but must have specific skills in order to manage his or her budget. A technician may need only to be aware that the finances get managed according to a budget, which determines the resources and equipment he or she gets.

Some managers and leaders may need to set organizational goals; others should be able to develop a clear and specific implementation plan to achieve those goals. Some operations employees should be aware of implementation plans and goals, and others should be able to perform the skills needed to implement the plan at very high levels. Your challenge as leader is to ensure that the people you select have, or are capable of developing, the level of skill required for the expected performance level.

Performance Conditions

Performance conditions include the environmental conditions affecting the job. These may include factors such as the following:

- *Travel.* Does the job require travel, including overnight stays? What percentage of time?
- *Workplace location.* Is the position at corporate headquarters, or is it at a manufacturing or research center? Is it a local assignment, or does it require relocation?

- *Working alone or on a team.* Does the job require teamwork or autonomy? To what degree?
- *Working independently or under supervision.* Does the job require delegation and independence, or does it require close coordination and cooperation with you?
- *Possible relocation, expatriation, or repatriation.* Is the role part of a career or experience path that will require one or more major personal or family moves over a specified period?

In summary, by analyzing each role to define all the aforementioned factors, you can begin to determine whether you currently have the leadership talent necessary to achieve your vision. Almost all organizations have professionals trained in human resources and talent management who can assist you. This may begin with your performing a detailed role or job analysis. This analysis can help you identify role requirements and select the leadership you need, and it will also serve as a basis for assessing training needs as well as setting performance expectations with your people.

Determining What the Individual Brings to the Position and Management Team

Having determined the functional-technical, leadership, and emotional intelligence competencies required for each job, as well as the expected level of performance and conditions under which a person will perform, you now can assess each person's ability to meet those requirements. (See Just Promoted Leader Tool 6, Selection Model for Determining What the Individual Brings to the Position and Leadership.)

One of the best predictors of future job performance is past performance. Even though experiences may not be identical, the core competencies needed for success in one situation can help predict success in other positions. Some managers and leaders feel that the core management competencies are of sufficient value and that a technical knowledge of the work is not essential to manage and lead effectively. Others argue that a leader who knows the basic work, the related technology, and procedures is better equipped for the job, gets up to speed more quickly, provides more decisive leadership, and makes better decisions. Either way, past performance is an excellent predictor of future performance.

Selection Model for Determining What the Individual Brings to the Position and Leadership

		Candidate's Demonstrated Abilities			
		1. Functional-Technical and Leadership Skills and Knowledge	2. Emotional Intelligence Competencies	3. Ability to Work at Designated Levels of Performance	4. Ability to Work under Designated Conditions of Performance
Job Responsibilities	A. The Role's Functional-Technical and Managerial Tasks and Competencies				
	B. The Role's Emotional Intelligence Competencies				
	C. The Role's Required Levels of Performance				
	D. The Role's Required Conditions of Performance				

Use multiple approaches to evaluate the present and potential members of your management team.

1. *Use interviews to assess their competencies, skills, and attitudes.* With the leaders already in place, use a variety of settings. Conduct formal individual interviews in your office; discuss an issue briefly in their office or the hallway; or take an informal coffee break or lunch together. Attend a meeting, or travel together. Get to know how individuals think and work.

When possible, also talk with your leaders in groups to compare their knowledge of issues, the quality of their thought, their group problem-solving abilities, and interpersonal skills.

The following sample questions will help you assess an individual's qualifications and attributes:

- What unique knowledge or skill does this person have that contributes to the strength of our management team?
- How has this person been utilized? What initiatives has she demonstrated in her present or previous positions?
- In what environment or assignments did this person thrive or not do so well?
- Of this person's top achievements, which ones relate to what we need? To our future needs?
- How does this person like to work? What is her work style? Does this person fit in with our culture and with my style?
- What are the strengths, weaknesses, and areas that this person is presently developing?
- How do this person's personal goals, desires, and aspirations match what we need?
- In summary, what does this person bring to the job and to our leadership team?

2. *Observe performance on the job.* See who gets the job done and who misses deadlines or has to redo work. Review documents the candidate has authored and programs he or she has developed. Observe internal candidates at staff meetings; watch them work with their staff at meetings and informally in the department. As you discuss work with the candidates' direct reports, be alert to suggestions of problems or strengths, and follow up on them.

3. *Ask people you trust to refer candidates to you.* Attend professional meetings, and talk to people with their own networks of strong candidates. Your colleagues and contacts outside the company have seen potential candidates in a variety of settings over a period of time. Ask for counsel and advice. Also ask people in your department to make recommendations. If you use this approach, be cautious in your discussions, particularly as they relate to incumbents. It is easy to start unnecessary rumors and create uneasiness in your organization.

When the requirements of the job match the employee's qualifications, you likely have a strong candidate. This is true when you select leaders, managers, and professional and support staff. As mentioned earlier, take particular care in choosing your administrative assistant. He or she should become one of your most important staff members and one of the individuals with whom you will work closest on your leadership team. Where gaps exist, assess a person's present and future ability to perform the job. Knowing the gaps allows for custom designing of learning and development plans for employees. Being aware of these gaps will also help you determine where to go within or outside your organization for help or where to make internal adjustments in work and managerial assignments.

Deciding Whether to Keep Everyone

On occasion, an incumbent does not rate well over an extended period of time and after thorough appraisals. If you are contemplating termination of an employee, seek the advice of legal counsel with expertise in employment and labor law and your organization's specialist in human resources and employee relations.

Today's laws can be complicated and laden with difficulties. However, you must not let your understandable reluctance to get involved in the legal and personal complications of a termination deter you from selecting, building, and developing the best management team possible. Do not keep marginal people because of sympathy or false hope. If you have a substantial doubt about an individual, mutually work on a performance improvement plan over a reasonable period of time. This plan could include a different work assignment that more closely matches a person's abilities. But it may be necessary to terminate individuals. Marginal performers will ultimately affect your own performance and your organization's success.

Sound ethics and good business practice should guide your treatment of employees who are barely holding on or those who should be terminated. Make every effort to see that the company helps them reestablish their careers elsewhere (including providing severance packages and outplacement counseling). These employees should be assisted in preserving their personal integrity, psychological well-being, and, within reason, their financial stability. Professional outplacement services and your human resources department can provide excellent guidance in structuring support services and equitable severance packages for terminated employees.

A very useful resource in helping to assess the relative value and managerial options relating to current team members is called the Team Integrity and Capability Grid, and it can be used with teams in various stages of team functioning and maturity. We see Just Promoted Leader Tool 7 as a valuable tool for use when leaders are transitioning into their new roles.

JUST PROMOTED LEADER TOOL 7
Team Integrity and Capability Grid

Constructing the Grid[2]

On the Team Integrity and Capability Grid, capability is the vertical axis, ranging from low to high, and integrity is the horizontal axis, also ranging from low to high.

Capability refers to a person's task-level credibility: How knowledgeable is she? What is the depth of her understanding? Does she add value in discussions? Do her ideas, concerns, and issues turn out to be valid? Is she good at what she does? If the answers are positive, she has high capability on the vertical scale.

Integrity refers to character, intention, and sincerity. Does she act on behalf of the company (high integrity) or only in her own self-interests (low integrity)? Does she purposely bias information, practice deception, sabotage, misrepresent data, tell you what you want to hear, or run a private power pocket? If you think she is an expert in a subject but you don't trust her motives or sincerity, you will be skeptical about the advice she provides.

On our grid, the horizontal scale of integrity (low or high) and the vertical scale of capability (low or high) form four quadrants into which you can sort the people in your organization. Let's look at people who fall into each of the four quadrants and focus on the implications for how you might view and manage them.

Note: *The Just Promoted Leader Tool 7 Team Integrity and Capability Grid is used with the kind permission of Dr. Martin Seldman.*

TEAM INTEGRITY AND CAPABILITY GRID

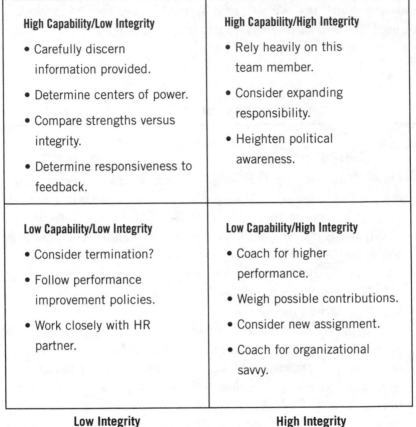

High Capability

High Capability/Low Integrity

- Carefully discern information provided.
- Determine centers of power.
- Compare strengths versus integrity.
- Determine responsiveness to feedback.

High Capability/High Integrity

- Rely heavily on this team member.
- Consider expanding responsibility.
- Heighten political awareness.

Low Capability

Low Capability/Low Integrity

- Consider termination?
- Follow performance improvement policies.
- Work closely with HR partner.

Low Capability/High Integrity

- Coach for higher performance.
- Weigh possible contributions.
- Consider new assignment.
- Coach for organizational savvy.

Low Integrity   **High Integrity**

The Team Integrity and Capability Grid is most useful once you know enough about your people to make informed assessments about them. In the grid below, privately place the names of your team members and possibly other essential personnel in your organization in the quadrant that you feel best represents their relative competency and trust assessment. This view of your team should aid you in determining the appropriate utilization or alternative actions to consider on a person-by-person basis.

TEAM INTEGRITY AND CAPABILITY GRID

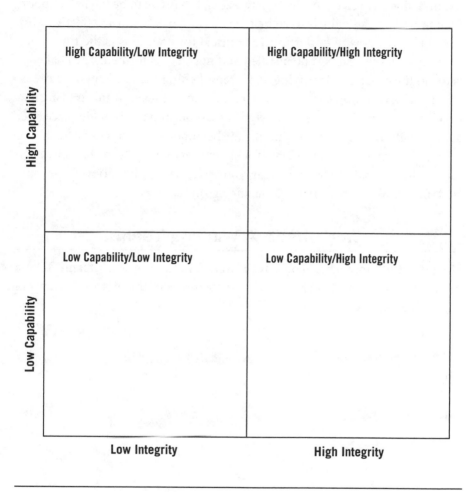

High Capability

High Capability/Low Integrity

High Capability/High Integrity

Low Capability/Low Integrity

Low Capability/High Integrity

Low Capability

Low Integrity

High Integrity

Building a Strong Leadership Team and Strong Teamwork

As you decide whom you want on your leadership team, you should also be thinking about how to shape them into a cohesive unit. Building a strong and committed work team is fundamental to the success of the newly promoted leader.

You have a great opportunity and challenge to transform the independent and sometimes disjointed efforts of professionals and managers into a well-oiled, dedicated, and directed leadership team. More than any other period, the first nine to twelve months of new leadership prove to be the most opportune period for individuals to come together and mesh into an effective work team. This window of opportunity is critical for you. This is the time when new expectations can best be instilled and new habits formed. The challenge is to aid the group in identifying and strengthening the fundamentals necessary to achieve a motivated, focused, and dedicated team. If this transformation is not well under way early in your transition, and if it is not in place after approximately nine to twelve months, it becomes increasingly difficult and sometimes impossible to effect. If a strong leadership team has not been formed by the end of your first year, your success may be seriously jeopardized. Let's look at what can be done during this early period.

Worksheet: A Winning Team

How do you know when you have a well-functioning work team? Take a moment to list 5 to 10 characteristics or attributes of the best work teams of which you have been a part.

1.

2.

3.

4.

5.

6.

7.

8.

9.

10.

The teams that have consciously worked on making themselves strong tend to be the backbone of their organization. They exhibit positive characteristics and become the framework to build high achievement. They consistently out-perform less focused, less energized work teams.

Common Characteristics of Well-Functioning Work Teams

An effective leader fosters a well-functioning work team. Characteristics include the following:

1. The team understands and supports the organization's vision, purpose, strategies, and goals. If the team is formed early enough, it can work collaboratively to actually help create or provide important input into the vision, strategies, and goals.
2. The team shares a small, focused, well-understood set of beliefs or values about such topics as how the organization should work, quality, customer service, and the organization's role in the community or world.
3. The team is aware of, and works to improve, its process and/or how it operates. This includes issues such as how decisions are made (generally by consensus); communication (open, direct); leadership styles (collaborative, situational); membership (flexible); and norms (shared).
4. Members listen well to each other and pull for each other.
5. Conflicts are managed constructively rather than stifled. People openly express feelings and ideas. Win-win conflict resolution is a norm, and both sides can accept the outcome.
6. Group decisions are often made through consensus, as opposed to a majority vote or minority power plays. As necessary, those with authority make tough decisions when consensus is not possible or a decision needs to be made now!
7. Assignments and responsibilities are clear and accepted by members.
8. The team effectively manages influences from external forces such as policies, regulations, procedures, politics, and constituents or customers.
9. The team gets results: high-quality products, in the shortest time frame possible, requiring the fewest wasted resources. High-performing work teams focus on results. Results are their constant target.

Team-Building Experiences

The purpose of team building is *to develop a more effective work team* to achieve the organization's vision and defined goals. In his practical book *Working in Teams,* James Shonk identifies five factors that influence team effectiveness:

1. *Environmental influences: The impact of influences outside the team*
   Policies and procedures: Corporate, client, government regulations
   Systems: Rewards and communications
   Organizational structure: The hierarchy
   Outside demands: Customers and government
2. *Goals: What the team is to accomplish*
   Clarity of goals
   Ownership and agreement of goals
   Specific and measurable goals
   Sharing of goals among team members
   No conflicts regarding purpose and goals
3. *Roles: Who does what*
   Understanding the need for clarity of roles
   Agreement and ownership of roles and responsibilities
4. *Processes: The way in which the team accomplishes work*
   Collaborative, win-win decision making
   Consensus seeking
   Open communications
   Efficient, effective meetings
   Collaborative, situational style of leadership
5. *Relationships: Quality of interaction*
   Expression and acceptance of feelings, attitudes, and emotions
   Open airing of interpersonal issues[3]

Shonk's model is helpful for understanding the key factors in team effectiveness, and it is useful for building organizations. You must act in ways that ensure strength in your team, and you must set up means to continuously evaluate your team's health and effectiveness.

More recently, Patrick Lencioni identified the five dysfunctions of a team. Each of these dysfunctions can be avoided with well-timed, high-impact team development efforts combined with excellent leadership. These dysfunctions can also be reduced or eliminated with professionally facilitated team-building processes:

1. Absence of trust
2. Fear of conflict
3. Lack of commitment
4. Avoidance of accountability
5. Inattention to results[4]

Team-building efforts take many forms, from a short, manager-led discussion about important team issues to a consultant-facilitated series of meetings or off-site "retreats." The overarching goal is usually the same: to become a more effective work team in order to achieve desired results and the ultimate vision of your organization. Leadership teams that work on improving themselves increase both their diagnostic and problem-solving abilities. Team members are conscious of their behavior in groups and are striving to improve their group performance. The team members' abilities to analyze and improve their team and the broader organizational and business processes are worked on and valued. We will visit the opportunities and challenges of organizational diagnostics and analysis in Chapters 6 and 7.

Situations in Which Team Building Is Most Useful

1. Formation of a new team:
   - New department, or a new district or region.
   - New offshoot function of an established department.
2. New people joining an existing group:
   - New director who wants to establish new work standards moves to an existing function and inherits a staff.
   - New team members join the organization, possibly with an existing leader in place.
   - Corporate reorganization results in new members or a reorganization of roles and responsibilities.
   - New school superintendent or school principal is selected.
   - Staff is expanded for a growing organization.
   - Staff is reduced, which results in a new management team.
3. Revitalization of a stagnant staff or a staff in trouble:
   - Corporate team is having no growth in its market share. The group is defensive, balky, and unhappy.
   - Staff is attempting to build new procedures and practices into the organization.
   - A staff that has performed inadequately or has not competed successfully is being rebuilt.
   - Staff is seeking to become more effective while under constraints of budget and potential staff reductions.
4. Building greater strength into an existing healthy team:
   - Twice yearly periodic "preventive health" team building to identify and remedy small problems.

- Creative problem-solving training designed to strengthen teamwork within the organization.
- Interdisciplinary work team meetings for three days off site to plan progress and to build teamwork.
- Annual retreat for the leadership team to decompress, keep each other informed, and to plan and problem solve.

5. Building strong teamwork between two or more functions:
    - Increasing collaboration between a marketing organization and the sales and research organizations.
    - Strengthening teamwork and coordination in horizontal, cross-functional processes such as those found in supply chains.
    - Building a stronger working relationship between the organization and a contractor or vendor responsible for fulfilling contract specifications.
    - Building trust and teamwork between a home office executive staff and management in regional branch offices.
    - Creating teamwork between a corporate headquarters of a global company and its regional or national teams in different parts of the world.

Guidelines for Team Development

You can learn much from other leaders' team development successes and failures. Here are some guidelines for success.

1. *Have a clear, simple goal for the team building.* Be clear about what your leadership team is to accomplish—that is, its *task*. Task objectives identify changes in what the organization does. The leadership team should be clear on what to develop, such as a new set of organizational goals, new products, a new organizational structure, a new set of standard operating procedures, a new image or ad campaign, a new technology, or a more efficient work flow. A leadership team of an insurance company recently worked on its accountability for key tasks as a way to improve how it develops new products.

2. *Solicit involvement and input before beginning.* Participation builds commitment. Get team members involved in planning the sessions. Get individual and group input on membership, where to get information, issues to address, communication, and decision making. Make sure you have developed

a climate of support for the process itself and how the process is to proceed. Do not start without the support of key opinion leaders.

3. *Create conditions for candid discussion, honesty, and objective feedback.* Model constructive behaviors that help establish a successful team. These positive behaviors focus on behavior and performance, not judgments and opinions. Be descriptive rather than judgmental. Describe the *effects* that behavior and practices are having on the organization rather than their motivation or rightness or wrongness. Keep things objective, based on observed performance and effects, not labels.

4. *Stay work oriented; use solid data.* Team building, because it requires analysis and feedback, is often seen as risky. People may get angry or hurt. They may let out their emotions. Whenever possible, use projects and responsibilities as the basis for team building rather than having the team analyze only communication and dynamics. People are more willing to try new approaches and behaviors within the context of work.

While focusing on work, the astute group leader can help the group members build awareness of their individual behavior and performance to strengthen their effectiveness.

5. *Don't expect changes overnight, but do expect changes.* Most of our organizational and personal behavior is ingrained. For most of us, change is difficult, even when we want it. Team building should be thought of as an ongoing process, not a single event. Your constant attention to the process of team building, modeling helpful behaviors, providing feedback to team members on their successes and failures, and maintaining positive expectations that teamwork will improve—all of these will help team members unlearn dysfunctional ways and foster improved teamwork.

6. *Do not raise expectations that cannot be met.* Credibility and trust, gained through a positive team-building process, are difficult to earn but easy to lose. Be careful of promises that are not directly under your control. Organizational and political constraints frequently are limiting.

Gary, an experienced manager, brought his leadership team together at a retreat every three months, determined that they would strengthen their working relationship and solve organizational problems. By the fourth retreat, they had strengthened personal working relationships, and they had addressed most of the issues they could affect. As they continued to meet, it became increasingly apparent that their organization's real problems were originating from the outside—inadequate resources, poor quality from their suppliers, and inefficiencies in their support organizations. They were powerless to improve these problem areas, and the team retreats only served to remind them of their powerlessness and their unmet expectations.

The major benefits that should be touted from the beginning of the process are better group and individual performance, ease of collaboration and communication, the pride of being part of a winning team, and preparation for future challenges.

To a large extent, organizational improvement is gained through role and goal clarification, better communication, and teamwork. Keep a realistic perspective. Team building will improve the things you can control, but you can't control everything. Here are typical responses that we have heard from individuals who have been involved in team building:

> "We understand each other's roles better."
> "Our purpose, goal, and direction are clearer."
> "We are clearer with one another. Most important, we learned how to listen to each other better."
> "I realize that *my* success is dependent on *our* success."
> "I realize the importance of group process, not only for our team but in my interaction with my customers."
> "We realized that there are many alternatives, not just one right answer."
> "My eyes really were opened around the issue of conflict. The principle of win-win problem solving is now a part of me."
> "We realized that teamwork helps us to compete better."
> "I am more accepting of others' points of view."
> "We learned not only to observe surface behavior but to see and hear several levels down."

7. *A time investment must be made.* Whether it is one meeting, a series of sessions, or an off-site retreat, people should think of the effort as an important investment in the organization's health. This is no trivial expenditure of time, effort, or money. It is not a holiday. Rather, it is important to leading your organization.

Strong organizations are characterized by leaders who develop strong managers and professionals. Strong leaders invest time in their people—in their training, their daily coaching, and their development. These are purposeful activities designed to create a better organization. All management, which is primarily the management of people, requires time—yours and theirs.

8. *An outcome of team building should be realistic solutions and action plans that are followed up, monitored, and rewarded.* A poster on an office wall read, "When all is said and done, there is usually much more said than done." Team building means commitment to keeping the best that we have and improving areas that need to change. This requires responsibilities that are "owned" by the team and supported by a commitment to review and reward progress. A manufacturing leadership team created several effective ways to build on a three-day, off-site, team-building retreat that was critical to turning that organization around. They agreed to the following:

Each participant included at least one team effectiveness objective as part of his or her annual personal performance plans.

At least 15 minutes were spent during every staff meeting discussing recent behaviors that built on the team effectiveness retreat.

The management team agreed to a follow-up meeting in six months. For part of the meeting, the members would review group and individual team progress related to teamwork objectives established at the original team-building meeting.

The director's behaviors and practices were internalized by his staff. In turn, each of the director's immediate reports replicated a similar process within their own work units. This leadership team went from having little or no time to consider how to operate, to creating a period during which to experiment with new team behaviors. Today this group has become a well-functioning team that has helped the organization achieve its business goals. The leader of this team kept a small frame on his desk with a favorite motto of former president Ronald Reagan. It read: *It can be done.* This is, in fact, precisely the spirit by which he led his team from his first day.

9. *When feasible, enlist the aid of a skilled group and organizational consultant to facilitate the team-building process.* Over the last several decades, the field of organizational development has established itself as a valuable tool

for leaders. Some team-building efforts can be led by the organization's leader, and occasionally, a task force composed of a cross-section within a management group can conduct its own team building. However, it is often wise to enlist the help of an experienced organizational consultant to add structure and an unbiased eye to the process. In addition to infusing expertise, an internal or external consultant will free the leader in charge to fully participate with his or her team in the development activities.

GETTING THE MOST FROM YOUR PEOPLE

"Know your people." This is a decades old adage that is as true today as it was many years ago. Despite the advent of technology to aid in so many work and leadership processes, what always ends up being one of the most critical factors for individuals in high-performance teams is the extent to which they are strongly motivated and engaged in their role and responsibilities. Unfortunately, according to a 2010 report published by the Conference Board, U.S. employee satisfaction, which is closely linked to measures of employee engagement, is at the lowest level it has been since their study began in 1987. Only 45.3 percent of Americans today say that they are satisfied with their job, down from 61.1 in 1987, the first year the study was conducted.[5] A vital role of leaders at any stage in their career is to create the conditions for high levels of motivation and engagement for those on their team and in the broader organization. There is no time when this is more important than during the first 12 months when a leader assumes new team and organizational responsibility.

Skillfully coaching and spending individual time with your team members to understand what really lights their fire at work can pay off many times over. We call this effort to really understand your people "creating Motivational Profiles." One of the most frequently asked questions in this regard is, "What do I really need to know about my people to be the best motivational coach with my people?" This tool helps you deal with this question in a very practical way.

Developing a Motivational Profile for Each Team Member

Motivational Profile: A Method of Personalizing Motivational Coaching

Instructions

This Motivational Profile worksheet is used by managers or team leaders as a way to creatively think about how to establish the conditions for high motivation for their associates.

Use one worksheet per associate. Fill in whatever information you can about the associate upon whom you are focusing. Just completing this step can serve as a quick diagnostic to determine how much you know about this person. Provide a copy of this template to each of your team members and ask them to also prepare for a discussion with you. Consider discussing some or all of the incomplete topics with your associate in order to work with him or her more effectively.

Note: The "deeply embedded life interest question" refers to the article "Job Sculpting: The Art of Retaining Your Best People" by Timothy Butler and James Waldroop (*Harvard Business Review*, September–October 1999). It is recommended that you read this article.

Questions

Associate name: _____   Date: _____

- What are your key competencies and/or abilities?
- What are your personal and professional goals and aspirations?
- What development opportunities interest you?
- What professional values do you possess that could be utilized?
- Do you have any concerns and/or personal constraints—for example, start or end of workdays?
- What are your deeply embedded life interests?
- If you could craft or sculpt your role, what would you like to add, change, or delete from your responsibilities, if possible?
- Is there anything that you would like to change about the way we work together?

TRAINING AND DEVELOPING YOUR WORK TEAM
Rationale

In this chapter, we have looked at issues relating to the selection of your work team and team building. A third pillar needs to be added consisting of training, development, and coaching your people.

Individual and departmental training and development needs should have surfaced as a result of the diagnostic work that you began as you took over your new position. These needs may be functional-technical or managerial or leadership in nature. Functional-technical needs relate to the content or expertise of the work itself (for example, sales training, upgrading financial or computer skills, and increasing scientific knowledge to a state-of-the-art level). Managerial or leadership training may include topics such as managing performance, employment and selection, planning, delegation, motivation and engagement, organizing work flow, and time management. All training is designed to improve one or more of the following:

1. Knowledge of information, procedures, principles: What people need to know
2. Skills: What people actually do to apply knowledge
3. Attitudes and feelings about things and people: The way people approach their work and their colleagues

Move quickly to establish people development as a primary organizational value. During the first months on the job, you should have signaled the importance of good talent selection, orientation, training, and development.

Context for Your Learning and Development Initiatives

1. You are setting new, often higher expectations for people and their work.
2. New employees may be entering the organization. They will need to understand the mission, the functions, services or products, and day-to-day operating procedures.
3. Rapid change in work means today's skills will be quickly outdated. Learning must be timely and continuous. New operating procedures and skills are the norm.
4. Competition is ever increasing. Developing skilled contributors and managers is a key competitive strategy.

5. Organizations will have underutilized, marginally performing, or problem employees. In work units, there can be gains of at least 10 percent in individual employee performance given skillful job matching, training, coaching, and overall leadership. The previous director of a major department was convinced that he had to have a staff increase of 15 percent just to "stay above water." When replaced, the new director not only did not increase staff but also, in concert with the employees, set higher performance standards for each position in the department. This effort was part of an overall performance improvement program that the new director initiated and led, a program she had begun during the three months after moving up to her new post.

Learning and Development Guidelines

Both employees and those in management and leadership roles should have learning and development expectations. Some key ones are as follows:

1. The primary responsibility for the employee's professional development always rests with the individual. Individuals must take the initiative to identify and request development and activities, feedback, and appraisals from which they can grow. Make clear to them in written policies and, most importantly, in your interactions that the people who report to you have the primary responsibility to identify their own strengths and weaknesses and determine their developmental goals and activities. Foster initiative and responsibility.

2. You have the following minimum expectations of employees:
   - Solid job performance in present assignments.
   - Commitment to ongoing professional development and assessment, including expansion of existing strengths or remediation of performance problems.
   - Networking and gaining knowledge of the needs of one's own organization, as well as other organizational functions. As appropriate, getting experience in areas outside of the employees' primary responsibilities. Substantial progress toward completing the organization's formal training curriculum or relevant external training is a foundation for further development.

3. The secondary responsibility for professional development rests with the employee's immediate manager, who must provide at least the following:

- Joint agreement with the employee on establishing developmental goals and support for a professional development plan.
- Candid discussions of the individual's performance and career potential.
- Ongoing coaching and feedback.

Examples of Learning and Development

Learning and development activities come in a variety of formats, including the following:

1. On-the-job coaching from a manager or senior coworker who is a master or mentor (This is sometimes most useful in a just-in-time mode.)
2. Job rotation into a job where a new skill must be learned and practiced
3. Project teams and special assignments that help the employee apply new skills and knowledge
4. Replacement assignments during vacations, illnesses, and so on
5. Lateral transfers to practice different skill sets
6. University executive education programs
7. Functional-technical skills training
8. Management or leadership training
9. Opportunities to make presentations that require research or analysis
10. Attendance and involvement in department, division, and staff meetings
11. Serving as leader-teacher, instructor, conference leader, or trainer
12. Coaching from specialists in the organization
13. Self-study of bulletins, reports, and printed material
14. Attendance at selected conferences, symposia, and workshops
15. Participation in meetings of professional and technical societies
16. Personal coaching
17. University course attendance, study groups, and in-house courses
18. Operating responsibility for a new function or task to practice new skills
19. Social Web 2.0 learning opportunities
20. Just-in-time access to knowledge resource centers
21. Podcast and webinar opportunities
22. Learning in the moment through accessing social networks and communities of practice

Coaching

Coaching is a powerful, flexible approach to elicit your employee's self-assessment, which, when combined with the manager's feedback, results in mutual understanding, commitment to mutually accepted goals, and a specific plan of action for achieving the goals.

Coaching encourages continuous improvement and reinforces solid work performance. It can also be a terrific tool for improving specific areas. Because coaching skills open communications and ensure ongoing feedback, employees generally value the approach. The open flow of communication reduces the tension of more formal performance reviews because there are no surprises. Employees know where they stand on a daily basis. Coaching is one of the most useful tools in building the helping relationships and empowering behaviors that improve job performance. From the many models for coaching that we have seen used in organizations, we have regularly utilized and have taught others the following six-step process. Its strengths are simplicity, ease of use, and consistently positive results.

The Coaching Process

1. *Establish climate.* Mutually identify specific or discrete performance objectives to meet, and define the performance to be discussed.
2. *Attain the employee's self-assessment.* The employee should discuss his or her performance with the manager including the following:
   - What have I done that I feel has contributed to the achievement of my own, or department, performance goals and/or standards?
   - What, if anything, have I done that I could change or do differently to achieve my performance goals and/or standards?
   - If I would change anything, how would I go about addressing my performance goals and/or standards differently?
   - How can my manager best help me?
3. *Provide feedback.* Supplement, correct, or credit performance cited in the employee's self-assessment. Reach a mutual understanding of any differences.
4. *Confirm agreement of necessary performance changes.* Explore alternatives to support changes, and redefine or restate expected performance levels.
5. *Establish an action plan.* With the employee, plan the developmental activities to help him or her reach the objectives.

6. *Plan for monitoring and review of performance.* The employee's developmental progress should be monitored on an ongoing, planned basis, with frequent and open opportunity for feedback and coaching.

If performed well, coaching should be a positive experience. It should strengthen the working relationship between the leader and employee and become a natural part of your repertoire of management and leadership skills and behaviors.

SEVERAL IMPORTANT POINTS YOU SHOULD KNOW ABOUT YOUR OWN LEADERSHIP AND PROFESSIONAL STRENGTHS

Key Principle
You should leverage your strengths while not overusing your strengths.

In the spirit of your own ongoing professional and leadership development, there several points you should know about your strengths:

1. Every person has his or her own strengths profile. We each have several top leadership and functional-technical strengths. Some may come naturally to us, and we have probably worked hard to develop them.
2. Strengths serve us in many ways. They are the main source of our professional success, and they have helped us get over some of our hardest times and challenges.
3. In many ways, strengths are like habits. We use them "automatically." We are unconsciously competent in these areas. We barely have to think about accessing these strengths when we need them.
4. Every strength has a potential "shadow side." For example, strong decision making taken to excess is autocratic and insular in nature. A results-oriented person can become overly demanding and abrasive. Concern for others can become overly "people process oriented" with everything needing to be decided through consensus. Some with superb functional-technical skills can become too narrow and see things with a limited perspective and may not be effective working in cross-functional teams.

5. Every strength can be overused, and most frequently this occurs during periods of stress, pressure, and anxiety. There are many times during the first year of a leader's new role when stress, pressure, and anxiety are present, and sometimes they can be dominating feelings.
6. Overused strengths are almost always personal blind spots. Others usually experience the symptoms of the overused strengths well before the leaders themselves do.
7. Awareness and "early warning systems" are mitigating factors. Understanding the overused strengths concept is essential to preventing problems. Overused strengths are potential career derailing factors. This behavioral pattern is a dangerous one because it is like an insidious disease. It can be a quiet killer. Once aware, the leader can be sensitive to the likely situations in which his or her strengths might be overused and how people react when they are.

JUST PROMOTED LEADER TOOL 9
Strengths and Overused Strengths Exercise

List Your Top 3 Strengths (For Example, Functional-Technical, Managerial or Leadership, or Intra- or Interpersonal)	How (a) You and (b) the Organization Benefit When You Use the Strength Well	Symptoms That the Strength Is Being Overused
1.		
2.		
3.		

- What are your top strengths that you can leverage as you navigate your leadership transition?

- How might these strengths be overused? Under what conditions do you need to be most alert?
- What can you do to alert yourself that you are starting to overuse your strengths?
- How can you use this knowledge in your role as a leader-coach of your team?

SUMMARY

In this chapter, we have looked at the importance of selecting, building, training, and developing your leadership team and work unit. Doing this well is among your most important activities during your first year as a leader. To a large extent, people selection and their development will determine the pace of bottom-line improvement and overall team effectiveness. We have also introduced the concept of overused strengths and how you can avoid inadvertently getting yourself into performance trouble by being aware of how your top strengths can also become a problem for you.

Quick Reminders to Keep You on Track

- Several of your most important responsibilities during the 12 months following your appointment include selecting your leadership staff, molding this group into a highly productive and confident leadership team, and making available the best possible training and development opportunities for your people.
- The choice of your team members is the first pillar of your team's effectiveness. The approach you use to establish your team will be based on a number of factors, including these:
  1. Your organization's mission and the ultimate vision you hope to achieve
  2. The type of work that exists and that will likely exist in the future
  3. The present type and variety of management and leadership talent
  4. Your assessment of how the present staff members work together
  5. The talent outside your organization that could fill gaps in or strengthen your team

6. Your evaluation of the extent to which staff members have or will align themselves with you as leader of the function
7. Your prediction of which managers and staff members will choose to leave on their own during the next year, possibly because they didn't get your job or other important positions
8. The organization's ability to attract talent based on its prestige, compensation, or opportunities

- Having considered the preceding points, you can assess the organization's needs for key leaders and individual contributors and begin to determine whether to retain or select new individuals for your management team. Using the Team Integrity and Capability Grid tool can be very helpful.
- Remember that selecting talent is usually the single most important thing you can do to create a strong organization.
- The selection process should begin with a detailed definition of the job, its requirements, and its key factors necessary for success.
- You must determine what incumbents and candidates for positions bring to the position and leadership team when compared to the key factors necessary for success. Often a difficult decision to make once you have started in your new position is, "Should I keep everyone?" If you decide to terminate someone, remember that you have ethical and legal responsibilities that you should review carefully with legal counsel and your human resources partner.
- If you do decide to terminate one or more people, try to preserve their integrity and self-concept. Whenever possible, provide outplacement counseling and a generous severance package. Such treatment helps the people, but it also communicates a lot about you to others.
- You will not only need to select your leadership team but you will also need to help the members of your team work well with each other. This is a second pillar of your team's effectiveness.
- Certain factors characterize well-functioning work teams. These factors can become goals for team-building efforts. You might want to have a skilled organizational development professional or external consultant work with you in your team-building efforts.
- There are situations in which team building is most meaningful. This is especially true when there has been an absence of teamwork or when the organization has undergone considerable change.

- A third pillar of your team's effectiveness is the training, development, and coaching of your people. There are many approaches to this responsibility, and they need to be carefully chosen and tailored to the individual learning and development needs and aspirations of the team members.
- Utilize the Motivational Profile to help create the ideal work and development conditions for each of your direct reports.
- You should leverage your strengths while not overusing them.

BEGINNING TO CRAFT YOUR VISION AND DIRECTION

The best way to predict the future is to create it.

—Peter Drucker

If you have an important point to make, don't try to be subtle or clever. Use a pile driver. Hit the point once. Then come back and hit it again. Then hit it a third time—a tremendous whack.

—Winston Churchill

Creating a "fire in your belly" mental picture of what your organization is capable of becoming and its reason for being is essential for you and your people. You will need to accomplish the following:

- Understand and help others understand the concepts of organizational vision, mission, and values. The current synonym for the term *mission* is "purpose" or the phrase "organizational purpose."
- Develop your vision, mission, and set of organizational values for the organization.
- Skillfully involve others in helping you create and carry out the organization's vision, purpose, and values.
- Be able to communicate enthusiastically your organization's vision, purpose, and values.
- Become a role model of your organization's vision, purpose, and values through consistent and reinforcing actions.

In this chapter, there is useful information about the following:

- The concepts of organizational vision, mission, and values
- Seeding your vision, mission, and values into your organization

- The importance of the group's quest for vision, mission, and values
- Key planks in your platform
- Acting consistently: Developing good public relations for your positions
- Questions to consider in your development of the organization's vision, mission, and values

CATERPILLARS AND SPOTLIGHTS: THE CONCEPT OF ORGANIZATIONAL VISION

Processionary caterpillars feed upon pine needles. They move through the trees in a long procession, one leading and the others following, each with his eyes half closed and his head snugly fitted against the rear extremity of his predecessor. Jean-Henri Fabre, the great French naturalist, patiently experimenting with a group of the caterpillars, finally enticed them to the rim of a large flower pot, where he succeeded in getting the first one connected up with the last one, thus forming a complete circle, which started moving around in a procession that had neither beginning nor end.

The naturalist expected that after a while they would catch on to the joke, get tired of their useless march, and start off in some new direction. But not so.

Through sheer force of habit, the living, creeping circle kept moving around the rim of the pot—around and around, keeping the same relentless pace for seven days and seven nights—and it would doubtlessly have continued longer had it not been for sheer exhaustion and ultimate starvation. Incidentally, an ample supply of food was close at hand and plainly visible, but it was outside the range of the circle so they continued along the beaten path.

They were following their instinct . . . habit . . . custom . . . tradition . . . past experience . . . "standard practice" . . . or whatever you may choose to call it, but they were following blindly. They mistook activity for accomplishment. They meant well, but they didn't achieve anything.[1]

Like processionary caterpillars, many organizations seem to go in circles; they lack overall direction, purpose, meaning, and a true sense of their mission, values, and future. These organizations rarely innovate and are almost always followers in their industries.

The caterpillar analogy can help us understand aspects of individual behavior at work too. Under conditions where direction, common work values, goals, and accountability are lacking, employees generally will do what they must to get by. A type of "group think" characterized by a "we versus they" and "we've always done it that way" mediocrity takes over. Like processionary caterpillars, habit, embedded traditions, and practices become a way of life. Energy is low, and creativity and cooperation are lacking.

Mission statements and vision statements are developed for both employees and customers. A *mission statement*, often called a *purpose statement*, describes an organization's core purpose, identity, and business principles. A *vision statement* is a broad aspirational picture of the future. Both mission statements and vision statements can provide focus and energy when used to drive the organization forward. Organizational *values* are deeply intertwined with vision and purpose. Usually few in number, often three or four, values support the aspirations of an organization's vision and its reason for being described by its mission or purpose statement. Together, vision, mission or purpose, and values make up an organization's belief system.

We cannot emphasize strongly enough that if vision, purpose, and values are simply the products of your thinking and writing rather than the products of your actions, they inevitably will become framed hallway and conference room artifacts of your failed attempts to provide leadership direction. To avoid that outcome, these guideposts need to be developed by you and your team with abundant input from others in your function or broader organization. And then they must be modeled and acted upon by you, your team, other leaders, and employees throughout the organization. Modeled in this way—day after day, week after week, and month after month—your culture, guided by important aspirations, purpose, and values, will begin to form and be regularly reinforced.

Vision, purpose, and values become instilled in an organization when people squint their eyes to look outside themselves, put aside individual interests, and capture what they want their organization to achieve and be like. Having a widely accepted organizational vision can make a real difference. When committed leadership with a strong belief system of the future makes itself felt, great things can begin to happen. People quickly develop a clear understanding of what is most important to the organization. Strong and consistent commitment to common vision, purpose, and values has an industrial-strength impact on individuals and the team or organization as a whole.

The combination of vision, purpose, and values works like spotlights on a runway. It points in a direction and can guide people to a desired endpoint. Through word and deed, strong leaders who are passionate about their organization's beliefs and who model what is important obtain needed resources, hold people accountable, and recognize and reward people appropriately when their actions and contributions are aligned with their organization's or team's vision and purpose. Importantly, they enlist the help and support of employees at all levels in the organization. Employees realize that they are part of the action, that what is good for the organization can be good for them as well.

Employees who have the opportunity to work with visionary, purpose-centered leaders begin to share a similar notion of where the organization is heading and what success means for them and others. They tie their success to that of the organization. While individual responsibilities and accountabilities exist, the language of work becomes spiced with the words *we* and *our* as described in Chapter 2. People begin to "own" problems and work together for excellent solutions.

Most importantly, employees feel that what they do matters and that their efforts contribute to something worthwhile and valuable. They feel that they can affect the course of events, and they take responsibility to see that the right things happen. Employees find that they enjoy sharing in a coordinated, aligned work effort with common purpose. The feeling is similar to an orchestra playing in beautiful harmony or an athletic team executing their plays as they were designed. This is a form of "possibility thinking," and it is described beautifully in the book entitled *The Art of Possibility* written by Rosamund and Ben Zander.[2] Ben Zander is the conductor of the Boston Philharmonic Orchestra, and he is a frequent speaker on leadership and organization topics. Shared purpose—a vision of what an organization is capable of becoming—can be a powerful and positive force. Some employees have trouble describing what a vision is, but they all know when it's there.

Healthy, high-achieving organizations have their heart and soul in their vision and purpose. Used in this sense, the term *organizational vision* has been an important part of leadership lexicon. The idea of creating organizational vision is not new. The importance of pulling together for a deeply felt common purpose and sense of the future has served nations, organizations, and humanitarian causes for many years. Revolutions in the cause of freedom that resulted in democracies in the United States, Poland, and South Africa are but three examples. Unified efforts across many scientific communities around the world to find the cause of, prevent, and cure deadly infectious diseases such as small pox, polio, and HIV/AIDS resulted from leadership with deeply committed vision and purpose. President John Kennedy challenged the United States in the race for space by creating the vision of landing a man on the moon within the decade of the 1960s. This image galvanized not only the scientific community but the whole country. President Ronald Reagan, who was a master communicator, captured the spirit and the symbolism of freedom in his famous and often-quoted speech at the Berlin Wall: "Mr. Gorbachev, tear down this [Berlin] Wall." Reagan's speech was a very significant step in the final actions that resulted in creating a free, reunited Germany.

It is *power*—the power of people who feel important and involved, of people and organizations being all that they can be—that makes visionary and purpose-centered leaders so valuable. In areas as different as business, education, politics, and sports, visionary and purpose-centered leaders have demonstrated an ability to unify and drive their organizations to greater heights by unleashing the energy and drive of their people. Thomas J. Watson led the building of IBM. Bill Gates envisioned easy-to-use computers and applications in every home and classroom and later, with his wife, Melinda, established a foundation whose purpose it is to eradicate disease in underdeveloped countries. So powerful is the vision and purpose of the Bill and Melinda Gates Foundation that Warren Buffett, arguably the most successful and discriminating of the world's large investors, has begun an extended process that will donate much of his life savings and estate to the Gates Foundation. Steven Jobs is legendary for his visionary leadership of Apple, which has developed such iconic products as the iPod, iPhone, iPad, and the Mac computer. Roosevelt's and Churchill's combined efforts to preserve freedom in the 1940s and Martin Luther King's efforts to ensure civil rights during the 1950s and 1960s are famous examples of visionary leadership. Sports dynasties were established in New York, Boston, and San Francisco by John McGraw, Joe Torre, Red Auerbach, and Bill Walsh, all of whom practiced visionary and purpose-centered leadership. Their successes were due in large part to the motivation and synergy of athletes' working together to achieve great goals.

As we move through this century, an increasing number of organizations of all kinds strive to identify and achieve their vision, mission and purpose, and core values. Some organizations emphasize their vision, others stress their mission and purpose, and yet others, their values. Some organizations emphasize all three. Some examples follow.

IBM's Vision

The vision statement of International Business Machines (IBM) has changed somewhat through the years. Its mission and vision statement is this:

> At IBM, we strive to lead in the invention, development, and manufacture of the industry's most advanced information technologies, including computer systems, software, storage systems, and microelectronics. We translate these advanced technologies into value for our customers through our professional solutions, services, and consulting businesses worldwide.[3]

Southwest Airlines' Mission

> The mission of Southwest Airlines is dedication to the highest quality of Customer Service delivered with a sense of warmth, friendliness, individual pride, and Company Spirit.

> ### To Our Employees
> We are committed to provide our Employees a stable work environment with equal opportunity for learning and personal growth. Creativity and innovation are encouraged for improving the effectiveness of Southwest Airlines. Above all, Employees will be provided the same concern, respect, and caring attitude within the organization that they are expected to share externally with every Southwest Customer.[4]

Colgate's Core Values

> Our three fundamental values—Caring, Global Teamwork, and Continuous Improvement—are part of everything we do. They are the foundation for our business strategy and are reflected in every aspect of our work life.

> ### Caring
> The Company cares about people: Colgate people, customers, shareholders, and business partners. Colgate is committed to act with compassion, integrity, honesty, and high ethics in all situations, to listen with respect to others and to value differences. The Company is also committed to protect the global environment, to enhance the communities where Colgate people live and work, and to be compliant with government laws and regulations.

Global Teamwork

All Colgate people are part of a global team, committed to working together across countries and throughout the world. Only by sharing ideas, technologies, and talents can the Company achieve and sustain profitable growth.

Continuous Improvement

Colgate is committed to getting better every day in all it does, as individuals and as teams. By better understanding consumers' and customers' expectations and continuously working to innovate and improve products, services, and processes, Colgate will "become the best."[5]

McKinsey & Company

The McKinsey Group describes its purpose and values in the following way:

What We Believe

We believe we will be successful if our clients are successful.

We believe that solving the hardest problems requires the best people. We believe that the best people will be drawn to the opportunity to work on the hardest problems. We build our firm around that belief. We believe you can't do one without the other. We believe these two parts of our mission reinforce each other and make our firm strong and enduring.

We believe in professionalism. For us this means to always:

- *Put the client's interest ahead of our own. This means we deliver more value than expected. It doesn't mean doing whatever the client asks.*
- *Behave as professionals. Uphold absolute integrity. Show respect to local custom and culture, as long as we don't compromise our integrity.*
- *Deliver the best of our firm to every client as cost effectively as we can. We expect that our people spend clients' and our firm's resources as if their own resources were at stake.*[6]

The Mission and Values of Amgen, a California-Based Biotechnology Company

Our Mission and Values

Amgen strives to serve patients by transforming the promise of science and biotechnology into therapies that have the power to restore health or even save lives. In everything we do, we aim to fulfill our mission to serve patients. And every step of the way, we are guided by the values that define us.

Our Mission: *To serve patients*

Our Values: *Be science-based*
                        Compete intensely and win
                        Create value for patients, staff, and stockholders
                        Be ethical
                        Trust and respect each other
                        Ensure quality
                        Work in teams
                        Collaborate, communicate, and be accountable[7]

Visions can also change over time as the organization matures and changes. Purpose and core values generally change much less frequently, if at all. Twenty years ago Apple Computer staked its future on its vision of making teaching and learning come alive in classrooms through exciting, highly interactive, computer-based learning. Apple's vision of the "Learning Society" was described in a speech by Dr. Bernard Gifford, Apple's vice president: "As a way of beginning, let me say that most educators seem to know that Apple's deepest roots are in education and that we've always been the leader in computer technology for education. What's less well known is the amount and intensity of internal conversation we have about teaching and learning, because this isn't a business for us. It's a passion!"[8]

Apple's current vision statement is much broader in nature: "To make a contribution to the world by making tools for the mind that advance humankind." This vision now fits Apple's broad reach into computers, telecommunications, and electronics.[9]

SEEDING YOUR VISION INTO YOUR ORGANIZATION

Even during your first day's remarks, you started to seed the early concept of your vision or possibly your deeply held points of view or perspectives that could serve as directional indicators of vision, purpose, and values. In generalized terms, you described your view of what the organization is capable of becoming. You talked about working *as a team*, shifting emphasis from *I* to *we,* the upcoming organizational self-diagnosis, and the goals of shared self-improvement. Determining, seeding, and beginning to establish your vision for the organization is a major objective during your initial weeks and months in your new position, and you need the involvement of others to accomplish these important objectives.

As you got to know your staff and conducted the early familiarization interviews and discussions, you asked individuals to share with you how they'd improve or contribute to a higher-performing organization. You shared with them your determination to improve the organization through mutual team effort.

At subsequent executive team meetings, department meetings, team meetings, and informal conversations with employees, continue to work on establishing the belief system of your team or organization—a vision and the purpose and values of what the organization can become. Talk about the key goals of the organization as well as problem-solving task forces and cross-functional task forces or teams. Begin to seek opportunities for growth and improvement. Ask people how they might solve particular problems or identify business opportunities. Invite their participation in the process. Invite others to share, broaden, or further develop your vision. Ask people to work with you in shaping thoughts and hope into a dynamic view of the future.

Ask your team to help make it happen. Share the responsibility for ensuring the function's success. Share your excitement, and ask people to volunteer their ideas with you and others. Affirm that these ideas will help create a highly motivating and inspiring view of the future. Vision, purpose, and meaning evoke passion and energy. Visioning should become a deeply felt, strongly valued process in which all of the organization can participate.

This sense of purpose is characterized by ideas and beliefs that bind people's efforts and energies. You must generate commitment to a vision. Such commitment is necessary because ongoing work must get done, and the process of identifying or working toward a vision will make extra demands on the organization's time and energy.

Three principles will help mold the organization's commitment to the process:

1. *People must believe that their commitment will simultaneously result in benefits to the organization and to themselves.* People must be able to identify themselves with a different, better, possibly broader view of the future. The

core of the vision can be generated by you, or it can evolve out of a group's work. Employees must believe that working together is genuine and that their efforts will make a difference between today's reality and tomorrow's growth or improvements. For others to own the process, they must believe that they are real and empowered participants.

Know in advance that you will encounter resistance from some people. For example, Coreen's often-expressed doubts had by now become tiresome to her colleagues: "But how will I get my regular work done?" "But do we really have the expertise to be doing this ourselves?" "But are we really committed to following through on the project?" "But do we have top management's approval to make some changes?" It was difficult to tell whether Coreen's concerns were her way of saying "I want some attention" or "I want to be consulted" or "There are some real problems here" or "I'm not going to like this work."

Alan, who felt he should have received your promotion, was passive-aggressive. He went along, verbally agreeing but not actively participating. Instead of making contributions at meetings, he made sarcastic asides. Asked for his opinion, he passed or made a humorous comment to deflect a serious response. His participation was only half-hearted, with no real sense of commitment or purpose.

You may want to reduce Alan's visibility because he puts a damper on the organization's commitment to your values of shared process and goals. You'd like to isolate him from power and control so you can ignore him. However, you know that won't work. Everyone will know why you have isolated him, even if they don't talk with you about it. More forceful action is sometimes warranted.

Coreen's boss met with her privately, gave her some descriptive feedback about her negative behavior, described how it annoyed him, described its effects on others, and described for her the more positive behaviors he'd like to see. He gave her some time to think about it, and he scheduled a follow-up meeting in about four weeks. The result was a change in her behavior. She showed her boss she really wanted to be a part of the group, and the future. Alan's case remained troublesome; he became increasingly isolated, and the problem ended only after he left the firm.

In order to move ahead, you must create enough critical mass to support the transformation. You must have commitment to the endeavor from the key stakeholders, opinion makers, and the leaders under you. Especially important is the support of your leadership team. Describe for them the steps in the organizational growth process. Collaborate with them on the design of the process, and ask them to assume leadership in developing various task forces and problem-solving groups. Do not move without them. But don't wait either until you have their total commitment, for this could be a long time in coming. Rather, focus your efforts primarily on those who are with you. Deal with the laggards as necessary. Always encourage people to be positive, to say "I wonder," "I wish," "I hope," and "If I could," and then help them to make things happen. We have learned from neuropsychologists that the word *imagine* is a powerful stimulus of creativity and emotional engagement. During your work to establish and communicate vision and purpose, use language such as "Imagine what we could do when . . ." or "Imagine what our contributions could be when we overcome this issue."

2. *You must keep driving toward achievement of the vision.* You must model real "fire in the belly" dedication. Your role is architect and crew chief of a process and a view of the future that touches people in a way they can embrace. But the heartfelt purpose around which people pull together is often intangible. Thus, the power of a committed vision and purpose is likely to include important principles or values, such as quality, excellence, or high levels of consistency or service. While potentially uplifting, the vision must be grounded in reality so it can be understood and achieved with hard work. It must advance your business or organization beyond where it is now and possibly beyond where it has ever been. But it must also target new and greater individual and group performance. The process is participatory: the organization shares its dreams, its resources, and the responsibility to act as one. Words will never be enough. Action and behaviors convince people.

3. *Keep top leadership commitment visible.* As long as people believe top leadership is interested, supportive, and participating themselves, they will maintain energy and commitment. Ask your boss to sit in on a few of your meetings, to address the total group periodically, to provide words of encouragement and appreciation. In short, keep your boss informed and visible in supporting your vision, goals, and values.

THE IMPORTANCE OF THE GROUP'S QUEST FOR VISION

Keep your vision focused on the team's power to accomplish great things. Together, *we* will create a powerful synergy. Two working together have the potency of three or four working individually. Whole organizations have almost limitless potential and energy. The dynamics of working together result in insights, creative ideas, leaps of logic, and associations that one often cannot attain working alone. New ideas are generated from people building on each other's ideas, constructively criticizing each other, competing, joking, and thinking together. People from different backgrounds, with different perspectives and viewpoints, will often strengthen the vision and positively alter it, much as plant biologists strengthen genetics through hybridizing. Trust the strength, power, and ability of the group. Trust your process, and others will follow your lead.

KEY PLANKS IN YOUR PLATFORM

You need to decide early on your key values because they will be the keystones of your vision. When Bruce was appointed vice president of finance and administrative services, he immediately faced a number of major challenges. His new areas had not been managed effectively. Even before he had an opportunity to delve into the functions, several problems were apparent. Several core financial and computer systems were out of date, and efficiency was lagging. There had been several cases of illegal practices and kickbacks in the two previous years. Lack of effective management and leadership was apparent throughout his division. There was much to be done.

Because of extensive briefings ahead of time by the corporate CFO, from the beginning, Bruce had a clear idea of his priorities and the role of his people, as viewed by his boss. Three major themes became the foundation of his early leadership platform. From his first day in the role, Bruce insisted on and involved his organization in (1) asserting the simultaneous value of individual initiative and cross-functional teamwork, (2) establishing sound standard operating procedures, and (3) implementing state-of-the-art information technology systems. Bruce felt that these issues were the foundation of his leadership platform and the seeds of his organizational vision.

Bruce realized that words alone would not be enough to emphasize his points, so he combined his written and spoken words with symbolic actions to communicate his priorities. Within a few weeks, there was no question in anyone's mind about what Bruce felt was important and what issues would be emphasized before others. He spent a lot of time with people, individually and in groups, not only asking questions but also stressing his main themes. The decisions he made about employees, including the way he organized people in projects and how he assigned work, all conveyed his early priorities. In particular, Bruce effectively utilized an approach that we call *managing vocabulary*. He used several key words and consciously repeated them to emphasize the major points in his leadership platform. Words such as *initiative, teamwork, systems, integrity, ours,* and *we* became the symbolic lexicon of the division. This repetition of key themes was a valuable tool in Bruce's efforts to build alignment in the organization. During this early period, people began to adopt Bruce's thinking and direction. The early period is a time for molding and setting important precedents and for visionary leadership. It is a time when your key values must become part of the organization's vocabulary.

When developing your vision, think about these issues:

Leveraging Strengths and Opportunities

- What are your department's or team's key strengths, and how can you leverage them?
- What is the greatest contribution your function can make to the organization?
- What are the opportunities your department can leverage?
- What are your department's key success factors?
- What do your customers (internal and/or external) value most about what your department does?

Managing Weaknesses and Threats

- What are your department's weaknesses? How can they be overcome?
- What are the threats to your department's effectiveness?
- What, if anything, do your customers find difficult or don't like about how your department functions?

Looking Ahead

- What are the key services or products that require the most focus?
- Who are your clients now?
- Whom do you want to be your clients in the future?
- How is your department measured for performance?
- What is the culture you want for your department?

ACTING CONSISTENTLY: DEVELOPING GOOD PUBLIC RELATIONS FOR YOUR POSITIONS

As your direction and priorities become clearer, how you communicate and how you act as a leader become increasingly important. Seemingly well-conceived platforms and great visions have failed not because of their content but because of the way they were communicated. Effect should match intent. People have a desire and a right to expect consistency between word and deed. A governor of a western state was recently elected based on a well-articulated vision of that state's future, but within weeks of his election a firestorm of opposition arose because his administration's public remarks during his early days in office seemed inconsistent with his election platform. People felt betrayed.

People look for and trust consistency between what is done and what is said. If your vision includes the desire to share organizational power and control in the interest of the overall good, your actions must match the vision. It is not uncommon to find a 25 percent or greater gap between what top managers say about quality and how their employees see those words in terms of action and commitment. Inevitably, employees will become cynical if words and actions are not consistent.

On the other hand, John F. Kennedy's inspired challenge "Ask not what your country can do for you but what you can do for your country" developed an expectation that leadership would invite citizen involvement and greater empowerment in a vision of America's "New Frontier." Kennedy started highly visible, idealistic programs such as the Peace Corps and VISTA to help realize this vision, and such actions made him appear consistent, believable, and able to energize the loyalty and commitment of millions of people. Barack Obama's campaign for the presidency of the United States was built on a vision of large-scale change of many policies, practices, and even institutions. The campaign was successful largely because of Obama's ability to articulate and convince his supporters that this was a worthy and wise course to follow.

QUESTIONS TO CONSIDER

Consider the following questions as you plan your vision, purpose, and direction. Writing your answers will help you incorporate them into your overall first-year plan of action.

- In organizations you've worked for, did the leader establish priorities early? How? What was the effect? If he or she did not, what was it like to work there? Did you and others know what was important?
- Describe effective symbolic behaviors and signs you have seen. What are some of the things you can do to symbolize your vision or expectations?
- What are at least three ways that you, as a newly promoted executive, can help influence and organize your function's early mindset regarding your key priorities?
- In groups, certain people are the high influencers. During the first few weeks in a new position, how might you influence the influencers in the organization?
- Are there work assignments, special projects, and task forces that you can organize around a key issue that can further strengthen the direction of your function?
- How might you use your ability to recognize and reward efforts during your first few months in a new leadership position?
- How might you facilitate setting team, group, and individual goals in a way that promotes perceived consistency between your intentions and actions? How can you use recognition and reward in a similar fashion?
- How can you ensure that you are consistent in what you say and do?
- Over the next several months, can you pick people for special responsibilities, assignments, and promotions based on their willingness and ability to work within your platform and vision? Remember to act in such a way that others in your organization can see the relationship between your selection of people and your commitment to certain goals and directions for your organization.
- How can you make the people around you feel like winners? What can you do to continue this feeling? If they don't feel like winners, why not? Together, how can you turn this feeling around?
- As a means of building consistency, some leaders periodically update a top-priority to-do list. For example, twice a year one director mobilizes people around those key problems and opportunities that are viewed as gateways to success. How might you apply this approach? What are its possible uses for concentrating people's attention on what is really important? What methods can ensure that all individuals in the organization are problem solvers, solution makers, and identifiers of opportunities? (Consider the incredible power of administrative

and executive assistants! Try unleashing their potency on several important problems.)

■ Are there work assignments, special projects, and task forces that can be organized around your goals and that can further strengthen the direction of your unit?

■ How can you make sure that you are effectively communicating your early priorities downward, upward, and across the organization?

The lesson is clear. Acting consistently on your stated positions, priorities, and values is a prerequisite for establishing acceptance of you and your vision.

Quick Reminders to Keep You on Track

■ Vision, purpose, and direction are what results when, together, people look outside themselves, put aside individual interests, and capture a common notion of what they want their organization to achieve.

■ A committed vision, purpose, and values together can serve as an organizational GPS. They can serve as a directional compass for your team or organization. People in high-achieving organizations have their heart and soul in their vision.

■ Another key to success is involving your people in developing ways to achieve the vision and purpose you are seeding.

■ There are important ways to seed your personal points of view into your organization, including the following three principles:

1. People must believe that their commitment to building a strong organization will simultaneously result in benefits to the organization and to themselves.

2. You must keep driving toward the initial identification and subsequent achievement of the vision.

3. Keep top management commitment visible.

■ Be a catalyst, a facilitator, and a model. Orchestrate the group's quest for vision and purpose.

■ Clearly identify, model, and manage the key planks in your leadership platform. Use symbolic behavior and language (*managing vocabulary*) to communicate your vision clearly.

■ Acting consistently—that is, having your actions match your intent and words—is the key to developing good public relations for your positions.

THE DIAGNOSTIC PROCESS
The Importance of an Effective Organizational Analysis

The major causes of problems are bad assumptions and solutions.

—Source unknown

To be successful in transforming your organization with the goal of achieving your vision, you must have an accurate picture of your organization's strengths, weaknesses, and other vital information within your first five or six months and, if at all possible, even sooner. You will need to accomplish the following:

- Ensure that your people understand the importance of accurate information in order to strengthen their organization and achieve its vision.
- Explain what an organizational analysis is.
- Involve many people in completing the organizational analysis while they continue their regular work.
- Facilitate the organizational diagnostic process with a sense of urgency.
- Complete the analysis and prepare to act on its recommendations in six months or less.

In this chapter, there is useful information about the following:

- Positioning the organizational diagnostic analysis within the overall problem-solving and transition management process
- The organizational analysis process
- The hazards of the process

POSITIONING THE ORGANIZATIONAL ANALYSIS WITHIN THE OVERALL PROBLEM-SOLVING AND TRANSITION MANAGEMENT PROCESS

The analysis allows the organization to assess itself for the purpose of strengthening what is working, improving what is problematic, and correcting what is wrong. Conducting a successful organizational "health check" is a key step in the organization's process of achieving its vision. This check usually takes from several weeks to half a year.

As a general rule, by the end of your sixth month in the job, and preferably sooner, the data collection phase should have been completed, solutions to problems and growth opportunities have been identified, and your plans have begun to be implemented. You need to move fairly rapidly. You have an agreement, which is ideally a part of your confirmed appointment charter, with your boss or bosses, who expect that you are going to make improvements. You've asked your staff to participate in self-renewal, and they will expect that once the diagnostic process is completed, the analysis and recommendations they've made are going to be implemented. You've set up expectations that you will take charge of the process, and it is time to move ahead.

The diagnostic process must go on while regular work proceeds. You will hear complaints that both cannot be done together. They can be, but it takes considerable work and committed effort. It is amazing what people can do when they are motivated to make things better. Performing high-quality work and completing the diagnostic process requires people to believe in what you are doing. A diagnostic phase as part of a transition management process is equally applicable for start-up organizations, in which there is generally less "history" to overcome but there are still challenges to meet in establishing a strong, sustainable organization.

THE ORGANIZATIONAL ANALYSIS PROCESS

An effective analysis can be conducted in a number of ways. We will describe a step-by-step process that we have found to be very useful. Precise steps and time frames vary by organization and circumstances. While we describe a process involving many people from your organization, we cannot emphasize enough the importance of your involvement as the chief diagnostician. You are as good as the information you get. Involve your people extensively in the process. But talk to people, dozens of people, in and out of your new function. We call it *360-degree input*, which is a type of feedback that is invaluable. Ask dozens of people dozens of questions if necessary to build your information base.

Sample Steps and Time Frames

A. Appoint a steering committee representing different levels and functions within your organization.   Weeks 2, 3, or 4

B. Designate the support and consultative resources, if applicable.   Weeks 2, 3, or 4

C. Create a statement of the steering committee's mission and scope of authority.   Weeks 2, 3, or 4

D. Develop a timeline and activity schedule for the process.   Weeks 2, 3, or 4

E. Steering committee identifies critical issues to be studied.   Weeks 4, 5, or 6

F. Delegate critical issues to task forces, designating leaders from the steering committee, selecting representative task force members from across the department or organization to complete the task force membership. (As a rule, steering committee members will serve on no more than one task force.)   Weeks 4, 5, or 6

G. Task forces develop and implement a timeline
and critical events schedule, within the steering
committee's deadlines.

    Task forces should complete three primary
functions:
1. Identify and collect data on the issues.
   For example,
   - Develop knowledge from within the task
     force.
   - Develop interview data from others out-
     side the task force who have information
     (often done by you and/or consultants).
   - Identify case studies and events that show
     the organization's strengths and weakness.
2. Analyze data and organize findings,
   conclusions, and recommendations.
3. Develop drafts of *critical issues papers* to be   Weeks 4, 5, or 6
   submitted to the steering committee for   through weeks
   discussion.   12 to 16

H. Steering committee reviews task forces' critical
issues papers and develops overall findings,
conclusions, and timing depending on
recommendations of preceding steps.   Weeks 12 to 18
I. Steering committee issues final report.   Weeks 18, 19, or 20

APPOINTING A STEERING COMMITTEE

To gain influence, you must give influence and empower those around you.
Appointing a steering committee is an effective way to gain power by sharing
power. The steering committee will oversee the organizational analysis. It will
coordinate and drive the analysis forward and develop and help implement
the solutions. The steering committee is critical to the success of the project.

    Appointing a steering committee helps accomplish many of the goals of
the analysis. A steering committee encourages participation in the diagnostic
process, building organizational buy-in and commitment. It focuses energy
on renewal, communicates a sense of "we-ness," and fosters the belief that
everyone can help make things better.

The steering committee membership should represent the part of the organization's structure that reports to you, functional reporting lines, levels of responsibility, and experience. But it should not be so large that decision making becomes unwieldy. Depending on the size of your organization, a group of 6 to 10 is an ideal representation and concentration of power. The larger the group, the more difficult it is to arrive at a consensus, and the more vulnerable the group becomes to the will of a strong chairperson, who tends to be the one with the most information. If you want to involve a larger number of your staff, you can ask them to work on task forces or on subcommittees.

Steering committee membership should also represent the department's formal and informal power structure. Appoint primarily those in designated roles of authority, most of whom will be members of your management team. Appoint people who are respected and can represent others. Appoint individuals that you plan to "stay on the bus" in important roles. That they have earned a leadership role or are viewed as influential means not only that they are generally knowledgeable but also, because of their power and influence, that they are key to implementing the committee's recommendations.

It is important to appoint key informal leaders at all levels in the organization, including those not necessarily in officially designated leadership positions but whom department members respect and listen to. Some of these people may be at different levels on the organizational chart, but they will create an informal constituency. They are, and represent, important stakeholders in your organization. These people can be expected to make strong recommendations and explain steering committee decisions to their constituencies. They will be able to build support for recommendations in which they participate. In some organizations, these people may represent labor, line supervisors or coaches, and managers of administrative staff.

The selection of steering committee members should be thoughtful; it should not be manipulative. Choose people on their merits, their potential as leaders and as energetic problem solvers. They should be respected and influential members of your organization. The recommendations that the committee generates and implements will affect the entire department or organization and must speak for all involved. People must feel that the committee was fairly selected and represents all viewpoints and constituencies, not just those that the established leaders may favor. Beware of stacking the deck.

Diversity of opinion will generate a better solution as long as the group members listen to each other and use effective group processes. A classic study of group dynamics in a historical setting was conducted on the Bay of Pigs affair. President John F. Kennedy felt that the Bay of Pigs disaster had occurred partly because of the limitations imposed by a small group of likeminded planners too insular in their thinking. Consequently, when he faced the Cuban Missile Crisis, he composed a large and diverse group of experts from government, industry, and academia. The successful strategy they devised was quite different from the strategies that the president's inner circle had proposed, and it was the product of lengthy and sometimes heated discussions. A superior consensus was achieved by a diverse group of problem solvers intent on an excellent solution.

Union members can be a particular concern if they are more preoccupied with defending the contract and their position in the union leadership than with resolving or improving the organization. Fortunately, labor-management tension has subsided somewhat in the recent past, as each has recognized its mutual dependency. Labor representatives generally are prepared to help strengthen the organization and thus help ensure that their jobs are safe within a viable organization.

You might discuss your preliminary selections with a few key associates and department members, partly to get some feedback and advice and partly to bring them into the process of managing the analysis. They can help you select committee members who will bring talent, energy, and effective representation.

Next have a series of brief individual or small group meetings with those selected. In these meetings you can describe the process, the members' responsibilities, and the time commitments, and you can make sure the members want to serve. At the same time, select and begin to brief the committee chair on his or her responsibilities and charter if you do not chair the steering committee yourself.

The steering committee chair, if you do not chair the committee yourself, should be someone with both formal and informal authority. He or she must have the respect of the department's or team's most experienced and expert employees, must be able to work with the most demanding and difficult people, and must be capable of moving the individual members toward consensus and implementation. It is a demanding and time-consuming task. The chair must also be someone with whom you can work, who can help keep the process on schedule, help committee task groups that are floundering, and move the process toward completion.

Since the organization will usually defer to your leadership, there will generally be little resistance to an appointment if the person has the organization's respect. People recognize that the committee chair will have to speak to you, negotiate with you, and represent you.

The steering committee oversees the five primary steps of the organizational analysis in close collaboration with you:

1. *Develop a statement of objectives or goals.*
   - State the objectives of the analysis. The objective of the analysis is generally to strengthen the function.
   - Describe activities and timelines.
   - Describe the expected outcomes and benefits.
   - Identify resources needed.
2. *Develop areas of study.*
   - Determine specific subtopics to be studied.
   - Identify critical issues to resolve or examine.
   - Specify the objectives, activities, and timelines for task forces.
   - Indicate potential sources of data.
3. *Receive, review, and analyze task force findings and recommendations.*
   - Receive task force findings and recommendations.
   - Analyze and prioritize findings and recommendations.
4. *Make final recommendations and design implementation.*
   - Review; approve, reject, or modify; and prioritize recommendations.
   - Plan implementation resources, activities, and timelines.
5. *Monitor and evaluate implementation.*
   - Oversee implementation activities. Ensure implementation, and in doing this, the steering committee works closely with you and your management team.
   - Troubleshoot implementation.
   - Fine-tune implementation to ensure that it achieves project goals and objectives.
   - Assess whether outcomes and benefits are achieved; adapt as necessary.

As the steering committee monitors and oversees the overall process, so should you monitor and oversee the work of the steering committee, consulting with the chair on managing the committee and with the committee on managing the diagnostic process.

Your role is not to control the steering committee's conclusions and recommendations. However, you need to be comfortable with its direction and goals. Candid discussions with the steering committee can ensure your support or communicate your discomfort with particular initiatives or goals. These discussions should begin as soon as possible.

You should know the diagnostic process as well as anyone on the steering committee (excluding internal or external consultants who may be involved). Use your knowledge and demonstrate your commitment to the process.

You know that participation should be broad and should represent different subgroups and the diversity of skills and experience in the organization. You also know the limitations of the analysis, if there are issues that cannot be touched (these should be very few, if any), and what the resource limitations are. These can often be identified early in the process and should be defined as the limits and boundaries of the organizational improvement process.

By selecting the steering committee and insisting on the "we-ness" of the effort, you can help ensure fair representation as the process continues. Through pronouncement and example, you can ensure that the problem-solving process is applied to all areas under you, that the *real* organization is accurately described, and that the task forces rethink and analyze the organization's functions and processes in a creative problem-solving mode. Similarly, the *ideal* organization, represented by the steering committee's recommendations, must be objectively considered looking at both alternatives and consequences. Get the groups started and give them plenty of room to operate. Intervene only when necessary.

Your primary role is to coach the steering committee. Much of your coaching will be done in private, with the steering committee chair and task force heads. Attend some, but not all, steering committee meetings. At steering committee meetings, ask questions. If meetings are problematic, redirect the group to stay on the agenda, to consider multiple approaches, to resolve its conflicts, and to develop consensus. Your more active input should be one-on-one with the chair, away from steering committee meetings so you don't undermine the chair's authority.

Develop a contract with the steering committee chair that describes his or her prerogatives and yours. Agree that if either of you feel the agreement is being violated, you may call "time out" before the problem festers. Project your own confidence and a strong sense that you understand the process. You should not be all-knowing of the "right" answers. Avoid giving the impression that you have been hired because you are the immediate expert and have all the answers. Project your commitment and strength by stating that you need and value all the help and input you can get. Demonstrate that you expect success, through your approach and your ability to ask the right questions. You will build confidence by making the tough decisions whenever needed.

The diagnostic process intentionally gives the impression of order. But it may create discomfort, some dissonance, and tension. There's a lot going on at once in addition to the organization's regular work. Reassure people. Build on each other's hopes for a stronger organization. Listen to what people are saying, to their concerns. Encourage your people. Give them your time. Remind them that the process works and, in the end, the organization will be stronger.

Designating Support and Consultative Resources

Consider the type, if any, of support services the steering committee or the various task forces may require. Consultants, internal to the company or from outside, can provide three types of key assistance: (1) help with the design of the diagnostic process, (2) help with technical aspects of the organization's work, and (3) help with conducting aspects of the analysis and implementation.

Consultants can provide assistance with the design of the diagnostic process itself. One of the steering committee chair's critical roles in the diagnostic process is facilitation. The chair's primary concern as a facilitator is to ensure that the diagnostic process is well organized, functions smoothly, and stays on schedule. A process or facilitative consultant can be assigned the following tasks by either you or the chair:

- Help ensure that the steering committee, and each task force, develops a reasonable approach and schedule and adheres to the schedule.
- Assist task forces and ensure that each member's input gets a fair and reasonable hearing.
- Help the steering committee and task forces resolve conflicts and develop consensus.
- Help ensure that the steering committee and task forces adhere to a problem-solving model, that alternatives are fairly considered, that solutions evolve from reasonably considered alternatives, and that recommendations fit the conclusions.
- Act as a source of ideas for creative problem solving and innovative directions.

The steering committee chair will perform the role of leader and process facilitator and function as a group member on issues where he or she has a strong opinion or input. Some people wear all three hats more easily than others. When the chair's process and facilitator skills are not strong, group members may feel railroaded, inadequately consulted, and forced to go along with things they do not support. A facilitator from outside, however, can safeguard the process by projecting an outsider's detachment and objectivity. The outside facilitator can coach the chair and help him or her stay in touch with the group's feelings and direction. A skilled facilitator will also be able to intervene in the group's deliberations, to reorient the group or draw attention to and help solve a developing process problem.

A second purpose of outside consultants is to provide needed expert information. For example, a steering committee or task force considering reorganization will profit from information on how other similar organizations are structured. Often, a consultant familiar with the industry has worked in a number of companies within the field and can describe different kinds of organizations as well as strengths and weaknesses of different structures and work flow patterns. Consultants experienced in the field provide a broad spectrum of what is happening in similar organizations and how you might improve your own.

A third role for outside consultants is to conduct parts of the analysis itself for the steering committee. Management studies by outside consultants are common because they provide an objective, independent viewpoint. One newly installed leader, for example, used outside consultants because she did not feel internal resources would look critically enough at an organization long accustomed to doing things the same way.

In another case, the consultant became the surrogate for a steering committee that had too little time to pursue all the sources of data required. In this case, the analysis was organized into subparts that were assigned to different consultants. One analyzed results of a questionnaire distributed among employees; a second conducted diagnostic interviews with all top managers and a sample of the first-line workforce; a third conducted interviews with people who had left the organization or declined offers to join it. The steering committee synthesized the three different elements of the analysis and directed the review and consolidation of consultant reports into a comprehensive critical issues paper, which included the final recommendations. The biggest disadvantage of such an approach is that it significantly reduces the involvement of the department or team staff in the organizational analysis. In turn, this may reduce the ownership of the data and solutions. Consultants must ensure that they do not end up owning the process, the findings, and the recommendations. They must help you to help the organization take responsibility for itself. Consultants who own the process end up getting the blame from organization members who do not support their recommendations. They often do a disservice to you and the organization if they do not work in a way that your organization owns its own data and solutions.

Issuing the Steering Committee's Mission and Scope of Authority

The steering committee must receive its charge from you, the organization's leader, for you control the committee's mandate, scope of authority, and resources.

At the committee's organizing meeting, announce the committee chair or that you will chair the steering committee yourself. Describe the role of the chair, steering committee members, anticipated task forces, other department and organization members, and how you will work with the steering committee.

Describe how you envision the diagnostic process. Broadly describe the data collection, analysis, and problem resolution process you expect the steering committee and each task force to follow. Be flexible, and encourage variations and new ideas. Describe the role of committee members, and outline the can-do behaviors each group member is expected to follow.

Stress that the analysis will position the organization to build on its strengths. On the other hand, few, if any, topics or issues should be off limits. The committee should analyze the organization's weaknesses, without defensiveness, to identify areas that need strengthening. Focusing solely on what's wrong simply builds defensiveness; rather, identify where the organization can improve while building on its inherent strengths.

Insist that the steering committee and its task forces address critical issues and growth opportunities facing the organization, including the sensitive issues. For example, include business projections not achieved; perceptions that staff work assignments are unequal; reporting relationships that are confusing or contradictory; project deadlines that are not adhered to; lines of communication that are not open; training that is weak; people's skills that are stagnant; and procedures that are inefficient and inconsistent.

Stress that no steering committee or task force issue is to be presented without a recommendation. This is the key. No one is to pass the buck. Findings, conclusions, and recommendations are to be issued in a *final report.*

Task force critical issues papers are to be submitted to the steering committee. These are then consolidated as the steering committee's final report, which is submitted to you. This will become a vital guide and tool for you. Review it in detail with your boss, and later summarize it for your organization as a whole. This last point is important because you will want to mobilize the organization and implement the steering committee's recommendations.

Developing the Timeline and Critical Events Calendar

The steering committee's timeline and deadlines are largely governed by your expectations and by the time required by constituent task forces. Typically, a task force will require about six weeks to four months to organize, collect, and analyze its data and draft its conclusions and recommendations depending on the size of the organization and the depth of the analysis. Add two weeks for organization and another four weeks for the steering committee to review the task forces' critical issues papers and then to develop final conclusions, recommendations, and a plan for implementation. The time frames depend on the size and scope of the study and the organization as well as the time available to members, who are also doing their regular work.

A critical events schedule marks activities that should be completed if the analysis is to be done on a timely basis:

- Whom to interview inside the function, with deadlines
- Which internal stakeholders and others are involved in horizontal work processes
- Whom to interview among clients, customers, and vendors and contractors, with deadlines
- Documents and products to be reviewed, with deadlines

Identifying Critical Issues

The diagnostic targets described in this chapter and more fully in Chapter 7 can define the task forces that will be required. There may be obvious problems or growth opportunities around which task forces can form. Take advantage of existing information and reports.

The task forces may be involved in the nine broad-based target areas described in Chapter 7, such as organizational mission and objectives, leadership, delegation, and culture. On the other hand, the steering committee may narrow the analysis to specific issues. One organization's task forces, each led by someone on the steering committee, were as follows:

- Evaluating the new product development portfolio
- Improving information and data management systems
- Reviewing a consultant's report on how the department's functions were managed in 14 different companies, and identifying recommendations for their own company
- Making recommendations for learning and development
- Considering workload distribution

Another organization's steering committee organized five task forces:

- Improving communications and procedures with the department from whom we receive our work, with particular emphasis on role definition
- Working on coordination between the home office and branch offices
- Improving computer hardware and management information systems
- Identifying career development opportunities for employees who will stay in place
- Improving the learning and employee development program and improving the performance management process

A third company identified three broad task forces: the planning process, the analysis process, and data management. Yet another company organized functionally, with a task force examining each business unit (product line). A broad array of potential targets is described in Chapter 7. With your coaching of the chair and direct involvement (as necessary), the steering committee identifies the scope of the analysis and the task force issues to be analyzed.

Organizing Task Forces

Task forces should be organized around growth opportunities and critical issues. As noted earlier, the diagnostic targets are identified by the steering committee. We have seen task forces that include no steering committee members, although this is rare. It is preferable that a steering committee member sit on each task force, and often that member will lead the task force. Task forces should include a variety of viewpoints among knowledgeable people. As with the steering committee, be sure to include formal and informal leaders in the area of the task force's domain, so recommendations will have organizational support. Task force members can include any employee from any role or position. They predominantly come from midlevel management and first-line supervisors, supported by individual contributors in the workforce. Task forces commonly consider how the work gets done, and they should be composed of people closest to the work.

Task forces should use a problem-solving process that encompasses issues identification, data collection, data analysis, consideration of alternatives and consequences, and selection of a solution. Task force deadlines and critical events should fit the steering committee's schedules and deadlines and should result in a critical issues report containing findings, conclusions, and a clear recommendation for each finding.

Like the steering committee, the task forces should draw input from multiple resources:

- A properly constituted task force will represent considerable information from within its membership, including individual contributors and first-line supervisors. Much information is available simply through discussions within the task force.
- Task force members may draw from consultants, who may work with other task forces or the steering committee, or from individual employees whose input helps shape the findings and recommendations. As mentioned previously, consultants may be retained to assist with or conduct the analysis for sensitive issues. If the steering committee retains a process consultant, he or she should sit in on task forces as needed, and possibly randomly, to ensure that the task force is functioning in an open and participatory manner.
- Task force members should draw on information not only from inside but outside the organization, including clients, customers, those who provide the organization with input or products, those who use the organization's output, and others who observe or interact with the organization.

Each task force should develop its own critical issues paper, describing methodology, findings, conclusions, and recommendations that will make the organization stronger. These will be consolidated or summarized in a final report of the steering committee, which is presented to you.

Developing Roles for the Functional Members of the Department

Broad participation in data collection is a way to gain support from across the department or function, and to profit from that work unit's diversity of knowledge and viewpoints. At the same time, it builds interest in the organizational improvement process and increases its visibility. As a rule, when management and employees participate in the process, they develop ownership for both the process and the outcome. The broader the participation, the greater the sense that people have been included, that they have gained recognition and status, and that their concerns were heard.

Some will serve on the steering committee. There are roles for others on one of the task forces, which usually have from three to six members each. Others will be interviewed by task force members as sources of information that can help the effort.

As with the steering committee, smaller task forces may collect data more quickly and possibly develop a consensus more efficiently. Larger groups, on the other hand, will be more representative and tend to have a greater richness of ideas.

Each task force should include a member of the steering committee. Steering committee members may volunteer to head particular task forces, even though the task force leader should be chosen by you and the steering committee chair. Select a leader who knows the task or function. Also consider a person's interest in the area. A senior leader will be most familiar with broader issues of mission, policies, goals, and objectives. His or her ideal task force members might be predominantly upper-level and midlevel management people who are familiar with looking at the organization from a broad, wide-angle view.

On the other hand, task forces that look at work flow and workforce issues should include people at an operational level: midlevel and first-line supervisors and experienced employees, who are more familiar with the day-to-day operations.

In general, the most experienced people will make the strongest contribution to task forces. They know the culture, history, how things got that way, intervening factors, and the solutions. More importantly, they know how to get answers, and they have the organizational resources to defend and implement solutions. On the other hand, a bright, less experienced person may add much because of his or her initiative and fresh perspective. A word of caution, however: overly frank newcomers, whose advice and observations are not always welcome by veterans, can get in trouble by being too direct. Participation on task forces can be a career maker or breaker for young people, depending on how they handle themselves. A little advance coaching can save young people from a lot of trouble.

A salesperson with six months of experience with a company was given the opportunity to brainstorm and problem solve the organization's learning and development program. She stated that the program was very weak in her division, that she was spending almost no time in the field, was left alone in the office too often, and saw the sales director and other experienced salespeople taking two- and three-hour lunches. It took only a few hours for her sales director's friends to relay what his new employee had said about him. After the closed-door meetings, department meetings, explanations, and memos, the new employee was transferred to a different site, fortunate that she still had a job.

What about your critics? By excluding them from the problem-solving task forces, you can deny them influence and power. In most information- and knowledge-based industries, information is a source of power. People without information are left out of decision making, and they lose power. But denying your critics access to decision-making authority can also harm you. Excluding them lessens your chance of bringing critics on board, giving them some stake, and turning negative critics into positive forces that can help both you and the organization.

We have seen it both ways—critics who came on board and were won over to the renewal process and critics who, primarily because they were angry, psychologically withdrew from the discussions or were difficult to cope with. It's a tough call. We generally suggest including a few known critics but choosing people who see things in different ways, not people with a personal ax to grind. You need diverse opinions, not negative attitudes. At the very least, convey a willingness to hear a true diversity of opinion. *No one* should ever be criticized or punished for his or her candor during a formal diagnostic process that you sponsor. Not only is such criticism unfair but it could damage your credibility permanently.

Broad-based participation can foster team building and the development of cohesion within the function. Two recently merged organizations used problem-solving task forces to get people from the different merged units talking to each other, sharing perceptions, experiences, and knowledge and building trust and commitment with each other. Another organization used creative problem-solving approaches to help four group leaders learn to work together. In the process, they shared definitions, perceptions, experiences, and objectives. They developed better working relationships as they shared mutual problems and carved out shared solutions.

THE HAZARDS OF THE PROCESS

Broad participation and group problem solving do not automatically strengthen your organization's renewal process. There are a number of hazards that can undermine the broad-based support you are trying to build.

One major difficulty is that of heightened expectations. Inevitably, someone's ideas will not be solicited, or his or her ideas will be solicited but not heard, heard but not heeded, or heeded but assigned a low priority. People will make suggestions that are not adopted. Hopes that pet ideas or suggestions will be adopted are dashed as decision-making committees sift through all the ideas and recommendations.

Unrequited expectations can defeat the process. If people begin to feel that they are not heard, or if they feel the process is a ploy to build support but that you'll do what you want anyway, your staff will feel used and manipulated and lose enthusiasm for the project and the process, and you will lose credibility quickly.

Endless task force meetings without decisions or a feeling of closure also sap energy. People begin to question why they are meeting. Participation becomes a burden. Task force meetings must have deadlines and milestones, and they must be conducted with purpose and an end in mind. They should give everyone time to be heard and to develop a consensus.

Another related cause of failure is the leader's overemphasis on process, to the detriment of results. To overemphasize process is to meet, participate, and deliberate without coming to conclusions and action. It is talk without action, participation without closure, deliberation without decisions. It is problem solving without solutions, without action. Nothing ever goes anywhere, and nothing ever gets done.

Leadership is the ability to set in place a change process for the group and to give employees an overall direction and vision without prescribing all the details. Leadership is setting deadlines, upholding your standards and expectations, and insisting on well-conceived results. It is being willing to confront or criticize when the outcome is not up to standards or is seriously flawed. It is also being willing, for the overall good of the organization, to accept good ideas with which you disagree. In Chapter 7 we will explore these issues in greater detail as we introduce the nine-target model for assessing organizational health.

Quick Reminders to Keep You on Track

- Conducting a successful organizational health check, an organizational analysis, is a key step in the organization's achieving its vision.
- The purposes of the analysis are for the organization to strengthen what is working, identify what is problematic, and correct what is wrong.
- As a general rule, by the end of your sixth month in the job at the very latest, the data collection phase of the organizational analysis should have been completed, with solutions to problems and growth opportunities identified, and implementation of your plan should be well underway.
- This diagnostic effort is part of the agreement, or appointment charter, with your boss that you have discussed and negotiated.
- You will want to involve your immediate staff and others, as appropriate, in the organizational self-renewal effort.
- Once completed, your employees will look to you to lead the charge in implementing the recommendations identified in the organizational improvement process. Your personal credibility and reputation are on the line if you do not.
- The diagnostic process goes on while regular work continues. Some will complain that it is too much to do. Keep the "open for business" sign out while you initiate the diagnostic process.
- An effective organizational analysis can be conducted in a number of ways. Regardless of approach, it always includes your active involvement as the prime orchestrator.
- You will need to ask many questions of many people in order to build your base of information (360-degree organizational feedback) and to check how different people view issues and problems.
- We recommend an approach that utilizes a wide representation of people from your function usually organized into task forces and a small steering committee to guide the effort.

ASSESSING YOUR ORGANIZATION'S HEALTH

The leader of the past knew how to tell; the leader of the future will know how to ask.

—Peter Drucker

Good is the enemy of great, . . . a Good to Great Principle.

—Jim Collins

To complete your organizational assessment, you have to know what to look for, what your targets are, and how to determine and ask the right questions. You will need to accomplish the following:

- Use the nine-target model to complete the organizational diagnosis and assessment.
- In this chapter, there is useful information about the following:
- The nine-target model: The organizational indicators of vision that are used in diagnosing (assessing) your organization:

  1. Purpose, values, planning, and goals
  2. Leadership, delegation, and accountability
  3. Politics, power, and culture
  4. Recognition, rewards, and incentives
  5. Relationships, communication, and teamwork
  6. Leadership development and talent management practices
  7. Resources and technology
  8. Innovation and continuous improvement

9. External factors including laws, regulations, community, and
   social and economic conditions

- Findings, conclusions, and recommendations

THE NINE-TARGET MODEL: THE INDICATORS OF VISION

There are a number of fundamental areas and processes an organizational analysis should consider. Whether the diagnosis is concerned with a single function or with all organizational functions that may be under your direction, you and the steering committee should consider which targets should be selected. There are nine primary organizational targets that determine the health of your organization. Once assessed, the present status of these nine areas should provide a clear picture of the overall well-being of your function. We call these targets *indicators* of vision because they are your starting point for what you want the organization to become. They indicate the number and nature of the organizational issues needed to achieve your vision.

Target 1. Purpose, values, planning, and goals
Target 2. Leadership, delegation, and accountability
Target 3. Politics, power, and culture
Target 4. Recognition, rewards, and incentives
Target 5. Relationships, communication, and teamwork
Target 6. Leadership development and talent management practices
Target 7. Resources and technology
Target 8. Innovation and continuous improvement
Target 9. External factors including laws, regulations, community,
and social and economic conditions

TARGET 1. PURPOSE, VALUES, PLANNING, AND GOALS

The *purpose*, or *mission*, is a succinct statement of corporate or functional purpose. It states why the organization is in business—what it is trying to achieve.

The purpose statement provides a compass for employee efforts beyond just making money. It also provides a philosophical touchstone to guide leaders and employees in determining and understanding the business they are in and how they should conduct business. As you learned in Chapter 4, *vision* is the statement of how you would like your organization to be in the future. Together, purpose, mission, and vision provide energy and direction for your department or function, and they must be aligned with the larger organization.

Here are a few examples of purpose or mission and values statements from several highly respected organizations. The first example is from Procter & Gamble (P&G).

P&G's Mission Statement

The Power of Purpose

Companies like P&G are a force in the world. Our market capitalization is greater than the GDP of many countries, and we serve consumers in more than 180 countries. With this stature comes both responsibility and opportunity. Our responsibility is to be an ethical corporate citizen—but our opportunity is something far greater, and it is embodied in our Purpose.

P&G's Purpose Statement articulates a common goal that inspires us daily:

Our Purpose

We will provide branded products and services of superior quality and value that improve the lives of the world's consumers, now and for generations to come. As a result, consumers will reward us with leadership sales, profit and value creation, allowing our people, our shareholders, and the communities in which we live and work to prosper.

Our Purpose works to unify us in a common cause and growth strategy. It is powerful because it promotes a simple idea to improve the lives of the world's consumers every day. P&G grows by touching and improving more consumers' lives in more parts of the world . . . more completely. While this statement defines our commercial opportunity, our culture reflects the broader opportunity of improving lives through and beyond our branded products and services.[1]

The Bill & Melinda Gates Foundation's Guiding Principles

The second example comes in a different format, that of "Guiding Principles." These principles provide the strategic, philosophical, values-based, and ethical direction for the Bill & Melinda Gates Foundation.[2]

Guiding Principles

The 15 principles below reflect the Gates family's beliefs about the role of philanthropy and the impact they want this foundation to have. The principles guide what we do, why we do it, and how we do it.

While many of them are fundamental to the way we operate, we will remain open to amending them as we grow and learn more about our work.

Guiding principle 1. This is a family foundation driven by the interests and passions of the Gates family.

Guiding principle 2. Philanthropy plays an important but limited role.

Guiding principle 3. Science and technology have great potential to improve lives around the world.

Guiding principle 4. We are funders and shapers—we rely on others to act and implement.

Guiding principle 5. Our focus is clear—and limited—and prioritizes some of the most neglected issues.

Guiding principle 6. We identify a specific point of intervention and apply our efforts against a theory of change.

Guiding principle 7. We take risks, make big bets, and move with urgency. We are in it for the long haul.

Guiding principle 8. We advocate—vigorously but responsibly—in our areas of focus.

Guiding principle 9. We must be humble and mindful in our actions and words. We seek and heed the counsel of outside voices.

Guiding principle 10. We treat our grantees as valued partners, and we treat the ultimate beneficiaries of our work with respect.

Guiding principle 11. Delivering results with the resources we have been given is of the utmost importance—and we seek and share information about those results.

Guiding principle 12. We demand ethical behavior of ourselves.

Guiding principle 13. We treat each other as valued colleagues.

Guiding principle 14. Meeting our mission—to increase opportunity and equity for those most in need—requires great stewardship of the money we have available.

Guiding principle 15. We leave room for growth and change.

BD's Core Values

The third example is from BD (Becton, Dickinson and Company), which is a global medical technology company with a very strong financial, ethical, and philanthropic history dating back to 1897.[3]

Purpose
Helping all people live healthy lives.

Envisioned Future
Become the organization most known for eliminating unnecessary suffering and death from disease, and in so doing, become one of the best performing companies in the world.

Core Values

We treat each other with respect.
BD associates act with respect toward each other and toward those with whom we interact. We disagree openly and honestly, and we deal with our differences professionally. Once we have made a decision, we act together in harmony.

We do what is right.
We are committed to the highest standards of excellence in everything that we do: on behalf of our customers, our shareholders, our communities, and ourselves. We are proud to work for a health care company whose products and services make a difference in people's lives. We derive our greatest sense of accomplishment from doing what is right—not what is expedient. We are reliable, honest, and trustworthy in all our dealings. We keep our promises, and if we make a mistake, we put it right.

We always seek to improve.
Superior quality is the "ground floor" of our organization. Upon it we continually strive to improve by developing, manufacturing, and supplying products and services superior to our competitors' and better

than the previous one. We study our progress and learn from ourselves and others how to do things more effectively and efficiently. Our commitment to quality goes beyond how well we serve our customers to include the way we deal with all people. How we do things is as important to us as what we do.

We accept personal responsibility.
We consider individual involvement and accountability to be both a right and a privilege and accept personal responsibility for everything that we do. We treat the company's reputation as our own and try to make wise use of our time and the company's resources. We expect access to the tools and information necessary to participate in any decisions that will reflect on our collective or individual reputations.

As management consultant and author Tom Peters has repeatedly stated, successful companies are shaped by their corporate philosophies.

Purpose and mission statements can take different formats. Russell Conwell, founder of Temple University in Philadelphia, was a nationally known nineteenth-century orator. More than 1,500 times during his lifetime, he delivered a single speech entitled "Acres of Diamonds." In booklet form, more than 1 million copies of the speech have been issued, and it is still in print today. The speech reflects the belief that America's genius is in the intellectual and social resources of all its people, including the poor and the immigrant; that our immigrant cities hold acres of these diamonds, who, given the chance to gain an education and given the opportunity of America, will shine like diamonds. The speech grew out of a mission Conwell gave his university, a mission that guides Temple administrators and faculty today, well over 100 years after its founding.

The purpose or mission statement should help shape how the company operates, how leaders lead, how the company works with its people and its external constituencies. It should be reflected in how work is done at the function or team level. Reviewing it and thinking about how it affects the function's priorities and activities should be an important part of the diagnostic process. How should the purpose affect what we do? What's not happening that should be happening? What are we presently doing that is not in line with the mission statement? Conversely, as a key indicator of your organization's vision, the purpose or mission statement should be reexamined periodically to determine if any changes are warranted and to make certain that the way the organization is functioning is consistent with its purpose. Changes in a purpose statement should not be made lightly, as it is fundamental in describing an organization's reason for being.

Another important point of this first diagnostic target is that of planning, including long-term goals and short-term objectives. Review the corporate or functional strategic plan. Does long- or even short-term planning exist? What should be your planning horizon? Historically, strategic plans were three to five years or longer. In some sectors today, three or more years could seem like an eternity. Is there contingency planning in which provisions are made for the unexpected or for emergencies? How do you address factors affecting risk and risk management? Do these plans help or stifle innovation or continuous improvement? In your judgment, will these plans hold up under the pressure of a crisis?

Compare emerging markets and product lines for synergy. Do they match? For example, in the 1990s, one large mainframe computer company saw no long-term future for personal computers while another mainframe manufacturer saw the PC as virtually its only future. The first of these companies does not exist today. In today's technology world, companies need to demonstrate the ability to turn on a dime yet use their planning and innovation processes to ensure a robust portfolio of promising products. One pharmaceutical company sees great growth in fighting infectious diseases as well as dementia and Alzheimer's syndrome. Another is committed to biological approaches to treating cancer and diseases of the immune system. One hospital's goal is to increase profits by testing drugs while another has established extensive diagnostic labs in communities it serves.

How does your function fit into the company's long-term goals? Make sure your long-term goals help achieve the corporate goals. Similarly, make sure your department's short-term and yearly objectives are specific, concrete, and measurable. Identify the signposts that measure how well they are achieved. Make sure there is alignment between your function and the broader corporate goals.

Comparing objectives is a spiral process. Departmental objectives should develop from divisional and corporate goals and strategies; work group objectives should evolve from departmental objectives; individual leader objectives should be related to work group objectives; and direct reports objectives should be related to leader and work team objectives. Goals and objectives from the most operational level upward should help achieve corporate objectives and longer-term goals. In today's team-based organizations, be certain that your function's planning and objectives flow smoothly and are aligned with horizontal team and processes such as supply and value chains.

Review corporate and departmental policies. Make sure departmental and work unit policies are in line with corporate policy. Policies provide additional guidance about how work should and should not be done. If policies are too restrictive, productivity can suffer. If they are too loose, legal, regulatory, and ethical breaches can occur. One need only look at the private, state, and federal bank lending and mortgage policies leading up to the 2008 financial crises and the subsequent deep recession as a clear example.

Many policies evolve over time and become habits. All policies should be reviewed periodically. Some need to be revised. Some simply add bureaucracy and may have no useful purpose. Other policies may reflect legal requirements. The diagnosis that is carried out by the steering committee should first review critical policies and retain the ones with the most impact on productivity and morale. Others should be eliminated whenever possible.

TARGET 2. LEADERSHIP, DELEGATION, AND ACCOUNTABILITY

A diagnosis should review departmental leadership. We have stressed the leader's importance as a diagnostician, problem solver, and leader of people, resources, and processes. Because of its sensitivity, this is one area that may not be the responsibility of the steering committee or task forces. It is an area that you may have to assess alone or with consultant help and with the assistance of your human resources partner as part of the diagnostic process. In other situations, you may be selecting a team from scratch such as in a start-up or a brand-new function.

Analyzing leadership includes issues such as the group's expectations of its leaders, the quality of the leadership, leadership's expectations of employees and the organization as a whole, the informal or earned power of your leadership team, and the efficiency of the reporting structure. How does the team expect leadership to behave? In the smokestack culture of 25 to 50 years ago, for example, workers expected management to be directive, arbitrary, and demanding, which led to divisive union-management relationships. In today's organizations, competencies such as vision, business acumen, fostering engagement, learning agility, and talent development are vitally important. Enabling and empowering employees is more the rule of thumb.

What is the organization's expectation? Examine the needs of the work team. What is expected by higher management? Consider the situational requirements of leadership. A young, inexperienced, relatively immature team may require close directive management. In contrast, a skilled, experienced, and mature workforce may resent close supervision, and such groups are often more productive in an atmosphere in which responsibility is more highly delegated. Assess the leadership expectations and needs of the team to ensure that your primary and back-up leadership styles fit the challenges at hand and the expectations of senior management as well as the team you are leading. Meshing your needs and preferred styles and those of your team may require you to "style flex" to create the best conditions for the performance of your team.

You must determine what you are able to delegate to your leadership team. What aspect of the day-to-day operations can you delegate? You must be comfortable that you have the leadership in place so that you can delegate appropriately and with confidence. If you cannot delegate to your team members with confidence, you will soon be overwhelmed with work—your own and theirs.

A manager for a large information organization had not sufficiently delegated responsibility to his direct reports, partly because he lacked confidence in them and partly out of his own compulsion to check everything and know all the answers. So he edged toward the 70-hour workweek (that's seven 10-hour days). He pressured himself to the point that it was affecting his health and family. He felt he had to know everything, be everywhere, and do everything. In the process, he created tremendous backlogs in the work. Deadlines were missed, customers upset. His own workforce became demoralized and angry as they found their own work scrutinized and often redone by their boss with little apparent improvement. This led to continued conflict between the employees and the manager. Ultimately he needed to leave the organization, and peace was restored with his former team under new and more effective leadership.

Your diagnosis should assess your middle managers' ability to demonstrate leadership as well as coach and develop managers and work teams. Do middle managers effectively lead capable people to whom they can confidently delegate responsibility? Review with your managers their direct reports, and encourage them to train or closely manage the performance of those about whom they have reservations. Chapter 4 has many useful tips in this regard. Transitions are a good time to make tough decisions, including those that could result in the termination of people who have been low performers but to whom your predecessor felt personal loyalty.

In this case, coach your direct reports on how to handle these situations with problematic or low-performing employees. Sometimes you may need to counsel the employee yourself. But do take straightforward, short-term steps to redress the weakness through training, coaching, or redesigning responsibilities. Careful performance improvement plans may need to be developed that could potentially lead to improved performance or, alternatively, lead to terminations. Your leadership team will be only as strong as its weakest link.

Also assess the key department tasks and who is accountable for each. In many organizations, people look puzzled or point in multiple directions when asked, "Who is accountable for a certain job or task?" Lack of clear accountability is a sure sign of trouble. Does the person who is accountable exert sufficient control over the work to be sure that performance meets standards? Efficient organizations work quickly, profitably, efficiently, productively, or by whatever criteria you set or approve as performance expectations. The more effective you are in selecting and developing talented team members, the less you should need to exert or expect others to exert a highly controlling approach with your people. In *Good to Great*, Collins describes a culture that reduces the need for bureaucracy and heavy-handed management practices by having carefully selected people with disciplined thoughts that lead to effective and disciplined actions.

The Informal Power of Your Leaders

Check the difference between informal and formal leadership. A manager of a data center had earned her position on the basis of diligence and hard work. She was the best technical data center manager in the group. Unfortunately, she was not very friendly or outgoing with peers and colleagues. She had earned neither their friendship nor respect. After her promotion, the group grudgingly followed her lead. Most of the time, they simply ignored her whenever they could. Before promoting her, her boss should have seen that she was not the group's informal leader. She had no informal power and no informal authority with the group. The leader of this group would have been better off promoting the group's natural leader or going outside the department.

An Efficient Organizational Structure

Also check the organizational chart. The reporting structure should help people work efficiently. Should it be a dynamic network or a more formal structure? We know one executive who runs the European region of a global organization and uses diagrams that look like connecting webs to represent how his teams should be working across business lines, functions, and countries. Structure should be simple and reflect the work flow and the way people really work together. Make sure the organization charts or more dynamic graphic representations reflect how people really need to interact, and encourage efficient work flow that maintains the standard for quality.

As we move through the first quarter of the twenty-first century, the rule of thumb is to keep organizations as lean, flexible, and fluid as possible, which can reduce bureaucratic organizational gridlock.

TARGET 3. POLITICS, POWER, AND CULTURE

When assessing the politics of your new organization, look for centers of power. Where is the informal and formal power? Who has networks of influence and can get things done, and who doesn't? Look at your organization's climate and culture and its values and beliefs. Make sure you work hard to build excellent working relationships with "high influencers" in order to achieve the goals and vision you have established with your team and organization. You can use the third Just Promoted Leader Tool (given in Chapter 2), Building Stakeholder Partnerships, to analyze your key stakeholder relationships and to identify ways in which you can enhance your relationship with critical stakeholders.

Formal and Informal Influence

One of the most difficult diagnostic problems is assessing the power of those who do not initially support you. Because they may have been in the function a long time, you may feel that they have more political allies than you. That may be true. But their having more allies does not mean they have more power. While they have informal power, you have the formal power, and, depending on how you build your vision and develop support and influence, you should be able to develop very strong informal power and influence as well. Chapter 2 includes a number of ideas that will be useful for you in this regard. The issue of power and allegiance to you is part of your diagnostic responsibility *and should not be delegated to a diagnostic* task *force.*

John was named to head the visual effects production department of a large information technology company. His first job out of high school was as a technician in the department, and he assumed greater responsibility as the department grew to more than 25 people.

Even though John was clearly the department's top performer and deserved a promotion, he had some liabilities. He was independent and strong-willed. He often kept to himself, and he was not comfortable with the give-and-take of group problem solving. His people were not sure he heard their concerns or even cared about them. In time, two of the earliest employees developed grievances about decisions that John had made. They decided to informally organize themselves to force John to face all the group's complaints and to share decision making with a "management board," which they felt they could numerically dominate.

John was willing to listen to the grievances and attempt mutual problem solving, but he was unwilling to share decision making with a management board. Because he had made that decision so firmly, his disgruntled employees had few options. They could disrupt the work, which they were partially able to do. But the ambivalence of other employees toward the disruptions and the general weariness of the employees caused by scheming, secret meetings, and gossip took its toll. The group's spirit and commitment to this quiet revolt soon soured. Within six months, the employees who had led the disruption decided to leave John's group or the company.

Formal power is the right to hire and fire, transfer, demote or promote, and reward. Informal power is the ability to persuade, influence, and be heard. Formal power is bestowed; informal power is earned through competence and relationships. In a showdown, formal leadership holds the money and power. Analyze the political climate of your department. Do those with formal power also have informal power? Who has earned informal power, and how do they choose to use it? Do they help or hinder your efforts? Do they help or hurt the organization's progress? Where are the power groups? If they are aligned along functional lines, such as cohesive work groups, your organization may be stronger for it. But if the political structure conflicts with the organizational structure, the conflict within work groups may affect productivity, employee engagement, and organizational effectiveness.

A marketing manager brought into a family-owned oil distributorship to increase sales suggested to the president (who was the founder's son-in-law) that his wife (the founder's daughter, who had worked there since she was a girl) was not organized and in fact disrupted office effectiveness. The marketing manager also suggested that one of the salespeople, who was the founder's son, was not productive and should be fired. He suggested that the company had hired too many friends and neighbors and that some should be let go because they were not productive. His observations were correct, but nonetheless within three months it was the marketing manager who was fired. He had missed the informal politics (the wife and son's real power) and, perhaps, misunderstood the culture (hire family and friends, help people we like, work with people we trust). The owners didn't really want the company to get big or highly efficient; they just wanted to be a little more profitable, a little bigger, and hire a few more friends.

Climate and Culture

Are the department's or team's goals in sync with the organizational climate and culture, and is the department's culture aligned with the best way to serve customers? For example, a bottom-line-oriented hospital management corporation decided to conduct research for pharmaceutical companies. However, when it comes to drug research, cost is not the highest concern for most pharmaceutical companies. Given the medical risk to patients, government regulations, the company's sense of ethics, the impact that negative publicity can have on a company's reputation, and the cost of product liability, most pharmaceutical companies value quality and speed far above cost. In general, they believe that researchers concerned about the bottom line will cut corners and eventually get the companies into trouble. The obvious clash between the hospital company's cost conscious culture and the quality goals of pharmaceutical executives is based on the cultures and values of each. What does each value? What is important to each? Can the two work well together?

Cultures differ in other ways. Financial institutions can often be bureaucratic and tend to be conservative. Direct e-mail insurance companies tend to be very entrepreneurial, marketing oriented, and aggressive. When one buys out the other, there is bound to be a clash of values and culture complete with whining, complaining, and general disagreement. Cultures have to be shaped and cultivated; this is a process requiring hard work, dedication, and time.

Values and Beliefs

Look at the corporate values. Look at the examples of P&G, the Gates Foundation, and BD presented earlier in this chapter. What is really important to each of these companies? Does your organization's culture conflict with the broader corporate culture? Even in radically different organizations (for example, basic research and marketing), there should be a core of common cultural beliefs. For example, if a company's mission statement is "Respect for the individual, commitment to service, and commitment to excellence," it should permeate the beliefs and values of those throughout the organization, including those in different functions, such as marketing and research.

There are some beliefs you may question—that our talent should be home grown; that everything we sell should be invented here (the NIH, or not-invented-here syndrome); that we should never use subcontractors or outside consultants; that we should maintain only those products that support a certain return on investment; that we should always take the lowest qualified bid. You may question the organizational climate—the climate for risk taking, for marketing, for growth, for developing new products, for realizing better quality, better timelines, or the climate for leading and developing human resources.

Since you are in the diagnostic phase, see if individuals or the organization hold certain values for a good reason. Certain clashes of values by different individuals or departments may raise new issues, lead to reconsideration of purpose, and be ultimately helpful. Other features will conflict with top management. Before you decide that culture or values need adjusting, make sure you understand their role in the organization and the source of their support. We will take a much closer look at culture and politics and how you can use them to your advantage in Chapter 8.

Target 4. Recognition, Rewards, and Incentives

The use of rewards and incentives is an important issue that a task force should address. It is usually a target for which people have a lot of energy. How are people recognized and rewarded? Are they rewarded for performance, or do they get an automatic raise based on longevity or contacts? Does your organization have performance standards and goals, and do managers use the standards and goals when appraising performances and making financial rewards? Are performance goals specific and observable? Employees should not just be told "Do your best."

Check incentive programs. Are top performers rewarded not only financially but with attendance at meetings and conferences, special projects, high-exposure corporate committee or action learning assignments, awards, bonuses, public recognition, or internal promotions? Do incentives help build a sense of pride and accomplishment, or are they withheld and used to intimidate?

Are incentives used appropriately and creatively? An important area to look at is the basis for incentives. One large corporation rewards research and development vice presidents on the basis of the number of new products brought to the market, not on the basis of product success, which may take much longer to assess. Think of the message this goal creates for managers:

- Emphasis on short-term accomplishments, with pressure to produce before the yearly deadline.
- A tendency to focus on quantity before quality, to look for products that quickly get to market.
- A tendency to push aside marketability questions and market research in the rush to produce new products.
- Little attention to a product's profitability or return on investment. Because of the reward for total numbers of new products, the research vice president fights just as hard for a product with a small market or low margin as for the home runs.
- A tendency to focus on products that are easy to develop because the technology is known (often, by competitors as well) rather than focus on breakthroughs, which take more time and are more expensive to develop but often produce greater profits.

What are people rewarded for? Innovation? Quantity? Quality? Loyalty? Longevity? Performance? Profitability? Teamwork? Knowing the incentive system can tell you a lot about individual and group performance. The ultimate question is, does the design of the reward and recognition system place the organization in the best position to achieve its vision of the future?

TARGET 5. RELATIONSHIPS, COMMUNICATION, AND TEAMWORK

A task force can effectively analyze communication and teamwork. How well do people get along? Do they cooperate to complete a project? Do they informally share information? Are cross-functional "dots" easy to connect? Are there efficient mechanisms to share knowledge? What is the trust level? Will people disclose important information to others who need to know?

One of the key teamwork variables is the ability to effectively and productively deal with differences and conflict. Is there a powerful norm of conflict avoidance, or are differences put on the table to be dealt with by candor, clear communication, and respect? Another variable is feedback. When things go wrong, how do people express their feelings? Do they attack, or do they attempt to describe the problem and describe their feelings? Can they express anger and yet maintain trust, communication, and mutual respect? Can they use crisis to increase communication about behavior and feelings?

What is done to increase group cohesion? Are there shared events, like parties, teams, and recreational activities? How do internal teams and committees work to increase group cohesion? Does teamwork in your organization increase customer satisfaction? The Cancer Centers of America have built their reputation on great patient-centered research, medicine, and equally great patient-centered teamwork. This teamwork regularly occurs between physicians, clinical specialists, and therapists in numerous functions, and social workers who also consistently and compassionately interact with patients and their loved ones.

Turnover hurts communication and cooperation. The time it takes a new person to become an informal member of the group, which can be three months or longer, is a time of reduced communication and information sharing between the new person and the rest of the group. Excessive turnover affects the performance and productivity of work teams and the overall organization.

Historically, Japanese management approaches point to the slow promotion and lifetime employment in Japanese companies as a way to increase internal communication and problem solving. Long-time employees build up networks of contacts within the company that enable them to get things done quickly and efficiently, albeit informally. Another excellent example of this management concept is the U.S. Army, in which a first sergeant, with 10 to 20 years experience, can get just about anything accomplished through a personal network of sergeants in supplies, administration, the motor pool, communications, planning, the mess hall, building maintenance, and housing. Conversely, when the sergeant doesn't want to do something, he or she will go by the book and cite regulations. It is a smart captain who tells the first sergeant to "get it done." A good officer knows better than to tell a good sergeant how to do his or her job. "It will be done," the motto of the U.S. Fifth Army Corps, is no empty slogan for an army that runs on the savvy of its sergeants.

TARGET 6. LEADERSHIP DEVELOPMENT AND TALENT MANAGEMENT PRACTICES

An organization's human resources and talent management practices entail a wide range of processes, including leadership development, talent acquisition, retention of key staff and maintenance of staffing levels, learning and development, competency assessment, and employee relations. A task force can make an excellent appraisal of the effectiveness of an organization's strengths and weaknesses in these, and other, important business-related people issues. In addition, your personal observations and interviews of staff, individuals outside of your function, and customers and clients will provide valuable information.

Leadership Development

IBM, General Mills, McDonald's, and GE are four examples of companies viewed as models for developing leaders. In these and other companies that are respected for their leadership development practices, leaders regularly model the behavior that they expect from others. They are personally involved in the development of other leaders. There is regular attention at all levels of leadership to the development of a pipeline of emerging leaders. Leadership development programs and processes support the business strategy. Business strategy and leadership development are highly aligned. These companies have the development of leaders as part of their genetic material, and it is very much part of the way they think, act, and invest. Leaders teach, coach, and mentor other leaders and those who show promise as leaders.

To what extent do these practices take place in your organization and the function or functions you lead?

Competency of Your Managers and Workforce

The competency of managers, leaders, and the workforce is one of the strongest single determinants of your ultimate success as a leader. The extent to which you and your direct reports successfully lead and create the conditions for high engagement and motivation of your human resources will influence how well you achieve your goals. Your most important job is to lead and manage to ensure that your organization's goals and objectives are achieved. This begins with assessing your immediate staff and the overall competency of your workforce. Whenever possible, use the insights and experience of a task force to provide input, compare approaches to building competence with functions and competitors, and recommend new programs and services. Are there resources and technologies dedicated to help employees and leaders learn, grow, and develop? How do you compare to other organizations?

Your direct reports should, in turn, appraise the competency of their staff. Ask for a thumbnail description of each employee, including his or her respective strengths and weaknesses, training, experience, and history with the company. It may be too early to make personnel decisions based on a single reading, but as you gather data and gain perspectives on the competency of the staff, these thumbnail sketches will expand and help you decide how best to use critical and limited talent resources. When assessing your staff, include their technical knowledge (about the work) and their ability to lead others. Consider using the tools introduced specifically for this task in Chapter 4. Once you have done your homework, give your top people your impression about the quality of their key people after they have shared their assessments with you.

Read your organization's goals, yearly objectives, structure, job descriptions, and performance standards, if they exist. They will describe what the department is supposed to accomplish, its individual roles and responsibilities, the reporting relationships, and the chain of authority. These can help you make judgments about what people are supposed to do and their expected and actual levels of competence.

Performance Management

Performance management practices help ensure that leaders and employees do what is needed in the way it should be done. In too few companies performance management practices are used effectively. Often they are not taken seriously. Performance appraisals are generally considered a yearly ordeal that employees and managers alike endure. But if properly managed, performance management will be coaching, learning, and developmental experiences. They can also point to performance discrepancies, help set career development goals, and help the employee set interim and yearly goals that will help the department achieve its work. Contemporary management practices point to the need for situational uses of performance and developmental coaching and feedback as opposed to heavily evaluative performance assessments that all too frequently lack good communications and a helpful path forward. Feedback and coaching on how the job is done and on goal achievement should be the hallmarks of a performance management program.

Performance standards should be customized to the job and should provide information on the tasks and the standards of accomplishments for individual performers. As such, they are more helpful than job or role descriptions alone.

Reviewing the yearly performance plans of people in your new department gives a sense of their capabilities. What does their leader think they are capable of? Performance goals indicate which high-priority department tasks must be accomplished within the year. Update these tasks with your direct reports. Are projects on schedule? Will project members accomplish their goals? Is the project still worth doing? *Where confidential personal and human resources information is involved, you or your managers should have the only access to employee information of this kind.* The task force working in this area should provide you with a candid evaluation of how the performance management practices throughout your organization are working and what can be improved.

Talent Acquisition and Staffing Levels

Is your company an employer of choice? Within the company, is the team or the function you lead well respected, and do they attract internal and external talent? Does your organization and team have an attractive talent brand? What is the buzz? Check the recruitment and selection process. How is talent recruited? Is the talent acquisition process set up to recruit outstanding people? If not, why? What is the real cost of hiring just qualified or unqualified people (that is, in mistakes they make and in lost productivity to managers and trainees alike)?

Is there a human resources staffing plan? Does the human resources plan fit the organization's long-term plan? Does it anticipate the types of skills the organization will need to help the company meet its long-term plans? Are personnel being recruited to help achieve the long-term plan? In a small consulting firm, two-thirds of the business consisted of training programs and materials designed to increase the performance of their clients. But the firm's probable future strategic direction consisted of management and leadership development and data-based information systems. Who should the company be hiring: people for the old business, who could help with the present heavy workload, or people for the future business, for whom there was not yet a full workload? Should the company's top people be developing the new product line, or should they continue to lend the old line their strength and experience to keep it healthy and profitable while others develop the new products? What is the best use of resources? It is the fortunate organization that has a workforce and leadership for both the short and longer terms.

Another question is whether the function has analyzed its overall human resources needs and staffing levels. Are people regularly working overtime, taking work home, and missing deadlines? Do they joke or complain about the workload? Perhaps people don't want to admit that they can't keep up, afraid of giving the impression that they don't have what it takes. How many new projects are coming online in the next six to eight months, and is the organization properly staffed with enough of the right people? Worse, there may be no new projects scheduled in the near future. Are managers and leaders who would normally delegate certain aspects of their work doing it themselves to justify their time and salaries? Are other people fighting over the little there is left? One manager, told he should delegate the training of new employees in his unit, said, "But then what would I do?" Maybe people are not busy enough. Is there dead wood? When was the last analysis of human resources needs conducted? What has changed since that analysis?

Retention

Finally, look at retention. Does the function hold onto its talent and experience, or is there constant turnover, the constant need to recruit, train, and the accompanying costs of lost productivity to supervisors and new staff alike? Talk to some who have left. Why the turnover? One company found that it was the lowest-paying large firm in the industry; another, which hired mostly nurses, assigned them to travel 70 to 80 percent of the time, which many, especially those who had children, soon grew tired of. A third company's workforce consisted of an all-male executive team and an all-female midlevel and first-line management staff. It was the women who left.

TARGET 7. RESOURCES AND TECHNOLOGY

Look at the department's resources. Are there enough budget dollars to do the job? Analyze the adequacy of the budget, the line of credit in a company where cash flow may be uneven, and financial management and reporting systems. Are you using state-of-the-art technology to optimize productivity? Also review capital investments, facilities, and equipment. Do you have necessary supplies? Technology will not always be a panacea. GM has learned that in its most technologically advanced plants, labor costs and escalating costs in their supply chain have made their cost of manufacturing a competitive disadvantage.

Apple has taken technology to a new level. Apple has become a benchmark company by combining outstanding teamwork, a culture that fosters innovation and the unique use of technology to produce breakthrough products such as the iPod, iPhone, iPad, and their generations of unique and user-friendly Mac computers that are popular around the world with near cult-like allegiance from their owners.

Walmart has become the largest retailer in the world for many reasons. One of their distinctive competitive advantages is their world-class purchasing and supply chain processes and technologies. They recruit talent from the top engineering and supply chain universities and continuously build and improve their capabilities. In turn, this gives them cost advantages that can profitably be passed on to their customers.

TARGET 8. INNOVATION AND CONTINUOUS IMPROVEMENT

Sony, Apple, Genentech, Microsoft, Dell, Google, Amazon—what do they all have in common? They are all highly successful companies with strong innovative cultures. If you go to Sony's Web site, the first thing you see as it is loading is, "Believe that anything you can imagine, you can make real." What a tone setter! These and other innovative companies have forever changed society through their products and services. Imagine today's world without personal computers, high-tech audio products, and flat-screen televisions, breakthrough and lifesaving drugs, high-mileage, energy-sparing hybrid cars, the ability to instantly order products via the Internet. Organizations with high innovation quotients typically act in the following ways:

- Foster personal creativity
- Value curiosity
- Have a culture that seeks new solutions to both old and new problems
- Encourage tinkering and experimentation
- Scan the environment for customer needs and wants
- Look at problems and challenges in new and different ways
- Identify both cost-saving and revenue-generating opportunities
- Take risks, sometimes reasonable risks and sometimes big risks that

stretch everyone's imagination and tolerance for failure as well as success
- Become magnets for attracting hard-to-hire talent who want to be where the action is
- Use and produce technology in new and different ways

As a starting point, assess your team, function, or organization against these same innovation criteria. How do you measure up? Are there obvious areas for improvement or for smaller, yet still important, adjustments that could be made to improve innovation practices and culture?

Continuous improvement processes help to enhance innovation, and they are also the building blocks to strengthen existing practices. Continuous improvement efforts almost always positively affect financial performance and bottom-line results. A focus on continuous improvement within the culture and with specific tools is not glitzy. It is not glamorous. It is, however, a major asset for any organization that embraces it. It can be as simple as implementing worthy customer and employee suggestions. Over the past several decades, much more sophisticated approaches have been implemented very successfully, and these approaches have reduced waste and have trimmed steps in simple and highly complex work processes. They have also reduced variation in both manufacturing and administrative processes. In this regard, six sigma (reduces variation), lean (reduces waste and undesired effort), and lean six sigma (a combination of both of these approaches) are all proven continuous improvement approaches that usually succeed when implemented well.

Here are examples of actions that organizations have taken that have successfully implemented continuous improvement initiatives. Consider these and other examples that follow as you assess your organization. Which are present? Which should be part of your organization? What would it take in terms of human effort, time, and money to implement selected practices that would be of benefit to your organization?

- Define and communicate goals and milestones for quality outcomes.
- Adopt common process management tools and methods.
- Appoint process leaders or process champions to lead and be accountable for successful quality and continuous improvement targets and goals.
- Communicate and train others so they view their work from a continuous improvement perspective.

- Sensitize others to the impact of process and variation in their areas of responsibility.
- Involve, train, and enlist others to be part of continuous improvement efforts.
- Solicit continuous improvement ideas from customers and other internal and external stakeholders.
- Ensure that process and quality measures are current as well as compliant with government regulations.
- Use continuous improvement methods to streamline and remove waste and variability work processes.
- Use evidence-based data to analyze, measure, and improve work processes.
- Learn and implement changes from errors, breakdowns, and near-miss events.
- Learn and implement changes based on selected best practices from other organizations.

The following are additional ideas related to work flow systems and overall quality effectiveness. Consider these ideas as well as targets in your organizational analysis.

Work flow systems analyses describe how the work gets done. They are important to help ensure consistency and quality among those responsible for the major departmental tasks.

Examine written procedures. Are they up to date? Do they reflect departmental policy? Are they consistently followed? Do they seem efficient, and do they make sense? Does the work get done efficiently even though or because written procedures exist? Is the informal way of communicating procedures, from experienced people to inexperienced, adequate for getting the job done, or are there inconsistencies and inefficiencies? Are people confused about what they are supposed to do and how management wants it done?

Analyze the work flow. Trace a sample of work through the system. Follow the process. Does the work flow follow well-documented procedures? Is it efficient and on schedule? Are resources available when needed, and are they up to quality? Is output of the required quality, and is it on time?

What is the effect of breakdowns on quality, efficiency, and costs? What are the causes of breakdowns? Are people in the right place at the right time? Does the equipment function as it should?

Does your supply chain help or hinder you? For example, what are the downtimes and delays? Are parts, supplies, and other inventory available when needed? What types of inventory controls are in place? Is the work up to quality standards? Is raw material (input) of specified quality? What percentage does not meet specifications? Does the process make sense and result in the expected quality? Do individual procedures make sense? Is the workforce trained, and do workers follow procedures?

Do procedures result in the specified quality? What is the quality of the product or output? Where are the quality breakdowns? What problems are uncovered by quality control? What problems come back from the clients? What kinds of problems do long-term users have? What is the reliability record compared to other similar projects or products, or according to client expectations?

As part of the organizational analysis, consider three approaches to collecting data about work systems: interviews, observation, and data analysis. These three approaches can be useful for you and for the work of the task force assigned to look at this target. Through interviews with managers and, especially, with those who perform the job day to day, you can describe the work flow functions and the tasks that make up each function. You can also inquire about real and ideal timelines for task performance and determine the real and ideal quality standards. This information can be compared with industry standards or regulatory requirements.

Then try to graphically reconstruct the entire work flow, from start to finish, using documents such as reports and sign-offs from an ongoing or completed project. Compare actual dates for performance tasks against a theoretically ideal project management timeline to determine how long tasks actually take with how long they should take. Examine related documentation, such as correspondence, that would indicate start and stop dates and problems; check memos and other internal communications; and review committee actions. Compare work flow at different periods of time or for similar projects. Compare successful projects with problematic ones or failures. What are the patterns? Where are the problems? Hire a consultant to compare your operation against the competition or industry baselines.

Then observe the work flow yourself to the extent possible. For a production process, observe the different tasks and compare task performance to what you know should be happening from the expert interviews and document review.

Intellectual tasks are more difficult to observe, although you can attend work team and task force meetings and review current documents, reports, and other analytical displays. You can attend and observe key activities such as team meetings, project management activities, sales calls, and/or field visits. Review and analyze meetings, and compare what is happening against what should be happening.

Work location is a part of work flow analysis. Are the right tasks being done in the right place? For example, what are the consequences of validating or correcting field data at corporate headquarters rather than in the field? Should elements be completed off site by a subcontractor? Should tasks be consolidated at a single site?

TARGET 9. EXTERNAL FACTORS INCLUDING LAWS, REGULATIONS, COMMUNITY, AND SOCIAL OR ECONOMIC CONDITIONS

Many industries, including pharmaceuticals, medical devices, chemicals, food processing, insurance, banking, transportation, and manufacturing, are regulated by government agencies and laws. As regulations change, they affect the way business is done. To analyze the present regulatory climate and how your organization responds is a part of the diagnosis. For example, as health-care insurance, food labeling, and production become increasingly regulated, the laws will affect the way managers conduct both research and development and marketing.

Legal judgments strongly affect future performance. Up to 50 percent of the cost of many products (for example, lawn mowers and all-terrain vehicles) pays for product liability insurance to protect the manufacturer from lawsuits brought by misuse of the product. In the health-care field legal issues almost always affect product development and costs. The United States has limited capacity to manufacture vaccines for infectious diseases in large part because there is a small but real chance, or the perception, that children inoculated will contract the disease from the vaccination itself, with possibly fatal consequences. This was one of the reasons that there was a shortage of the necessary vaccines during the N1H1 flu outbreak during the fall and winter of 2009 to 2010 in North America. So even though the vaccine is of great benefit and required by local and state public health officials, the damages recovered by parents of those few children who have died from the inoculation over the years have forced the majority of pharmaceutical companies to abandon vaccine manufacturing. Recent changes in legislation to protect manufacturers from such suits may encourage more manufacturers to produce these vaccines.

The change in government regulations for approving the marketing of new drugs has, among other things, permitted drug companies to use foreign medical data to prove that their drugs work. As a result, many companies are conducting more research outside of the United States, and, in fact, many companies are requiring that research be conducted abroad so data can be included with U.S. data. A change in government regulations, then, has led to changes (and possibly opportunities) in how business is conducted outside and inside the United States. In addition to your work and that of an assigned task force, internal audits and regulatory inspection reports provide a wealth of data about your organization's compliance with laws and regulations.

Local, state, or federal regulations can create tremendous burdens that make a business's survival more difficult. For example, many states have regulated pricing for insurance and transportation. Environmental regulations, while necessary and well intended, increase the complexity of doing business and may close down some natural resources firms. The smart and effective companies not only deal successfully with today's reality but invest heavily to predict trends and patterns. This is certainly true in response to concerns about climate change. Increasing numbers of grants and tax incentives as well as venture capital companies are spurring the formation of "green" companies and investments in alternative fuels to reduce the country's reliance on fossil fuels. The same can be said about research and manufacturing incentives for hybrid and electric cars. The incentives are creating new opportunities for major auto manufacturers following their near demise resulting from the economic crises and recession that began in 2008. They adjust today and plan for the future. They are more fluid than stagnant and more flexible than rigid in their ability to adapt to changes around them.

Community standards can also affect a business. Concerns about safety have affected the tobacco, liquor, food, and auto industries. Concerns about student achievement affect the organization and management of schools.

Review economic and social conditions as well. The population is getting older. The first of the baby boomers turned 60 in 2006, and millions across the globe have followed. People are more aware of health and fitness. The population is more highly educated. Diagnose the economic and demographic trends that will affect your new business or function. What will increasing consolidation mean in industries as diverse as airlines, communications, pharmaceuticals, and banking? What will increased international cooperation and joint ventures mean in industries such as manufacturing, advertising, and construction? What will the increased emphasis on licensing and concerns about copyright and patent infringement mean in pharmaceuticals, electronic products, computers and toys, and the apparel industries? What will be the effect of technology on companies that are stretching the capabilities of their present hardware and software? How often will you need to replace the technology base of your business, organization, or function? What does a cheaper currency mean for a service industry? How can service companies do business abroad?

FINDINGS, CONCLUSIONS, AND RECOMMENDATIONS

The steering committee ultimately receives findings, conclusions, and recommendations from each task force and consolidates this input into its overall conclusions and recommendations.

The steering committee should start to develop preliminary findings. First, the steering committee should review the task force reports for adequacy and completeness. Was the analysis thorough?

Did it address the right questions? Was data collection adequate? Were the proper people interviewed? Was consultation with outside experts appropriate and sufficient? Were adequate documents examined? Were the customers, clients, and other outsiders interviewed significant to the work?

There are other common problems involved in the development of findings, conclusions, and recommendations. Review for issues such as the following: Do the findings seem reasonable? Balanced? Without bias? Do the findings and conclusions match your perception and the information you have collected in many private discussions and interviews? Do the findings reflect all data sources? Whenever possible, findings should be represented in objective and quantitative terms, in terms of percentage or proportions of those interviewed and using deadlines or milestones described in documents.

Individual comments are significant primarily as they illustrate a perception or observation made by a significant percentage of those interviewed, or a significant percentage of documents analyzed. But individual comments that are unrepresentative of the group consensus are not balanced and sometimes unfair. Be careful, however, not to discard individual comments indiscriminately. Sometimes an individual might provide valuable insight or, at the least, contrasting ideas that can be helpful for comparisons.

The steering committee should discuss each task force's report in detail with the task force chair. If the chair is a member of the steering committee, also include at least one other member of the task force. To undergird the morale of the task force, to underscore the value of wide participation, and to ensure that task force members are heard, they should have an opportunity to appear before the steering committee and discuss their report whenever possible. Steering committee members should have read the report and be prepared to discuss it. Discussion of the report should be the meeting's focus. The presentation by task force members should be limited, for example, to a 10- or 15-minute synopsis of findings, conclusions, and recommendations, followed by a discussion period. Moreover, as deliberations continue, the steering committee should keep the task force periodically advised of its thinking and status. It is easy for task force members to confuse extended deliberations or unforeseen delays with a lack of interest or rejection of their findings and recommendations.

For one agency, whose work was to evaluate the quality of products to be sold to the public, product evaluations were conducted by highly educated reviewers. Their recommendations to approve or disapprove the marketing of the product passed through three successive levels of management review. While the overwhelming bulk of the work was done by the first-level reviewers, who often invested hundreds of hours in their reviews, once the review was passed on to the next level of management, the original reviewers remained uninformed about whether their recommendations were supported or not and which of their analyses were rejected or accepted by the next-level reviewers. It was as if the product of their hundreds of hours of work disappeared into a black hole. It was demoralizing to them, and it contributed to successively less rigorous reviews. The first-level reviewers would have preferred rejection to ignorance. Negative feedback was preferable to no feedback. For the participatory process to be credible, people must feel that their input was heard, even if it was ultimately rejected. To feel ignored is worse than being turned down.

SUMMARY

The nine-target model involves many possible areas of study. Some include the leadership capabilities of your direct reports and other highly sensitive topics found in targets 2 and 3 and are assessments you will have to make with the help of your boss, possibly with consultant support, and certainly with your human resources partner.

Other areas, including target 1 and targets 4 through 9, can be reviewed by the steering committee or by task forces organized under the steering committee. Eventually, you will review their recommendations and be deeply involved at the decision level, but in most areas you can get considerable help.

Even in the largest organizations, it's unreasonable to study all functional areas, at least at one time. Doing so will overwhelm your organization's ability to collect and analyze information and to absorb and implement recommendations. With the help of your steering committee, you will ultimately derive conclusions regarding the areas of study and develop a plan of action that will build on your organization's strengths and correct its problems.

Quick Reminders to Keep You on Track

- In Chapter 6, we described the rationale and organization of the organizational analysis or diagnostic process. In Chapter 7, we outlined the nine-target model for focusing your diagnostic efforts.
- The nine targets are the organizational indicators of vision and direction. Under your leadership, your organization's data collection efforts will be key to describing the relative health of these target areas within your organization.
- The nine target areas are the following:
  Target 1. Purpose, values, planning, and goals
  Target 2. Leadership, delegation, and accountability
  Target 3. Politics, power, and culture
  Target 4. Recognition, rewards, and incentives
  Target 5. Relationships, communication, and teamwork
  Target 6. Leadership development and talent management practices
  Target 7. Resources and technology
  Target 8. Innovation and continuous improvement
  Target 9. External factors including laws, regulations, community, and social and economic conditions
- With the help of many people in your organization, you will draw a number of conclusions and begin to develop a plan of action that will build on your organization's strengths and remedy its problems.

FROM RESISTANCE TO RENEWAL
Building Your Leadership Team's Commitment

We must all hang together; or assuredly we shall all hang separately.
—Benjamin Franklin, July 4, 1776

Anticipate resistance to your efforts while planning for organizational renewal. In doing so, you can build real commitment through your management team. You will need to accomplish the following:

- Identify those factors in your organization that will help and hinder your efforts.
- Effectively overcome forces and factors that resist change.
- Develop and implement a change strategy that works.
- Learn from others' failed change efforts to increase your chances of your success.
- Deal realistically and effectively with the politics of change.
- Understand Your Personal Political Inventory and what to do with it.

In this chapter, there is useful information about the following:

- What you should know about your organization's culture
- Why people resist organizational change
- Key behaviors and principles of effective organizational change efforts

- The Big Three Implementation Strategies
- Learning from organization efforts that fail
- Anticipating the politics of change

Leading change is like defying organizational gravity . . . and gravity has never had a bad day. In this chapter we will look at the forces in organizations that tend to resist change and maintain the status quo. The process of problem solving and strengthening the organization will unnerve some and excite others. Some will fight, some will drop out, and others may try to ensure your failure. But others (your biggest supporters and strongest contributors) will "own" problems and share in the solutions. These winners will turn barriers and problems into opportunities for improvement and renewal. These are the people who will join you in a joint venture to achieve common goals.

A few people usually leave for other jobs after a new leader's arrival. This can be healthy for you and for them. You may lose experience and expertise, but you might also benefit because turnover has a way of unclogging career paths for your bright, ambitious people. It also allows you to recruit some new blood. Promotions and new assignments become possible. Those who want to advance have opportunities to grow. Even without promotions, turnover lets you enrich and expand existing job responsibilities because assignments and projects are left uncovered.

When people leave your organization, wish them well. The impression that you leave on those who stay will be positive. Help them see the opportunities ahead even though it is natural for individuals to feel the loss of their friends and colleagues and their expertise. In short, turn voluntary turnover into new opportunities for you and those working with you.

Just as some will choose to leave, some of those who remain will fight you. They will test your skills, strength, and clarity of purpose.

When Dick took over a major department in a financial management company, he felt considerable hostility from about a quarter of the department. Some felt that he wasn't qualified because he had come from another functional area. Moreover, his training was in another discipline. Yet he had proven himself a very capable manager and project leader in previous assignments.

Besides being talented and a hard worker, Dick had developed a strong relationship with an executive who periodically provided valuable guidance.

At least four internal candidates had applied for Dick's position and were not chosen. Dick dealt with the four straight on. He began to model the behaviors he expected of others. In group and in individual meetings with them, he stated that he valued their talent and experience and that he hoped that they could stay and join his team. Dick acknowledged their disappointment in not being selected and their need to sort out their individual futures. He felt that they could contribute and influence others to do the same.

Two stayed and became valuable members of the department and earned greatly expanded responsibilities. Over a six-month period, Dick had to come to terms with the third individual, who never bought in and never joined the transition. Nor did he demonstrate the management and leadership capabilities expected of the job. Following ongoing, documented coaching and counseling sessions, warnings, and finally a probationary period, Dick eventually terminated the individual.

The fourth individual was the toughest of all. In subtle, often sneaky ways, he not only resisted Dick's leadership but tried to undermine him. He held back and/or slanted information that Dick needed. Within and outside the department, he missed few opportunities to criticize Dick, but because he used humor rather than outright criticism, he was hard to pin down. He wrote memos pointing out "errors" Dick had made. When asked to contribute at executive team meetings, he passed, made a wisecrack, or criticized. Rarely did he build on an idea or contribute positively to the group. He wanted his friends in the department to support him and undermine Dick. But Dick's team members, first indirectly, and then more forthrightly, began to brief Dick on what was happening. They too were anxious that the department go forward. A second termination was imminent and was avoided only because the individual in question accepted a position elsewhere days before he would have been fired.

In Dick's example, two good people chose to help, and they positively influenced others' performance. Two others chose not to contribute. One clearly tried to impugn his new boss. Both would have poisoned the renewing organization.

Yesterday's actions were antecedents for Dick's present success. Dick directly confronted resistance, and as a result, he and the organization benefited. Dick insisted that team members must be committed, energetic, and creative. He communicated and modeled from day 1 his view of the people and organization he wanted. Dick knew what he expected of himself and of others—the type of work culture from which the employees and the corporation could benefit—and he succeeded. He got the type of people he wanted and got rid of the malcontents and nonperformers. Now let's look at how you can translate resistance to renewal.

WHAT YOU SHOULD KNOW ABOUT YOUR ORGANIZATION'S CULTURE: A PREREQUISITE TO ORGANIZATIONAL RENEWAL

In recent years the social sciences have viewed groups and work systems in new ways. One key finding has been that, like societies, businesses and other types of organizations have their own cultures. In its simplest form, one could define organizational culture by answering the question, "What's it really like around here?" In Chapter 7 we introduced culture as a key diagnostic target in helping you understand your new organization. As you assume leadership, you will have to understand your organization's culture in much greater detail. This knowledge is a prerequisite to organizational renewal and needs to be a priority as you move into your new position and continue in your first year.

The following three concepts are important in understanding organizational culture.

1. Whenever People Live or Work Together, They Form a Culture

Culture is a complex web of traditions, values, beliefs, behaviors, and expectations that exist on an everyday basis. Culture should not be mistaken for the organizational climate, which tends to be transitory and shorter term. Culture describes the social, emotional, and psychological foundation on which decisions are made and actions occur. Companies with strong cultures model by example, matching their guiding principles and vision with the reality of daily behavior. In your new leadership role, you have the opportunity to set the tone from the top, to act consistently with what you communicate to others. What you emphasize is important.

2. Every Culture Develops Its Own Behavioral Norms

Every culture has unwritten expectations and ways of doing things, called *norms*, that are major determinants of the behavior within that work culture.

Norms range from those that affect how people work together and how power and authority are used to those influencing how people are recognized and rewarded. Norms can also include subtle behaviors such as communication and signs of stress. Whether overt or subtle, understanding the undocumented, or "shadow," organization, as it is sometimes called, is a critical skill for the leader who is assuming new responsibilities. If organizational renewal and growth are to be maximized, the influence of norms on what, how, and why behavior and events occur must be understood.

The best time to begin influencing the climate and culture is during your first days, weeks, and months on the job. This must happen as you help people learn about and understand what is important in their culture and the positive as well as negative impact it has on them.

When Andrew was assigned as department head in a medium-sized accounting firm, he had been forewarned about the culture he would inherit. This department had been marginally profitable for the preceding four years. Management had been somewhat laissez-faire, more concerned with workforce job satisfaction and autonomy than with productivity. It was a very nice place to work. Predictably, the culture strongly resisted efforts to change:

- Most professionals maintained an eight-hour workday, regardless of impending customer deadlines or the workload. Members of the executive team typically were the only ones in the building after 5 p.m. Compensatory time was taken liberally, especially for travel. Some would travel only between 8 a.m. and 5 p.m., even if the travel time extended the trip by a day. If West Coast work required Saturday travel, they took the following Monday off. If Chicago travel would get them home after 7 p.m., some would stay overnight in a Chicago hotel, or travel late and take the next day off.
- Managers did not assign work; rather, they offered work to employees, who often felt free to reject it depending on their tastes, like or dislike of travel, and matters of convenience. Managers had to ask workers whether they would take on work, and they often had to practically beg people to take on jobs that required travel. Frequently managers ended up doing difficult or inconvenient jobs themselves.
- By failing at or otherwise resisting work they did not enjoy, some workers had carved out rather undemanding jobs for themselves. Since there was not enough of what they liked to fill a workday, these people were

only marginally productive. Profitability was the result of efforts of too few members of the workforce.

■ Because people expected to work autonomously, some resented attempts to train and manage them. They neither understood nor appreciated the value management brought to the product.

■ Some mid- and lower-level managers conspired to keep top leadership away from the work, fearful that management might try to control working conditions, work flow, staffing, or hours.

With a mandate to make his department profitable, Andrew had to confront the culture directly. First, he formed a leadership team with the four top managers. They identified the organization's strengths and problems, and they began working on the weaknesses. A new financial information system was installed that assigned hours to jobs and provided reports to top management that showed which jobs contributed to profitability. Weekly time sheets tracked the time of particular projects as well as administrative, sales, and product development time. Profitability took on much greater importance as staffing and pricing policies were revised. Employees and midlevel managers received monthly reviews of their hours and productivity.

Most importantly, Andrew met with employees individually and in small groups on a regular basis, asking, "What are you doing? What's difficult? How are projects coming? What are the problems? What do you need? What's next?" He did this once, twice, three times a week with members of his leadership team, mid- and lower-level managers, and line employees, and in biweekly department meetings. He touched base with everyone frequently, including the support staff and workforce, and he set an example for other managers to follow. He managed by walking around, listening attentively, and responding honestly and directly.

Gradually, the culture began to change. People became more attuned to profitability and accountability. Mid- and lower-level managers, more mindful of the expectations, began to ask for more work and responsibility. Perhaps most importantly, those who most strongly defended the old culture and resented the constant supervision, the accountability, the meetings, and the talk about profitability eventually left the company. Those who replaced them were selected partly because they had the needed work habits and skills and partly because in their interviews, they indicated that they expected a different culture. The company became hungrier and leaner.

Organizations with unhealthy cultures know it. The managers who are working long hours to pick up the slack left by those under them are resentful. Ambitious mid- and lower-level managers are concerned about the organization's health because their livelihoods depend on it—they have tuition, mortgages, and bills to pay.

Find these people. Build around them. Hire people who will support a new culture. You may have to weed out a lot of the old guard before the culture can change.

3. Cultures Are Powerful

People are capable of visioning and molding the cultures of which they are a part just as they are capable of being shaped by that culture. Often during the early phase of a leader's transition, the prevailing feeling of the organization is that problems will continue, that things really can't change. This sense of powerlessness is often found at all levels in the organization. A corollary is an individual's feeling that "others within the organization are better able to improve or effect change and renewal." It is common to hear a middle management group say that if improvements are to occur, then senior management has the power to make it happen. These same senior executives are frequently heard bemoaning their inability to get those below them—the employees, first-line supervisors, and middle managers—on board. After all, they reason, this is where the work is really done. Certainly, middle and first-line management is where the people are who can make ideas succeed or fail.

The employees, on the other hand, who have much more influence and power than they typically recognize, look upward and say, "That's *their* job. They set the rules, and they have the clout." The prevailing sense is that the power and responsibility lie elsewhere and that others are responsible for success. Some use this as a weapon to avoid responsibility and place the blame elsewhere. As Janet, an experienced manager, would often tell her bosses, "You people had better . . ., somebody had better . . ., nobody seems to . . ., somebody ought to . . .," as if everything that needed improving were someone else's responsibility.

In reality, power rests within all of the groups working together to synergize talent and energy with the goal of becoming stronger and better. Excellent leaders at every level of the organization fail to accept "that's the way things are here" or "that's the way it's always been" as the norm. They are able to identify and reverse the forces that resist positive movement and involvement.

When Robert was an assembly-line worker in a truck plant, he made frequent suggestions to his foreman for improving efficiency and quality. He didn't complain; he didn't file grievances with the union. Instead, he tried to work constructively with management. When an opening for a new foreman came up, he was promoted to foreman.

Again, he made a number of improvements to increase quality and efficiency, contributions that resulted in his being named head of quality control. From quality control, he was named director of customer service for western Canada. While visiting one of the regional offices, he spotted a request for bids from a large trucking company. Upon inquiring, he learned that the regional manager did not plan to submit a bid because the customer had never bought the company's products in the past. Robert asked the manager if there was any objection to his putting a bid together, to which the manager said no, there wasn't. Within a week Robert had prepared a proposal to sell the customer diesel trucks. For good measure he threw in a 100,000-mile warranty. The customer couldn't resist, and Robert shortly thereafter was made a district sales manager.

From there, his career went to plant manager, director of manufacturing, director of sales, and eventually to president of his company. What is special about Robert's experience is that it demonstrates that the initiative of one person, his own initiative, could make a difference. No matter what his job, on the production line or as a member of management, he made a difference, and he believed in his company and its products enough to want to try.

Rosemary, president of the largest bank in a large East Coast city, started as a teller. She wrote a training manual for the tellers in her branch. The manual brought her to the attention of management, which promoted her to director of teller training. In whatever job she had, she once told a reporter, she tried to do the best job possible. From there, the promotions just took care of themselves.

Managers typically have many more responsibilities and problems to solve than they can manage at any time. Managers, supervisors, and members of the workforce who step forward with suggestions, and who offer to get involved in implementing the solutions, are often rewarded for their initiative. Organizations need energy. They have too few problem solvers and too few people who are willing to make an extra effort and take some initiative to solve problems.

Those who take initiative, who take some risks to make things better, are usually rewarded for their initiative and leadership.

The real challenge for newly appointed leaders is to act on the belief that there is hope and power within the organization to renew itself. Both Dick and Andrew found their support from among those who wanted the organization to be more successful, stable, and secure. Robert and Rosemary saw things that needed to be done, and they did them. Every organization has those who recognize the need to change and to strengthen the organization. They are essential if the culture is to change. In renewal, the new leader can serve as a visionary, a unifier, and a catalyst of people to improve their organization, their team, and the culture that supports these structures.

WHY PEOPLE RESIST ORGANIZATIONAL CHANGE

The following forces that resist change need to be understood so that you can counter their negative effect on the developing culture. We will discuss ways to reverse these forces later in this chapter.

1. *Lack of involvement and ownership in problem solving the organization's position.* Many new leaders are reluctant to involve their people in organizational change. Certainly, to ask them to participate will cede to them some authority and power. Linda, determined to change her organization's work procedures and to improve the standards for performance and the quality of the work in an efficient way, rewrote the procedures over a three-week period and presented them to her group at a department meeting. There was an uproar. People were upset that she had revised them on her own, and they were even more upset when they read them. Some fought her. Others said that since she wanted to figure out the solutions, she could have *all* the problems as well.

The people who hold the organization's critical positions in management and the workforce must feel a sense of ownership for the organization's new ideas. They must participate in developing and implementing important ideas. Their input must receive consideration. Everyone must feel heard if he or she tries to contribute.

2. *Failure to identify the issues to be addressed and specific action steps to be taken.* A most difficult part of addressing change is to move from the identification of a problem (what's wrong) to the identification of a solution and the action steps, including timetables and milestones for improvement.

A human resources department in an aerospace company had been teaching a technical course for three years. Three trainers taught the course periodically. All three complained about the same problems with the course. They didn't like some of the activities, didn't think the instructor's guide was adequate, and felt the participant's manual was too sketchy. Yet in three years not one of them had made any changes. Nor had one even asked management for some time to improve the materials. They simply complained and continued to live with the problems. People need to stop complaining, identify the solution, and take responsibility for selling the improvement to others in the organization and for getting it done.

3. *Escape from accountability.* Given their choice, many people in low or moderately performing organizations would choose not to be held accountable for their work or for efforts to improve the organization. A small device manufacturing company had a serious problem with product reliability. Users blamed the manufacturer. Within the manufacturing company, the product designers, quality assurance and quality control technicians, project managers, and those who tested the product in the field each blamed someone else for the product failure. No one wanted the responsibility for creating solutions. To solve these problems required people to get involved and to take the initiative. They need to get work done and find even better ways to do the job next time.

4. *Not using positive peer support and peer pressure adequately.* Organizational change requires developing a culture that supports change from within. This means that the workforce must be convinced that its best interests coincide with what is best for the organization. Some of the most convincing arguments come from colleagues and peers who understand the positive implications in strengthening an organization. Unions are slowly recognizing this as they see jobs flee to Mexico and other countries. Managers need to see this as well.

Management too often keeps the organizational improvement process to itself, often reinforcing a we-they dichotomy that embodies the worst in labor-management relations. Management's authoritarianism and control led to the adversarial conflicts between labor and management in the period of the 1930s to the 1970s, especially in the autoworkers, steelworkers, and garment workers unions.

When the workforce distrusts management, it is very difficult to establish that cooperation. A group of professionals in a small advertising firm shared grievances about a lack of consultation on projects, job costing, the control of projects, allocation of company resources, and profit sharing. Once the group realized their common grievances and approached management with their concerns, management could essentially do nothing to placate them because things had deteriorated to the point that every response management made to solve the problem was viewed with distrust: "There they go again, trying to manipulate us."

One manager's offer to work more closely on projects was viewed as controlling. Management's offer of greater autonomy was seen as an attempt to distance themselves from the workforce. An offer to a sick employee of sick leave was viewed as an attempt to get rid of an aggrieved employee. A manager's friendly inquiry about a vacation was interpreted as an attempt to find out how soon the employee would return to work.

A common mistake is not getting the workforce involved in the organizational improvement process early enough. To get them involved after they have substantive grievances tends to encourage them to coalesce into a kind of mutually supporting group pitted against management. Better to get them involved early in the process, serving on committees *with* management, and *not* on worker committees that make recommendations *to* management. Build consensus, not conflict.

5. *Not exerting sufficient pressure on people to improve the organization.* Generally, the tension or pressure to change and grow is not strong in organizations. People will not change if there is little impetus to change. Organizations can benefit from pressure from within or outside the organization. This *structural tension* or *cognitive dissonance* is the tension that people feel when they realize the difference between what actually exists and what could be. The pressure can come from a variety of sources. External pressure comes from competition, from clients and customers, from leaders and stockholders. Internal pressure can come from leadership, from productivity or profitability data, from peer pressure, or from competition for internal resources.

Individuals often feel their own internalized pressure when they realize the difference between what actually exists and what should be. Those within the organization set internal standards and strive to live up to them. Without tension or pressure to improve, people tend to support the status quo.

Many managers share no productivity or profitability data with their employees. Sometimes the managers have no good data themselves. Some managers insulate their employees from the hard realities. Some don't tell because they don't want to give employees financial and productivity information when times are good, in fear of greater salary demands. Other managers don't want to alarm employees that their jobs, even their company, may be in jeopardy.

Organizations with little mid- and lower-level pressure to improve often provide employees with too little information. For an organization, especially one that is marginally profitable, to withhold profitability information from employees is to court disaster. Since employees have no reason to believe there is a problem, why should they change? To change their culture, they need to see the data themselves. Dissonance is created only by real, believable data indicating there is a problem.

6. *Doing too much, too soon.* Organizations are capable of managing only so much change at one time. Change disrupts the work flow, slowing or bringing things to a halt. Well-managed change affects the organization while not seriously disrupting the ongoing work. The opposite is also true. Organizational and business change efforts can be highly disruptive to ongoing business and priorities if they are not led effectively. This dynamic is not limited to businesses. For example, newly elected government administrations can become so preoccupied with priorities they choose to focus on, that other initiatives suffer. Some have argued that the war in Iraq during George W. Bush's administration and the ongoing focus on health-care reform during Barack Obama's first year as president prevented other important initiatives from being addressed effectively. When possible, a reasonable principle to follow is to work on one, two, or at the very most, three priorities at a time to build momentum and a pattern of successful implementation. The conclusions from your diagnostic work will provide a firm basis for your priorities.

The goals in the business plan that Morgan and his 14-person group developed were ambitious:

- Three new target industries, including one they knew little about but felt had parallels to their base business
- Three new products for old customers, including two that would need considerable organizational time to develop

- The purchase of personal computers for the staff
- A reorganization along product lines
- Naming of new product leaders

Launched with great enthusiasm, by the third month the effort had barely gotten off the ground. Committees no longer met, and Morgan's periodic attempts to raise the issues were met with uncomfortable silence. His organization simply had an inadequate mass of people and resources to do everything they wanted to do at once. They had spread themselves too thin and were overwhelmed. They should have focused their energies on a few needs at a time.

7. *Organizational homeostasis.* Like living organisms, individuals, groups, and organizations tend to level off at a steady state, or revert to earlier norms. This tendency to fall back is called *organizational homeostasis,* and it is common in all change efforts. Homeostasis manifests itself in several ways. One is the tendency for organizations that have improved their standard of quality to fall back from that standard. A group that has adopted a six sigma defects standard suddenly begins to find exceptions to the standard or to argue that zero defects is an unreasonably high standard that makes the product too expensive and that the customers will accept a slightly lower standard without complaint.

Homeostasis can also affect how the work is done. Many companies, having spent considerably on new IT hardware, software, and training, are stunned to find employees more comfortable with their old ways—including some programs that they have successfully used for over 10 years. In one sales group of eight, only two members were using the expensive new sales tracking system, and two of the eight had not even bothered to try it. Without consistent reinforcement and encouragement from leadership and revised work procedures to support the new, organizations tend to revert to former standards, procedures, and methods.

8. *Illusion of impotence.* People tend to attribute much greater power to others than they do to themselves. They often see themselves as isolated and unable to effect change. Individuals often see others as much more able to take action and to overcome barriers. Ironically, people will frequently identify each other as having much more power or influence than they see themselves hav-

ing. The key is for many in the organization to feel the ability to influence positive change and work with others to achieve it.

We've written about the effect the feeling of powerlessness has on an organization. Typically, each person feels someone else holds the power to change things. Even the leader may feel that middle managers, or even the workforce itself, holds the real power to change things.

Depression is a feeling of hopelessness. Nothing is fun or interesting anymore. We hate to get out of bed, to start the day, to go to bed. There is no energy, drive, or enthusiasm. Organizations, like the people within them, can experience depression. It is the hopelessness engendered by a feeling that nothing really makes any difference and nothing can get better.

Organizational depression is caused by a feeling of powerlessness. When we feel no individual or group has the ability to affect conditions, a gloom can easily descend over the organization. With power there is hope. Without power the workforce slides into depression. Organizations need people who take initiative, and initiative must be recognized, appreciated, and rewarded.

9. *Selective perception.* Simply stated, perceiving is believing. Perception gives personal meaning to what we experience. People filter the events around them through the selective screens of their needs and values. They will see and hear what they are predisposed to perceive, and they will believe their perceptions. It has been said that whenever two people interact, there are seemingly six people present:

- Each person as he or she sees herself or himself
- Each person as he or she views the other and the events around himself or herself
- Each person as he or she really is

As a force acting against change or growth, selective perception can be critical since people see what they want to see and what agrees with their perceptions. If people in your organization believe something, they will act as if it is true, whether or not it is actually true. You must deal with what is perceived to be true, not just with the objective truth.

A key to your success will be your ability to create a common perception of the organization's needs and its future. It will do you little good to reassure yourself that the group's perceptions of what exists are not accurate. People will act on perceptions as though they are true. And you must respond. You cannot ignore them simply because you know they are untrue.

10. *Rule of modeling.* Beginning in infancy, we learn how things are done through modeling, habit, and reinforcement. A type of programming occurs. The *rule of modeling* says that we tend to do first that which has been modeled for us. We will usually act as we have seen others around us behave in the past.

The young manager is fortunate who has worked for an excellent manager. A few months of observing and modeling the behavior of an excellent manager is more helpful than a dozen people with good ideas, or a dozen months spent in school.

Jessica had been on the faculty of a large state university for 12 years, when one of her former students offered her a job as vice president in his rapidly growing company. Eager for a new opportunity, challenge, and the chance to grow, she took the position.

To Jessica's great surprise, while she was brilliant at product design, sales, and service, she was not as skilled in managing and leading her function. Her university experience prepared her to be a self-starter and an independent thinker and operator. She was analytical, mentally nimble, quick to solve problems, and a good colleague.

But never in her 12 years of relative autonomy at the university had she ever been managed. Comfortable managing herself, she knew little about the role of leading others. She had never hired, supervised, trained, disciplined, or fired an employee, nor had she seen it done well. Never had she had a performance appraisal. She never had a performance plan, never managed one, and she didn't know how to plan work flow, the work of others, or a budget. While very concerned about her employees and their performance, she was essentially uncomfortable devoting a majority of her time to managing them. She was happier doing her own work.

Fortunately for Jessica, she reported to an experienced, professionally trained leader, who made management and leadership his career. As Jessica began to model some of her boss's behaviors, she was able to provide a better model for her own employees, and she developed not only a motivated but also a more organized, rational organization. To help your organization adopt new norms and behaviors, you will have to develop them yourself, and then model them, talk about them, and reward them in others.

11. *Vested interests.* It is often a shock to young managers to learn that people do not always do something because it is right and just. Instead, they often act out of self-interest.

When Vanessa became principal of an urban middle school, she was filled with energy for creating a school that would put the needs, concerns, and learning styles of students first. She wanted a new curriculum, new materials, new teaching methods, and new technology to help students. Proposing her ideas to her faculty, she was stunned by their negativity. She had expected they would greet her ideas enthusiastically. She was sure they shared her observations about the school's failures and that they would welcome changes that would do the right thing for the students.

But not every member of her organization saw her ideas as helpful. Applying their own self-interest, many saw Vanessa's plans as essentially disruptive to the organization and to their well-ordered and sometimes protected lives. They felt her ideas would require hours of planning, learning new skills, and new problem solving and that they would not improve student performance materially, or improve the school. They didn't see their own self-interest in the change.

Similarly, when Dennis decided to move his group to larger, more modern quarters, he encountered unexpected opposition from some of his senior employees. Many felt the new space was too expensive, was a longer commute, provided more space than was needed, and was more than the group could reasonably pay for. Again, senior group members did not perceive their benefit in the change, and they opposed it.

The most demoralizing experience of Suzanne's 10-year career was an organizational renewal effort initiated by Jay, her new boss. Jay, who had been a successful executive at a large West Coast industry leader, was recruited to Suzanne's East Coast–based company to improve research and development in an organization whose strength was primarily operations. Jay immediately began by naming six task forces to analyze the organization's strengths and weaknesses and provide recommendations to an executive committee of four. Suzanne's task force met once with Jay, then met on its own, weekly, over the next three months. Suzanne spent an additional four to six hours a week on the task force's work. Over the three-month life of her task, she devoted perhaps 120 hours to her task force, including some evenings and Saturdays that she spent catching up on her regular work.

Jay had not met with the task force during its deliberations, but at the three-month mark Suzanne's group had finished their report and presented their recommendations. And then there was silence. For three months her task force heard nothing. There was another meeting with Jay, and then nothing. No implementation, no feedback, no information about good or bad reaction to the report. Nothing. No explanation, no discussion. Suzanne felt she had been had. People in key positions, vested in the way the organization was operating, became very nervous.

Realize that power and influence usually rest with those who have worked hard to establish their niche in the organization. Those with established interest in the status quo will resist or fight change that might risk the loss of this vested position. Those who see their power unchanged or enhanced will participate in change. Be sure to spend whatever time is necessary to help those with existing interests and power to realize that they can also benefit as the organization changes and grows. To support change, they must believe it is in their best interests.

12. *Lack of monitoring, control, or evaluation tools to maximize follow-up.* Leaders must follow up on decisions, be accountable, and hold others to their responsibilities and agreements. Leaders who do not monitor implementation of plans, exert control when implementation gets off track, or evaluate effectiveness of the plans will fail. Without adequate monitoring and follow-up, all of the effort that went into the planning meetings, information gathering, problem analysis, solution identification, and planning is for naught. It is a waste of time. Worse, the people who invested so much time and optimism, the people who believed in you—believed in the process, invested themselves in it, and sought to persuade the rest of their colleagues to cooperate—will feel betrayed by your failure to ensure follow-through and effective implementation.

KEY BEHAVIORS AND PRINCIPLES OF EFFECTIVE ORGANIZATIONAL CHANGE EFFORTS

There are many approaches to changing an organization. Elizabeth, inheriting an agency in disarray, asked for everyone's letter of resignation the day she arrived on the job. She felt that by asking for mass resignations, she would have the leverage she needed to rehire only those she wanted to keep, in order to force immediate compliance with policies about which she felt strongly. Second, she felt it was easier to hire back selectively rather than to fire selectively.

One positive outcome of this tactic was that she captured everyone's attention in a hurry. However, she did not anticipate that work would stop and morale plummet. The threat of potential job loss caused great resentment among high and low performers alike. The high performers who were asked to stay were hurt and defensive that they had been forced to go through such an exercise. Many became distrustful, even though Elizabeth had had no intention of letting them go. What she did reminded them of their vulnerability and shook them from their feelings of security and complacency. Indeed, a number did begin looking for jobs elsewhere. A period of general malaise ensued, and Elizabeth had a difficult time reestablishing trust and support for herself. Some who stayed never did recover from the shock to trust her completely.

The most effective approaches to organizational planned change stress high levels of employee participation. The incoming leader will never have a more opportune time to build optimism and hope for the future than during his or her initial months on the job. Equipped with the knowledge of the typical forces that will undermine change, you can approach renewal with a core of practical principles. These *principles* should become goals of renewal as well as a *means* to achieve the objective of a fully functioning organization. They directly counter the dynamics and forces resistant to change. They include the following:

1. *Involve people.* Build from employees' individual and organizational strengths. Help them identify opportunities to develop solutions that will ensure higher productivity and organizational effectiveness. Your use of a steering committee and task forces during the diagnostic process should get you off to a good start.

2. *Model a true commitment to results.* Managed with energy, enthusiasm, and true leadership, high expectations most often beget high results. Leading for results must be a core value pervading all that is done well. There must be no misunderstanding that the primary goal is better organizational performance—derived from better results as individuals, as work teams, and as a total organization.

3. *Apply diagnostic problem solving.* As described in earlier chapters, people gain the best results when they work together on their organizational growth targets. A finely tuned diagnostic process will point you in the right directions. Identify and know what information you need. Devise effective and appropriate ways to identify your organizational and business needs, and then sight your vision and goals.

4. *Focus on changing norms and culture as a primary means to achieve desired results.* In the long run your results will come when people's attitudes, behaviors, and actions have changed.

5. *View your organization as a dynamic system.* Realize that activity, decisions, or problems affecting one area or person will almost surely affect other functions and individuals.

6. *Use positive tension and pressure.* Tension is essential for initiating and managing the movement toward change. The concept of positive tension, as mentioned earlier, is based on psychological principles that have been known for years—cognitive dissonance, discrepancy theory, gap theory, or structural tension. When people perceive a discrepancy or gap between an *ideal* situation that they value highly (for example, I *really* want to be valued by my team) and the reality of what is (they see me as passive, unhelpful), they will be motivated to change their behavior to achieve the desired state.

The organizational principle of positive tension is potent and releases enormous energy. When responsible employees, especially those who have high levels of influence with their peers and others, identify changes that will build a better place to work, you will have begun to build positive tension. They will want to reduce the gap between the way things are and the way they could be. A fabric of small groups woven together through collaborative effort is created, and the result becomes goals that are individually and organizationally attainable, valuable, and rewarding to individuals within the organization.

7. *View the role of the leader as catalyst, facilitator, decision maker, visionary, and leader of momentum.* This is the essence of moving up successfully and thriving as a new leader. It is also basic if planned change is to occur during the first year in your new role. The role is challenging and exciting.

It is your pot to stir. Remember, your leadership, power, and influence all count; use them.

8. *Lead with a "velvet hammer."* The most successful transitions by leaders seem to be characterized by the leader's well-developed interpersonal, and more broadly, emotional intelligence skills when they are combined with behaviors that are tough and courageous. The interplay involves blending the talents of helping professionals such as good listening, respect, and empathy, with those characteristics of results-oriented businesspeople. It is difficult but important to coach an employee, while in the next hour develop bold business plans or discipline or even terminate a chronically unproductive member of your group. This style is leading with a "velvet hammer." It is being able to show the best of your soft side and tough sides. Great leaders are simultaneously able to demonstrate their humility and ability to connect with their people while also clearly being determined, resourceful, and results oriented.

THE BIG THREE IMPLEMENTATION STRATEGIES

The eight behaviors and principles of organizational change work because they counter the forces that slow or prevent change. Here's how you can blend some or all into effective strategies:

Strategy 1. You can add positive forces, norms, or actions to the work environment where previously there was a void or unproductive activities.

Strategy 2. You can decrease or remove negative forces, norms, or actions from the work environment.

Strategy 3. You can add positive forces, norms, or actions while reducing or removing negative forces, norms, or actions (a combination of strategies 1 and 2).

Let's take a closer look at these core strategies.

Strategy 1. Add Positive Forces That Were Previously Absent or Too Weak to Help

Sometimes, something as simple as adding a valued professional or making a change in work location or equipment can dramatically affect an organization's performance. One small company simply hired an expert technician, which gave the rest of the workforce the confidence to pursue a certain line of business. Another organization increased training by 50 percent. One manager began an employee-led six sigma quality program; another initiated highly visible employee recognition and reward programs and employee appreciation days. Still another instituted a flextime program after studying successful and unsuccessful ones in 15 other organizations.

Strategy 2. Remove Negative Forces from the Work Environment

There are frequently obstacles that get in the way of good work by individuals and/or teams. Impediments could include certain conditions in the workplace, steps in the work process, certain reporting relationships, or even certain people. These impediments frequently can be managed by asking the following questions:

- What purpose does it (for example, policy, procedure) serve?
- Do we really need it or need to do it?
- Are anyone's behaviors (including my own) getting in the way?

If you find that impediments exist, reduce or eliminate them from your renewing organization.

Strategy 3. Add Positive Norms and Forces to the System While Simultaneously Reducing Negative Norms and Practices

A case involving a manager, Judy, demonstrates the effectiveness of strategy 3, which is the most potent strategy of all. When Judy provided much needed focused listening time to individuals at all levels in her department, there was a dramatic change in employee enthusiasm, morale, and productivity. Every Thursday afternoon, for 2½ hours, she welcomed employees into her office. Each took a number, and each was guaranteed at least 10 minutes with her to discuss his or her issues. She would then follow up with several of these employees whose ideas or concerns made a particularly strong impression on her. She would take them to lunch and have a less rushed and structured time to listen and interact with them.

Judy also helped communication with a regularly scheduled series of departmental lunchtime "table talks" started so that participants could vent feelings and informally generate solutions to persistent issues.

These sessions were designed to mix people from a variety of functions and different levels of work responsibility, which built stronger relationships and better communication across the department. Unlike her predecessor, when concrete suggestions were made, Judy wouldn't commit if she wasn't willing to begin implementing the idea within a short period of time. She always publicly credited the employee for the original idea. These actions resulted in employees' feeling valued, capable, and responsible for making things better. The overall effect was to reduce feelings of frustration stemming from poor communication.

Linda was selected as the western regional sales director for a thriving IT consulting organization. With five district sales managers reporting to her, she commanded a total workforce of 85 over a seven-state region. On composite measures for sales, productivity, and net profit, the region ranked last of six. Linda was hand selected by the national sales director following six years as a highly regarded account rep and district manager headquartered in the Sunbelt. Linda confronted some difficult practices when she assumed her new responsibility.

- Sales goals were dictated by her predecessor and forced downward to district managers and account reps, with little, if any, opportunity for feedback or negotiation. These people had become cynical about the goal-setting process and regularly undershot their goals. Goals were generally not reasonable.
- Communication within the region was poor. There was a strong feeling of "checking up" versus "checking in" with the account reps and district managers. This resulted in many inaccurate judgments about people and their dedication. Face-to-face contact was infrequent and usually problem or crisis driven.
- The performance management process was poorly administered. Recognition and reward was sporadic and based on loose criteria that the account reps felt were arbitrary and unfairly subjective.
- There was little sharing of "best practices" from person to person. If an account rep developed a new approach or a unique selling proposition, little was done to spread the technique or build on it with others in the region.

Within several days of her arrival as regional sales director, Linda began to implement a strategy of rapid information gathering and relationship building. Her diagnosis was already under way, as were her efforts to establish her presence and credibility. Linda knew of two very experienced district managers in her new region who were regarded as "old pros" with great loyalty to the company. Both were within several years of retirement and had maintained a solid work record. Neither had applied for the regional position, being content to finish their careers without the added pressure that comes with a more senior position. Everyone Linda spoke to in the corporate office said these two could be trusted as reliable sources of good ideas and valuable information.

Linda spent many hours with each of these two district managers during her first few weeks on the job, gaining important insights into the strengths and problems of her region. Without their help, it would have taken several months to gather this information. Both enjoyed serving as sounding boards for her ideas. As Linda began formulating an overall approach to improve performance in the region, she asked for their help. They became loyal and valuable resources for her, forming the nucleus of her leadership team.

Linda designed an approach that would simultaneously reduce negative norms while increasing positive ones. The approach included the following:

- Linda installed a goal-setting system for each sales district that began with a bottom-up approach. Each account rep identified sales targets, as did, in turn, each district manager. When these did not seem to meet a standard that Linda felt could be reached, she initiated a positive, win-win problem-solving approach to recalibrate the goal setting.
- Within 10 weeks, Linda had individual, face-to-face meetings with every employee in her organization. She was careful to listen more than speak. When she did speak, she conveyed a message of optimism and involvement. Within a short period of time, Linda had gained an initial impression of each person. She noted those who tended to complain but infrequently offered solutions or recommendations. They were usually part of her region's problems. It was easy to see who was positive and who made recommendations that could help. Early on, she began to break down the feeling of helplessness that her employees felt. She went right after the dynamics that had paralyzed her region. She was seen as a person with high standards and a willingness to empower the organization by listening and responding to her people's ideas. People felt energized.
- Based on an employee suggestion made in Linda's initial round of individual discussions, a "Regional Performer of the Month" club was begun. Linda asked five account reps and three division managers to develop objective criteria for selecting the monthly winners. From the

beginning, Linda invited successful ideas and realized the importance of recognizing people for their contributions.

- A small task force was formed to submit recommendations within two months on training, sharing of best practices, and meeting the communication needs in the region.
- Several other employees were asked to work on ideas that would improve the system for measuring and rewarding performance on a semiannual basis.
- Linda volunteered her region for a pilot evaluation sponsored by the corporation for the use of a new Web 2.0 social learning system that also included professional access to LinkedIn within the company. In doing so, she enhanced her image as an advocate and innovator for the region, getting her region new resources and recognition.

Today Linda has turned her region around. Sales are up. Her region has gone from sixth to second in performance within 18 months, and morale is up, as is productivity. People want to work for her.

In the process of renewing the organization, several employees were terminated, including two district managers. Linda's "velvet hammer" was respected because she had set high standards, listened, and acted collaboratively with her organization. Only the underperformers feared her. Linda's stock continues to rise in the corporation, where she is seen as firm, fair, and dynamic and as a supportive and highly effective leader.

LEARNING FROM FAILED ORGANIZATIONAL EFFORTS

For every success in renewing an organization, there are failures. While many elements are needed for success, to fail on just one or two key issues can undermine you.

Even a well-planned, thorough effort can fail. Lauren, with the support of a seasoned consultant, planned a comprehensive diagnosis that identified some obvious and some camouflaged problems. Her staff expended considerable time and effort in problem analysis, decision making, and action planning. The process was generally well designed and executed.

However, one problem was not addressed. Lauren was reluctant to confront her two most strident resistors. She was unable to resolve problems caused by their vested interests. Neither Lauren nor her supporters were willing to be as tough as needed. Conflict avoidance is a killer for leading change. Also, win-win conflict resolution wasn't useful because the resistors didn't want to compromise. As Lauren hesitated, her opponents simply stiffened their resistance. Ultimately, time and circumstances demonstrated Lauren's "velvet," but she could not use the "hammer." While some improvements occurred, the pace and depth of change was disappointing to her and her boss. Ultimately unable to control her organization, she was passed over for promotion and eventually reorganized out of her job.

In addition to wasting valuable time and money, unsuccessful efforts can escalate existing problems and further entrench negative norms, apathy, and frustration. Some of the most common traps follow.

Lack of Senior-Level Support

As your organization's leader, you have to be fully committed, skilled, and strong enough to improve or turn around your organization. Your boss must also provide unflinching support. If you are hesitant or if your support from above is ambivalent or weak, you stand a better chance of failing than succeeding.

Perpetuation of Win-Lose Behaviors

Moving an organization is difficult enough without people sabotaging the effort. Decisions that chronically result in winners and losers encourage people to drop out or stand in the way of progress. Once you are sure that you have the right people, then do everything in your power to use I win/you win (no-lose) problem solving as issues, barriers to success, and problems arise.

Some organizations use the Quaker concept of consensus before action. A Quaker meeting does not adopt a decision until all assent. This is time-consuming and not always appropriate or even possible. However, consensus decision making can be very powerful. It helps ensure that the decision has been thoroughly discussed, and it has a good chance to be supported up and down the organization. Organizations need people who can combine championing good ideas and helping to shape a consensus.

Inadequate Involvement of All Levels of Employees

Time and time again we have seen the status quo perpetuated because employees resent an effort of which they are not a part. Employees at all levels need to help plan and become involved in (not just hear about) the change process. As leader, you can design intra- and inter-level and cross-functional discussions, task forces, and meetings to engender the communication, problem-solving, and information exchange processes.

Forewarned is forearmed. If people are not describing the renewal process as "ours," look out! Also, make a special effort to involve your support staff, such as administrative and executive assistants and other hourly or nonexempt workers. Never underestimate their ability to help or hinder an organizational change effort or project. They are well positioned and are often more knowledgeable on certain issues than those to whom they report.

Inability or Unwillingness of Employees to See the Big Picture

Because they lack information, don't believe in the vision or purpose, or are blinded by selective perception, many fail to understand the intent and rationale of a renewal effort. Make sure employees develop a clear understanding of why and how "we" are proceeding as "we" are. Explain the vision, purpose, and process informally and in scheduled functional and team meetings. Encourage questions. Offer information. Concentrate on communicating the big picture as you work on the various pieces. Repetition of a consistent message will help your efforts. Over and over, offer the vision and the purpose and explain the process. If you believe in the goals, other people will usually believe in what you are trying to accomplish as well.

Falling Victim to Entropy

Organizational energy is hard to define and even harder to measure, but very easy to feel. Energy is essential if you are going to help the organization move forward. Regularly remind yourself of the following twist of a basic law of physics: *An organization in positive motion won't automatically stay in positive motion.* Earlier, we called this tendency to regress *entropy*. Once you have started the process of individuals and groups identifying ways of growing and developing, work doubly hard to perpetuate the effort. At some point, your organization will achieve and be able to maintain a new level of healthy functioning. Until the organization locks into its new level and pace, keep your foot on the pedal. Manage momentum by continuously tapping the sources of energy within your people.

Insufficient Attention to and by First-Line Managers and Team Coaches

As the linking pin between you and the workforce, your first-line managers and those who lead and coach work teams occupy a unique position. On a daily basis, they are accountable for the performance of the people doing the work. Accordingly, they need to be fully involved in renewal. When you think that you have integrated them into your plans, go one step further. Involve, inform, listen, recognize, and reward them frequently. If they haven't internalized their commitment, if they talk about "they" and "you" rather than "we" and "our," expect breakdowns in the renewal process.

Inappropriate Levels of Expectation

Changing the way things are—the culture, policies, and procedures—takes time. Short-term "highs" can be experienced in training courses, retreats, work team meetings, and individual and group problem-solving sessions. But you are seeking longer-lasting results. Depending on the issues uncovered during the diagnostic process, it takes anywhere from 6 to 12 months and sometimes longer to see results that can be sustained. *Set goals just out of reach but not out of sight.* Organizations that stretch are organizations that grow.

Anticipating the Politics of Change

Politics are part of any organization. University professors lobby for tenure, special research projects and grants, and preferred teaching schedules. Executives jockey for promotions and assignments to key task forces. Airline flight crews want favorite routes and departure times. Teachers and school administrators lobby for assignments to better schools, classes, and rosters. Politics is the process of ensuring, in a human organization brimming with feelings, perceptions, and competing needs, that you get what you want (hopefully not at the expense of others).

For the leader moving up, there are numerous opportunities to take advantage of the political environment. However, the road to political success is strewn with obstacles that can derail your career. Perceptions that change is imminent and the aftershocks of new leadership often heighten political behavior. People jockey to gain influence over resources, decisions, and perceptions. The early and continued influencing of people is of prime importance from the announcement of your appointment.

Earlier we talked about a new general manager who, within a few days of starting his new position, was totally engulfed in public and private controversy. His inability to manage the politics of his position inevitably led to his early exit.

Routinely assume that political forces are at work. *Never assume* that being a solid manager or leader and a strong performer alone will result in your success. Nurture, strengthen, and reinforce your support from direct reports and the team as a whole, your peers, your boss, and your boss's boss. Be part of their support and networks. Trusting relationships can go a long way toward ensuring your success. Always remember, however, that *your success depends first on the quality of your work and the quality of your relationships with key stakeholders.* Your work and these relationships are your starting point.

We have spent considerable time in this book emphasizing how to build support. You must be able to analyze the political situation, build a strategy to address the prevailing conditions, and implement a specific plan to make the politics work for you. Managed well, you can develop advocates who work in your behalf. One vice president of manufacturing said, "My people began to carry me. I previously had to drag them screaming. Turning it around was hard, but worth it!"

JUST PROMOTED LEADER TOOL 10
Your Personal Political Inventory

Try the following activity. Inventory those organizational political factors that could help or hinder your transition. Your awareness of these factors or patterns should help you develop a clear strategy and action plan to better manage the politics of your transition.

Complete this assessment as soon as you have some information about your new role, certainly no later than two months after assuming your new position. If possible, do it before assuming your role. Then repeat this inventory every three months during your first year on the job and once or twice a year thereafter. Do it alone or preferably with a confidant or consultant you trust.

Part 1

Instructions

Your Personal Political Inventory extends the stakeholder analysis you completed in Chapter 2. It is designed to help you accomplish the following:

Take a personal inventory of the key people and stakeholders and their influence on you.

Assess various political factors that may be in play that could affect your success in your new role. (See Figure 8.1.)

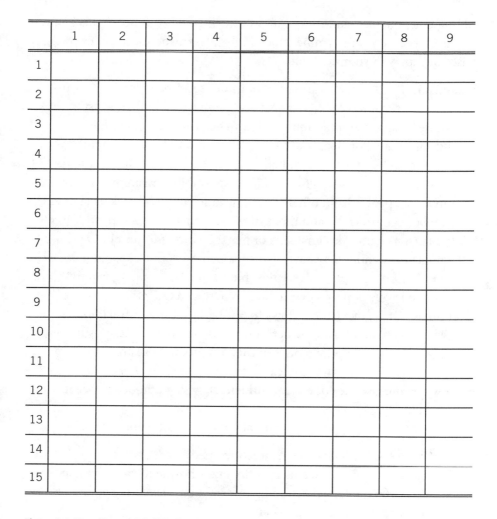

Figure 8.1 Your Personal Political Inventory

The inventory will allow you to capture in graphic or table format a considerable amount of important information that can provide you with valuable insights that can help you understand key relationships and organizational dynamics when viewed with a political lens. Part 1 consists of compiling data in a variety of categories. The instructions for each category correspond with a numbered column in Figure 8.1. Part 2 of the inventory consists of integrating the information, searching for patterns of political activity, and identifying potential opportunities or areas of vulnerability. In turn, this analysis can assist you as you determine which high-integrity political tactics you may wish to employ in your new role.

Column 1. List the names and titles of the 10 to 15 people in the organization who seem most able to affect you politically. Limit your list to those whose behavior or intentions can influence your success or failure during your transitional period. The individuals you list could hold any position and might be individuals from outside your team or that part of the organization for which you have responsibility. Examples are, but not limited to, people from other functions or locations, clients, customers, suppliers, consultants, and those in professional societies. In addition to the person's name, designate his or her title or role. A number of those whom you identify may have also appeared on your stakeholder analysis.

Column 2. Code that person's relationship to you. For example, B = your boss, C = a colleague or peer, DR = a direct report, and O = other (describe).

Column 3. On a scale from 1 (low) to 5 (high), rate each individual on his or her ability to influence others' opinions of you, whether positively or negatively. As with other codes in this inventory, these are subjective measures. However, they indicate how you perceive others' intentions toward you. Use the code I (for influence), with a number beside it (for example, I4).

Column 4. Code each person's general approach with you:

P   *Passive, laissez-faire.* Seems unconcerned.

PA   *Passive-aggressive.* Seems friendly but is hostile toward you beneath the surface, often withholding information, evaluating your work, or using humor at your expense.

RA   *Responsibly assertive.* Generally acts in an active, up-front manner. This person generally meets his or her needs without infringing on yours.

S   *Supportive, friendly, loyal.* Someone you can count on for support, who gives constructive and discreet help.

A   *Aggressive.* Generally goes after what he or she wants with little or no regard for your rights, needs, feelings, or position.

O   *Other* (designate).

Column 5. Place a YMR in column 5 for the five people whose work contribution *you most respect.* Limit your coding to five individuals. Do the same with the five whose work *you least respect* (YLR). In parentheses next to the five YMR and YLR codings, indicate rank on a scale of 1 to 5. For example, YMR (5) indicates the person whose work you most respect, and YLR (5) indicates the person whose work you least respect.

Column 6. The information in this column is the converse of column 5. Your coding will depict the five people who you believe most and least respect your actual and potential contribution. Use MRY for those who you perceive *most respect your* work and LRY for those who *least respect your* work. Rank order the individuals as you did in column 5.

Column 7. Identify up to five individuals who have access to very important information that could affect your performance. Code with an INF for *information*. You may also wish to rank order these individuals (for example, INF (1), INF (2), and so on).

Column 8. Identify up to five individuals whom you perceive as having access to critical or important resources other than information, such as people, money, or materials. Code with an R for *resources*. Again, you may wish to rank order the individuals.

Column 9. Using an SM (for *support me*), identify the three to five individuals listed on your inventory that you most want to have on your side (that is, supporters of your leadership efforts). You may already have the support of some, and you may need to develop the support of others. Now turn to Part 2 and pull your data together.

Part 2

Instructions

Integrate the information from Part 1 to assess your present political environment. Take some time to study your chart. Look for the connecting threads between two or more columns or the items within a column. A useful way to do this is by completing one or more of the following unfinished sentences as you review the information. Feel free to use any of the sentence stems more than once. Try these:

I learned

I relearned

I am aware

I was surprised

I was pleased

I was disappointed

I wonder

I hope

I am concerned

Complete at least five of these unfinished sentences. Take your time to look for the many patterns that exist. The following are examples:

- I realize that I have the support I need from my boss and direct reports but not nearly enough from my colleagues.

- I am aware that some who have access to the resources that I need to be successful are people whom I do not respect in terms of the quality of their work and with whom I do not have a good relationship.
- I was surprised to see the number of opportunities that I have to increase my influence with others.

Next Steps

- How would you describe the political impact of your new role? Who are those who might be positively affected by you in your new role? Who are those who might be negatively affected by you in your role? Who are now or who may become allies, fence sitters, or resistors? Who might even try to prevent your success? Are there others who may be affected by your appointment? How can you align yourself so that others become supporters, or at least neutral in their stance with you?
- Is there a key individual in whom you can confide or who can aid you during the early days? This person may be your boss, a confidant, a consultant, an HR partner, or someone you trust in your new organization. Many organizations have a wily veteran who has survived the comings and goings of many leaders, who is wise in the politics and operations of the organization, and who knows to keep information confidential. This individual can be a source of great political help and support.
- The type and timing of your oral and written communications will affect the political winds. Whom can you trust to help you bounce around ideas? Who can provide candid critiques? How should you best use his or her talents?
- For purposes of stability, what shouldn't change during your transition into your new role? People? Work assignments? Organizational structures? Certain aspects of the culture? Highly valued or potentially volatile symbols?
- Who are the organizational high influencers—that is, the opinion molders? How can you earn their support?

In this chapter we have looked at many issues relating to building your management team's commitment and effecting positive change. In the next chapter we examine ways to stabilize your organization after active periods of change to avoid future stagnation. We also begin to look at work and personal life issues that can benefit you in the process of moving up.

Quick Reminders to Keep You on Track

- Individuals, groups, and organizations usually are comfortable with the status quo; they often resist change. Understanding why is fundamental to being able to plan and execute actions that will improve and strengthen your organization.
- The primary aspect of resisting change centers on the resistance to your leadership agenda. There will always be some people who would prefer someone other than you at the helm and a different set of priorities.
- Understanding your organization's culture, that is, "what it's really like around here," is critical to your early success.
- Several concepts are important in understanding organizational culture:
  1. Whenever people live or work together, they form a culture.
  2. Every culture develops unwritten expectations and ways of doing things, called *norms*, that are major determinants of the behavior within that culture.
  3. Cultures are not stagnant; they change.
- The most effective approaches to organizational planned change stress high levels of employee participation. Your first year in managing a function will provide you a great opportunity to build involvement, optimism, and hope for the future.
- Important principles to adhere to in your effort to achieve the objective of a fully functioning organization include the following:
  1. Involve people and build from their individual and organizational strengths.
  2. Model a true commitment to results.
  3. Apply diagnostic problem-solving concepts.
  4. Focus on changing norms and culture where appropriate.
  5. View your organization as a dynamic system.
  6. Use positive tension for initiating and managing the movement toward change.
  7. As a leader, assume the role of a catalyst, facilitator, decision maker, visionary, and leader of momentum.

8. Lead with a "velvet hammer," that is, a personal blend of well-developed interpersonal skills combined with tough and courageous leadership.

■ Three strategies utilize these principles to effect organizational change:

Strategy 1. You can add positive forces, norms, or actions to the work environment where previously there was a void or unproductive activities.

Strategy 2. You can decrease or remove negative forces, norms, or actions from the work environment.

Strategy 3. You can add positive forces, norms, or actions while reducing or removing negative forces, norms, or actions (a combination of strategies 1 and 2). This strategy is usually the most effective.

■ Organizational improvement efforts fail for important reasons. The just promoted leader can learn from the unsuccessful experiences of others in order to avoid making similar mistakes. These mistakes include the following:

1. Not developing senior management support
2. Perpetuating win-lose behaviors in the organization
3. Not adequately involving all levels of employees
4. An inability or unwillingness of employees to see the big picture of organizational improvement
5. Falling victim to homeostasis—not achieving or maintaining momentum to change and improve
6. Not creating or maintaining high levels of expectation to improve the organization

■ Organization politics are always at work. They can work for you or against you. You need to employ legitimate approaches that will aid you.

■ Your personal awareness of the politics that could affect you is very important. Complete Your Personal Political Inventory several times during your first 12 months as a leader.

9

SETTLING INTO YOUR RENEWING ORGANIZATION

Nothing is as temporary as that which is called "permanent."

—Anonymous

By about the ninth month of your new leadership role, you should be able to begin helping your organization settle into a much higher level of performance compared to when you started. Also, throughout your first year, there are very important parts of your life outside of work that will frequently be stressed because of the time and effort that you are devoting to your new role. You will need to accomplish the following:

- Achieve a new, higher, more productive organizational "steady state" as you approach the end of your first year.
- Evaluate how you are doing and whether you actually like the new role you started less than a year ago.
- Step back and assess how you are working with your boss and other key stakeholders. Are you helping your boss, and is your boss helping you?
- Understand how you can manage the new responsibilities of your work life and personal life so that they effectively complement each other.

In this chapter, there is useful information about the following:

- Preventing future stagnation
- Fine-tuning your leadership role and your organization
- SOARING: Sharpening the way you think about your work and personal life

Preventing Future Stagnation

We have emphasized the just promoted leader's need to renew the organization. To do so requires great effort. In most cases, however, skillfully led renewal has an uplifting effect. People feel part of something worthwhile. You might even hear barely audible individual and group sighs of "Finally!"

But planned organizational growth does take a toll in time, effort, and money. People get tired of meeting to plan and implement change. There comes a point when they want to get back to doing their jobs full time and slow the pace of change. This cooldown usually comes after some of the major change goals have been achieved and while enthusiasm for the new vision, purpose, and direction is still strong. In many cases, the cooldown occurs during the later part of your first year. Subsequent changes will fine-tune the major changes already made, and they will not jolt the system as much as they did during the more intense period experienced earlier in the year.

In his 10 months on the job, Jim, the director of a high-tech research and development center, had overseen the radical streamlining of his organization. He had selected and personally involved himself in the development of his new executive team. Two of his five direct reports were new. The executive team had revised the business plan, which resulted in a reprioritization of the project portfolio and reallocation of financial and human resources. Resources formerly devoted to postmarketed product redesign were shifted to new product development teams.

The work flow was reorganized, and some formerly consolidated functions were decentralized. The planning, design, execution, analysis, and documentation of research projects were divided into five work functions, to be performed by specialists in each function. People would specialize in what they were good at, rather than being responsible for all functions.

Work flow procedures were redesigned, and the standard operating procedures were revised to reflect the new work flow. Much of the new design was technology driven. All professional and support staff were supplied with new software. New workstations were introduced into key design functions, and tasks formerly completed in person were now being done virtually and with the help of state-of-the-art technology.

The executive team met every two weeks for updates on the renewal. Each executive team member was involved in at least one task force. Even though consultants were used to facilitate the task forces and conduct much of the information gathering, analysis, and solution identification, the effort had nonetheless consumed about 30 percent of the executive team members' time and about 20 percent of the task force members' time. After eight months, they were dizzy from the pace of change, and many were feeling a discontinuity from their work. Few in the department fancied themselves professional managers. They were successful researchers who had been promoted to leadership positions, and they were anxious to get back full time to their newly streamlined research projects.

Fortunately for Jim, renewal was manageable. He had an experienced and stable workforce, good executive team leadership, and the support from above that allowed him, within reason, the resources and consultants needed to improve the organization.

Rob, named director of new product development, also hoped for a smooth transition as he took over his responsibilities in a telecommunications equipment manufacturer. But after a preliminary assessment of the 75-person function, he was less hopeful. Pitted against tough competition from Asia, India, and Silicone Valley competitors, he felt that major shifts in the existing approaches to new product development were in order. Projects were in early development that could jump the competition, but to bring them to market quickly, Rob would need a major infusion of cash in order to hire the right talent and provide the technology and equipment to attain this goal.

Under pressure from investors to reverse recent quarterly losses and a drop in share value of stock, Rob's management was reluctant to provide him the resources essential to the renewal he knew was needed. One top manager said, "We all have to manage with what we've got. We can't do more than we can pay for."

Rob's direct reports knew that in a competition between maintaining the product flow and rejuvenating the organization, product flow would receive top management's support. Overwhelmed by their own product deadlines, for which Rob's bosses would hold them accountable, they had little stomach for a major renewal effort. Like Jim's organization at the end of the renewal process, Rob's was exhausted as well—but it had not yet begun the effort. Already working long hours and under lots of pressure, they had no patience for the extra time and effort needed for examination and renewal.

Based on Rob's needs and the contrasting demands of his leaders, Rob realized the dilemma he was in. He lacked a well-designed corporate renewal strategy, with agreements from top and middle managers in key functions to make it happen. His strategy would allow the operations people to plan for a slightly longer wait for new products, while product development rebuilt itself. Rob's lesson was painful, one he should have realized before he took the job. In organization renewal, the pace and timing of change are often as important as the buy-in and involvement throughout the organization. Sometimes two feet are needed on the accelerator to strengthen the organization. Other times intermittent cruising speeds or even pauses will be in order, while the organization tends to the work.

Both these leaders, Jim and Rob, were faced with similar issues. Jim's was how to prevent stagnation in an organization wearied by the organizational improvement process. Rob's was how to overcome stagnation in an organization exhausted from the day-to-day work. Managing the ongoing change will be one of your most difficult challenges, and there is no driver's manual to ensure success. Here are a few rules of thumb that can help, however:

1. *Try to achieve the difficult balance between, on the one hand, combating the forces of stagnation and, on the other hand, overextending people.* This takes constant attention to timelines and progress, communication about delays and problems, openness to suggestions, and sensitivity to people's needs.

Juliette knew her group of data analysts was seriously backlogged, yet she knew they needed to have a better way to manage the work. So she decided to ease them into a process of change. They started with a series of once-a-week working lunches in the conference room, which Juliette paid for out of her travel budget. After two meetings, a core group of interested people formed, who continued to meet once a week for Juliette's lunch; others were invited to the open meeting, but Juliette's group committed themselves to continued meetings. As they discussed their needs and wants, they slowly began to develop a set of goals, and as interest grew, Juliette encouraged them to set a timeline.

She was able to gain agreement from another function in IT to provide some part-time assistance to work on needed data analysis and keep important projects on track. Additionally a consultant was especially helpful at analyzing alternative solutions and helping the group select and implement the best course of action for them. Two visits were scheduled to other companies to benchmark certain procedures and see new software in action. Juliette continued to ensure consultants' help, and she maintained the hiring and training schedule. By doing so, she was able to contribute to the broader change effort in the organization being carried out by a task force. She remained open to task force suggestions about delays and help with problems. She took their suggestions, and she maintained gentle pressure to complete the task. She did not want them to lose momentum, but she also didn't want them to be overwhelmed. She was sensitive to everyone's needs, and was able to keep daily work flowing while gradually adopting changes.

2. *If you are going to miscalculate, err on the side of overpacing, zealousness, and overcommunicating.* Goals that make people stretch are motivating. Unreasonable goals are demotivating because people feel they are impossible to attain. Set somewhat challenging time goals, and stay in close communication with the task forces. It is easier to throttle back than to throttle up.

All leaders and managers face daily urgencies, and the urgencies, because they have to be handled immediately whether priorities or not, tend to crowd out real priorities. A phone call, for example, is an urgency that is often not a priority task, yet it interferes with priorities.

Tighten time schedules, and pay attention to them so that work on the task force becomes a priority. If task force members know you are concerned about deadlines, task force work will become priorities and urgencies. If, on the other hand, you exert no pressure, the deadlines will slip in the face of other priorities.

When Kevin told his managers and task force members to get the job done "as fast as is reasonably possible," he gave them an open-ended invitation to prolong the task. Impatient about their slow progress, he gave them a deadline. Keep people very well informed about the change process. If anything, overcommunicate.

3. *Be aware of the tendency for things to revert to the way they used to be, if left untended.* Look for the signs of "organizational dry rot." You see them,

the growth-stultifying disease of "things as they were before, or things as usual." Continue to explore different ways to help people move toward goals.

Be wary of comments such as these:

- "We're not ready for this yet. Maybe we should slow down. Things are changing too fast."
- "Why spend the money? It's too expensive. We have spent a lot of time and money, and we are not much better off."
- "That's not our job. So-and-so ought to be doing that."
- "Things were better before the changes."
- "Why try this? We considered it three years ago and rejected it. It didn't work."
- "We've never done it this way. I'm not sure it's better."

Keep interest in the changes high. Reinforce them. Alert your team to watch for signs of slippage and to nip them. Where a change is not working out, be prepared to raise the issue rather than to just let things drift back. Actively manage the implementation so changes are reinforced. Identify implementation problems, and handle them promptly so those problems do not discredit the renewal process. Be prepared to intervene yourself or to get a direct report involved in solving burgeoning problems.

4. *Always use your diagnostic and problem-solving skills to "sniff out" what is going on.* Stay visible, and listen, listen, listen! Get into the work areas. Know your people's names. Be familiar with work processes and equipment. People will appreciate your skilled ear, and you will accumulate valuable information to help you lead your organization more effectively.

5. *Organizational health maintenance is essential!* Never forget that what you have gained in the first year of your renewal can be lost in a few weeks if you allow old habits to return. We have seen that bad habits, individual or organizational, are very hard to change. They also easily return. Just as reformed smokers quickly can again become smokers, so can organizational disease quickly recur.

The last several decades have seen an emphasis on personal disease prevention, wellness, and health maintenance. Organizational leaders can learn much from these social phenomena involving personal health management, wellness, and prevention. It is much easier to *maintain* organizational health than to incur the discomfort of organizational surgery and long-term therapy. Organizational health wellness and maintenance involves uncompromising standards and never-ending, everyday effective management. It also involves embracing the value of continuous improvement for your team and organization.

Derek had worked hard to reorganize the service at his deli restaurant. Working with his experienced employees, he had established guidelines for customer service. Some of the guidelines included these:

- Because customers like to be acknowledged and they like to order quickly, approach them with a smile and a menu as they are sitting down.
- Take their order as quickly as possible. Regular customers usually know what they want. People hate to wait.
- Get the order immediately to the kitchen. Put your name on the order form so the cook can page you.
- Water, bread, butter, and beverages fill the time while waiting for the order.
- Check on the order from time to time with the cook. Don't let the order get lost.
- If the order is slow, talk to the customer. Assure him that he has not been forgotten.
- When it is busy, divide the tables among servers so no customers are overlooked.
- If you see a customer looking around, inquire, even if it is not your table. Help each other to keep the customers happy.

In spite of these guidelines, there was constant slippage in service. Derek had to constantly monitor the floor, even with his best servers, to make sure they did not slip back. It required constant vigilance and supervision to maintain the new standards.

Fine-Tuning Your Leadership Role and Your Organization

As you near the end of your first year, step back from your day-to-day responsibilities to reflect on your new role. Reflect on what you have accomplished. Moving up is never easy. You've had to tap dance on a lot of marbles! Personal reflection often results in a new awareness: "I didn't realize that we had done that much."

Regular reflection and high levels of self-awareness should be standard fare for leaders moving up. Self-analysis is part of being a good diagnostician, problem preventer, and problem solver. Questions such as the following can help you reflect on your organization's progress and your own personal progress:

- How am I (are we) doing?
- Where do I (we) wish to be in the future?
- How should I (we) get there?
- Are there pitfalls of which I (we) should be careful?

At the six-month mark, Suzanne reflected on her accomplishments and disappointments as the leader of a small sales team. She had made three new hires. She had structured and led them through a comprehensive training process. They were reasonably confident they could work with new clients, were actively involved in developing proposals and contracts, and had mounted and successfully carried off an exhibit at the industry's major trade show.

However, Suzanne's list of disappointments was much longer than her list of accomplishments:

1. The sales reporting system was virtually nonexistent. Even though she had designed a system and she required weekly itineraries and weekly reports on contracts and proposals, her people were not accounting for their time and accomplishments. In addition, the operations department had insufficient information to plan for the upcoming workload.
2. In spite of weekly sales meetings, Suzanne did not have good data on her people's activities. One seemed good at managing old clients but seemed to have no new leads. One seemed to spend too much time writing sales materials. All seemed to avoid phone work. She felt uneasy that the reassurances she was given at sales meetings did not seem to be operational in daily performance activities.
3. In spite of the added sales resources and the fact that she had divided her marketing leads among her sales force, the actual number of sales proposals had not increased from when she was doing the job by herself. To some extent, this was because her salespeople were managing old contracts up for renewal and managing the professional conferences, activities formerly completed by operations staff. This in itself was an indication that her sales force was not sufficiently oriented to new sales.

4. Their reports from sales trips suggested customer interest in a single low-technology, low-priced product. She suspected the salespeople were not confident or knowledgeable enough to sell the more complex or higher-priced products.

At the six-month mark, Suzanne began a round of monthly assessments with her direct reports. All were frustrated that neither the sales information system nor the sales activity reports were automated. Similarly, they felt the proposals and contracts were not standardized enough and required too much effort to complete.

One salesperson, who had formerly been in operations, confessed his discomfort with the sales lead process. Another admitted not having enough leads but placed the blame on the excessive time required to generate contract renewals, product descriptions, and managing the industry trade show. They had few complaints about Suzanne's own style, except that each felt she was blind to other's lack of accomplishments.

These impressions had become increasingly clear to Suzanne, as her level of discomfort increased. Her six-month self-appraisal was an opportunity for her to turn her heretofore vague discomfort into clearly stated accomplishments and disappointments, to be objective about the disappointments, and to begin the problem-solving process. Clearly stated as problems, she proactively addressed the problems and avoided getting blindsided by them later on.

Her instincts to formally assess her performance were correct. Her boss and the operations managers were already aware of the problems in Suzanne's department, especially the lack of information about sales activity and the lack of new proposals and contracts. Suzanne's formal self-appraisal allowed her to surface these problems with her boss and solve them *before* he came to her with some ultimatums. Indeed, this six-month assessment may have saved her job. She demonstrated to her boss that she was aware of the problems and was managing them, which allowed her to solicit his help and the help of the operations managers in solving the problems.

At the six-month mark and especially as you near the end of your first year, review your performance, highlight your successes, and spotlight the areas that need improvement. Self-awareness is a core element of emotional intelligence. An employee's candor and proactive identification of challenges and areas for improvement will build the boss's confidence in the employee. This confidence buys time, which is what newly promoted leaders need to achieve their agenda.

1. *Prepare a written performance summary without being asked to do so.* As noted above, list your accomplishments, disappointments, strengths, and areas for improvement. Send it to your boss without being requested to do so, and schedule a meeting with him or her to discuss it. Show your initiative, interest, and insight in your abilities, and describe how you are doing overall. You'll be helping your boss to help you. It is your responsibility to help your boss be your coach, mentor, and sponsor.

2. *At the six-month performance review meeting, be prepared with questions for which you genuinely desire feedback.* Again, help your boss to help you. Be open to his or her ideas and suggestions. Ask specific questions for which you genuinely desire feedback. General questions usually result in generalized feedback. Demonstrate your ability to accept criticism if it is forthcoming. Don't be defensive. Listen, and try to understand. Learn from this experience. Show your enthusiasm and pride in what you have accomplished. Thank your boss for all the help, support, ideas, and feedback.

3. *Selectively solicit input from direct reports, peers, and others in the organization.* By asking for candid feedback, you create a potential reservoir of insight and recommendations. It is okay to be vulnerable with others. In fact, showing a limited amount of vulnerability can sometimes reveal a leader's humanity and can actually increase his or her credibility. In this way, leaders are viewed as authentic and, therefore, believable. Another useful approach is to reserve 15 minutes at the end of your direct reports' performance reviews to ask for ideas on how you can better help them and your organization in general. If you have done a good job establishing rapport and open communication, you will typically receive a wealth of useful ideas.

4. *Consider the following questions as a guide for introspection:*
   - How do I feel about my job now?
   - How do I like the job of leader?
   - Am I underchallenged, or do I feel over my head?
   - Can I do the job the way I feel it should be done?

- Whom have I affected for better and for worse?
- How have I developed? What do I need to work on next?
- How does the job fit into what I really value in my life, my family, and my lifestyle in general?
- What would I change most about the job? Am I able to make changes in the job to achieve a better fit?

5. *Reserve at least a week each year in your busy schedule to participate in a professional development seminar, workshop, or retreat.* These events might be technical and concern the content of your job. Strengthen areas where you feel less confident, and broaden areas of strength. Develop your management and leadership skills by attending an executive education program at a respected graduate business school such as Wharton, Kellogg, INSEAD, Stanford, or IMD (a business school based in Switzerland) or through an organization like the Institute for Management Studies, the Center for Creative Leadership, the American Management Association (AMA), or the National Training Laboratory (NTL) Institute.

SOARING: SHARPENING THE WAY YOU THINK ABOUT YOUR WORK AND PERSONAL LIFE

Successful leadership also means sharpening your mental outlook and the way you view yourself, your job, your family, and your friends. SOARING is a creative approach to thinking and viewing your personal and professional world, and it suggests seven points that successful managers can live by:

S **Superior** leadership is your daily goal and primary work value.

O **Opportunities** to succeed abound—you can make them happen, and every day they come your way.

A **Achievement** and success require a positive mindset that you can learn and develop.

R **Respond** to problems positively and energetically.

I Inform yourself about the common work problems and personal pitfalls of leaders who are moving up.

N **Never** fail to develop as a leader.

G **Gain** an understanding of the impact of moving up on your family, health, and time.

Superior Leadership Is Your Daily Goal and Primary Work Value

To be a superior leader brings us eye to eye with our true selves—our strengths, weaknesses, concerns, and dreams. To strive to be superior is simultaneously enriching, energizing, and challenging. To perform at the upper limits of our ability requires complex knowledge, skills, attitudes, and behaviors.

Superior leaders have a master plan, a vision of what they wish to accomplish. Accomplishing that plan is akin to eating an elephant—just one bite at a time. Superior leaders create and make operational their vision, with activities that, one at a time, help them constantly upgrade their abilities.

Feedback from direct reports, peers, and her boss helped make Carla more aware of her strengths and weaknesses. The weaknesses were, in particular, preventing her from becoming a superior leader, and she knew they would slow her success and promotion.

From her subordinates she learned they needed better systems and procedures to automate elements of the work that were repetitive. They wanted Carla to provide more frequent and specific feedback and to tell them when they did a good job more often.

Managers of other departments said they needed better information on her group's work, so those who handled the work knew it was managed in time, and those to whom she sent her work (her clients inside the company) could better plan for what was coming. They also said she was making too many last-minute requests of them, which created timeline pressures that interfered with their normal work.

The feedback from Carla's boss was the most critical because his impressions would affect her salary, bonus, career advancement, and in fact, whether or not she would continue in her job. At the six-month appraisal, she found her boss had already heard the complaints from her peer managers, who had been going to him with their complaints rather than to her. They felt when they went to her that she listened but didn't change anything. So in frustration they hoped he would be able to get through to her.

Her boss had some suggestions about her personal attire, the stacks of papers and unfinished work on her desk and sometimes even on the floor, and her office furniture. To him, these were symptoms of the lack of organization and planning cited by Carla's fellow managers. He also wanted more accountability from her, so that when he was asked about her work he could report exactly on productivity and short-term accomplishments.

As a result of the feedback at the six-month review, Carla was able to develop a plan of action to strengthen her leadership, which in turn would strengthen her working relationships with her boss and comanagers.

Superior leadership, Carla's aspiration, requires a master plan, and it is difficult to develop that plan without feedback, especially from your boss and your fellow managers who talk to him or her. Rely on others to tell you what you are doing well and what you need to improve. In the final analysis, it is their perceptions of your effectiveness—what they think—that will affect your present and future success.

Superior leaders seek to constantly improve their leadership abilities. For them, leadership effectiveness is a strong value and goal. Bob regularly strives to improve his leadership abilities either by practicing them or reinforcing them. He often listens to books and courses that he downloads to his iPod while doing his morning exercises. He rereads his favorite books on management and leadership every year, and he puts a short synopsis of the ideas he is working with on his BlackBerry and laptop computer. Every day he is aware of and applies in his work the skills and abilities of a superior leader.

Superior leaders like Bob exercise their best abilities many times a day. They are steady and consistent in their approach to their work. They are logical, consider alternatives, listen to others' ideas, and weigh consequences, yet are confident enough to override logic when their intuition is compelling. They trust their judgment and intuition. They learn who the others are in their organization whose logic and intuition they can trust and from whom they can learn.

With an unflinching commitment to their beliefs and values, superior leaders set high standards for themselves and others, and they have a low tolerance for anything less. Most importantly, they live up to their standards. When they are unable to meet their own standards, they figure why and work to improve. Bob's daily performance is shaped by his beliefs about good leadership. He constantly strives to live by his values to achieve his goals, and he maintains a remarkable ability to help others do the same. Superior leaders touch people's lives. Bob has the ability to make every person with whom he comes in contact feel better, more important, more competent, and more valuable and responsible. He knows when to take charge and when to get out of the way. Superior leaders seem better prepared and work harder and smarter than just about everyone around them because they are well grounded in the values, beliefs, purpose, and principles by which they live.

Opportunities to Succeed Abound—You Can Make Them Happen, and Every Day They Come Your Way

Opportunities are the constant. The ways in which each of us thinks, feels, and acts are the variables. We can control the way we view ourselves, others, and the world around us. Opportunities will be there, and we can grab them even when they surface as problems.

Superior leaders are extremely positive. They are energetic when others are complacent and calm when others are frenzied. Being "on the line" is a challenge to superior leaders who choose to be accountable to themselves first, feeling that if they can manage that hurdle, the rest will fall in place. They look for and find opportunities to shine.

For Brad, every business encounter is an opportunity. Contacts are opportunities for new business. He is always seeking an opportunity to determine which customer's needs the competition has not identified, is not aware of, or is not meeting well. "You know, Brad," said one potential client, "if I could combine your knowledge of the field with your competitor's technical expertise, we'd have a perfect program." This piece of information gave Brad insight into his competitive strengths, information on where he needed to improve, and an opportunity to suggest a joint arrangement that would get him a part of a contract he thought he had lost.

Another winning attitude Brad has toward his losses is the persistence to know that in a little while his lost contacts will see his competitors' shortcomings and be open to reconsider working with him. So, in effect, all contacts are potential successes, to be maintained.

Similarly, Brad sees lost business as an opportunity. Early in his career, he learned that most angry customers want to be heard. They do not necessarily want you to go away. Rather, they want you to hear their complaints and find a solution. They have already invested much time and effort selecting you, and they do not want you to fail. So Brad uses his company's failures as opportunities to meet with the customer, listen to his or her grievances, solve the problem, and keep the customer apprised of the progress. One unhappy client said, "Yes, I was very unhappy with the job your company did, but I thought your project manager or you would call back. I thought we'd try to analyze what went wrong, and we'd learn from it." Another client said, "Yes, it was a disaster—but it was really our fault. We simply didn't know what we wanted, and we didn't manage you very well. You should have called."

Within Brad's own organization, both successes and failures are similarly an opportunity to grow. It is primarily from his failures that he learns where things should improve. Failure is his most painful feedback, which shows where improvement is needed. A competitor's successes provided Brad with the impetus to pressure top management for more resources and new products and to pressure his own organization to improve. For him, both positive and negative experiences and feedback are opportunities for growth, improvement, and strength.

Achievement and Success Require a Positive Mindset That You Can Learn and Develop

Achievement and success depend upon a positive mindset that can be developed. Whether it is inborn or learned, some people seem to approach life with an outlook characterized by undefeatable optimism. In the face of disaster they, like Brad, have the knack of finding solutions for turning problems into opportunities.

More pessimistic leaders tend to view difficult situations as obstacles. They are often more prone to responding negatively to pressure and are often unable to convert tension and anxiety into energy. Those with a more negative mindset often have not learned to control their inner state.

The positive thinker tends to handle stressful situations with positive internal messages such as these:

- Yes, this is a difficult situation, and a solution is out there waiting to be found ("Yes, and," versus "Yes, but"). I need to focus, to think, to control the problem, but the solution is there.
- Solving difficult problems is like walking a tightrope, one careful step at a time.
- I am going to do the best I can even though this is going to be a difficult situation. I will be courageous. (A nationally known news anchor, in a recent interview, confessed to almost daily feeling the fear of failure, the fear in his job. But he also said that success is the ability to fight and, for one more day, overcome the fear.)
- I choose to reduce tension and anxiety by positively focusing on the part of the task I am working on today. John Wooden, the legendary coach and all-time victory leader in men's college basketball while at UCLA, always told his players not to focus on the goal but on the steps.

Do each of the things we stress well, and the larger goal (success) will take care of itself.

- If for some reason I didn't do well today, I will do so tomorrow. My best is the best I could do today, and tomorrow I will strive to do better.
- I will be the ultimate judge of my performance. I am not working to please others, but myself. I work to my own standards of excellence.
- I love difficult challenges; the tougher the circumstances, the better I perform. Challenges provide me the opportunity to develop new capabilities, to discover powers I didn't know I had.
  No matter what others say and do, I am always a capable person.
- What is the worst thing that could conceivably happen if I fail? And then what? And what is the likelihood that it will occur?

Respond to Problems Positively and Energetically

Here are some reminders that have proven helpful to leaders:

- No matter what, I will accept each challenge and my reaction to it. I will work with what life sends me and try to make the best of it.
- I will try to approach my toughest challenges aggressively. I will play to succeed. I want to win, to be the best, to do the best work, to be trusted by my customers to do the best work possible, to get the work. I will work to the best of my capabilities and succeed.
- *Though my enemies attempt to slay me and I am in fear, I shall put down my fears and live to fight another day.* (Saint Anselm's Prayer, posted on the desk of former President Richard Nixon.)
- I will include others in my success. I will gain their commitment by giving of myself and helping to empower them, and by giving them credit. I will gain influence and power by sharing it with others.

Inform Yourself about the Common Work Problems and Personal Pitfalls of Leaders Who Are Moving Up

While the snares seem endless, an important study has summarized 10 key reasons for leadership derailment.[1] Here is how they play themselves out.

Ignoring Specific Performance Problems with the Business

Leading well is a process of empowering your organization to continuous improvement by your working with your organization to identify specific performance problems and implement solutions. No business can be stagnant. Change is a constant of business. Even as things go well, you must keep your eye on the horizon, on the next generation of goods and services. You must ensure that your organization prepares for the future even as you succeed in the present.

Being Insensitive to Others: Using an Abrasive, Intimidating, or Bullying Style

Contrary to the business press myths about successful bullies who win through intimidation, few bullies ever make it to the top. The reasons are that they make too many enemies on the way up and they expose their Achilles heel, which is their inability to build a stable, strong, capable staff.

There are different kinds of bullies. The stereotype is of the yelling, stomping, threatening bully. But overcritical managers are also bullies as they over-scrutinize their employees and second-guess their decisions, creating in them the fear to criticize, to make suggestions, or to do anything beyond what they are told to do, for fear of being wrong.

Less recognized but having the same effect are the psychological bullies. These can be kind, humane, often personable managers who treat employees like children. They judge the employees' ideas (good, bad) rather than building upon ideas or brainstorming with them. They fine-tune others' ideas in such a way that these bullies end up assuming ownership and credit for the ideas. Their people feel like children who are seeking approval of their work and their ideas rather than colleagues who have valuable input and advice to offer.

All bullies—the loud and brash, the overcritical, and the psychological—have the same effect. They make people feel powerless, childlike, and dependent. They generate resentment and undermine the organization's ability to develop strong capable leadership.

Being Cold, Aloof, or Arrogant

Cold, aloof leaders think they have to maintain some distance from their workforce. In fact, however, successful managers and leaders are accessible, friendly, solicitous of their employees' opinions and input, and grateful for their assistance. Successful managers acknowledge that the best ideas frequently come from the workforce. Aloofness cuts managers off from the crucial information needed to manage well. Arrogance cuts managers off from the hybridization of ideas that form strong organizations. The arrogance that "I am right and only my ideas are good" discourages employees from taking the initiative to identify and solve problems. They will say, "It is his organization, all the ideas have to be his, so let the problems, the solutions, and the consequences be his too." Arrogant managers end up with all the problems and all the responsibility because they are cut off from needed information.

Betraying Trust

If an employee comes to you with a request, observation, or confidential information, you must honor the request for confidence, even while you feel compelled to initiate some action. Similarly, not trusting experienced and capable employees undermines their confidence in themselves. "Damn it," said one long-time employee to his boss, "I am 52 years old and a graduate engineer with over 30 years' experience in the field. I need to feel trusted to do this well."

Overmanaging: Failing to Delegate or Build a Team

One of Jo Ann's problems as a manager was that she couldn't let go, didn't delegate. The decisions she got involved with ranged from the trivial to the substantive. She selected the computers, the keyboards and screens, decided who needed training and who didn't, signed the checks, edited the product descriptions, made the presentations to major customers, and directed all the firm's most important projects. She hired, fired, supervised, trained, promoted, and reorganized. She was her small organization's leader, accountant, HR professional, trainer, purchaser, head of the support staff, and supervisor of buildings and maintenance. Jo Ann did it all, and she was exhausted, angry, and resentful of the load she was carrying.

And carry it she did—not because others couldn't take responsibility but because Jo Ann couldn't let go of responsibilities to say, "Okay, it's not the way I would have done it, but it's okay."

In the short term, Jo Ann was making excellent decisions that were helping her organization. But her reluctance to delegate severely constrained her organization. People were reluctant to make decisions on their own because they felt they would get a better decision from Jo Ann. As a result, responsibility upon responsibility and decision upon decision, both trivial and significant, were piled upon her desk. She became a bottleneck to growth, as projects and decisions awaited her attention. By helping, she was unwittingly sitting on the organization's energy, creativity, and competence.

Being Overly Ambitious: Thinking of the Next Job or Playing Negative Politics

One of Estelle's problems was thinking of her own promotion ahead of the welfare of her organization. There was a perception that she sought influence and contacts very carefully and with great persistence. It seemed to her employees that her current assignment was merely a steppingstone to her next promotion.

Whether her employees' impression of her was accurate or not was immaterial. This was the impression she gave. What did she do? She served on too many corporate and industry committees. It seemed to her employees that she spent more time in meetings outside the department than within the department. Much of the time she did have for the department ended up as time at her desk, preparing reports for her many committee memberships and doing departmental administrative work.

Her people saw little of her, and she didn't have much informal time to chat and brainstorm about problems. Furthermore, her direct reports felt that the amount of time she did spend with them was inadequate. She seemed more interested in responsibilities outside the department than in her department's work. How she used her lunchtime also affected those perceptions. Many lunches were so-called power lunches with top and middle managers who could help her career. Rarely did she lunch with direct reports and never with her employees. When no power lunch was scheduled, she preferred to eat at her desk, working.

She spent little time chatting with those on her team or other employees. There were few "free-floating" discussions about the work. Encounters were planned, to the point, purposeful, and functional. Things seemed so impersonal, so businesslike. Her people did not feel she was involved with them, their concerns, or their work.

And she got overly involved with the negative politics of the organization. Much of what is called "politics" is actually the behind-the-scenes gossip, criticisms, second-guessing, and politicking to advance a particular point of view. When politics are self-centered, they are often personalized, focusing not on the merits of the idea alone but explicitly or implicitly on the person advancing the idea to the benefit of himself or herself. In contrast, politicking can be used also in a savvy, well-intentioned way that advances good ideas for the benefit of the team, organization, and business.

Negative politics undermine face-to-face, direct, and open communication. Estelle's broad network involved her in corporate politics, even those that would not have normally been her concern were she not so intent on advancing her career.

Failing to Staff Effectively

Many top leaders say that the single most important factor in the quality of an organization is the quality of its professionals and leaders. Remember the *Good to Great* principle of "first who, then what." Hire the right people, provide them with the resources and support they need, and then get out of their way.

Staffing is the flip side to delegation. It is difficult to delegate when you feel the quality of the work will be problematic. A leader needs people whose judgment and quality he or she trusts. If you don't have them, get some new help.

Joyce, an extremely successful leader, formerly of a Fortune 500 company, built her success primarily through the quality of her hires. She got the best people available—even if they cost more. She hired the best—graduates at the top of their graduating class, from the best schools, alumni from top companies who could bring those companies' procedures and winning strategies to her organization.

Within a year of taking over her organization of 50 people, a third of the professional staff was new. Veterans who were not productive, who were not team players, or whose work required constant supervision were eased out. The new workforce not only had an improved work ethic but its members also had skills that reflected where Joyce thought the organization should be headed. Without surrendering any present capabilities, she was able to hire replacements who expanded the capabilities and quality of the organization's products and services.

Not Thinking Strategically

A successful leader must be capable of planning for the future, as well as managing the work at hand. Strategic thinking means thinking in terms of one-, three-, and five-year plans. You have goals for your organization's products and services, and you have operational plans to achieve those goals.

To think strategically also means to think about the future needs of customers. It is the ability to extend products and services in ways that build customers' loyalty and their interest in your products and services. It is the ability to keep customers coming back for repeat business, for future product ideas and needs. In the process, customers will bring their good ideas, which will provide a wellspring of product extensions and new product ideas. Sometimes customers will even help develop those ideas when the first customer contract is signed.

Anticipating competitive threats, planning for likely scenarios, and positioning your organization to cope with them are also essential to strategic thinking. Continuous improvement, an eye to new technology, and listening to customers are the keys.

Not Adapting to a Boss with a Different Style

We have repeatedly returned to the central issue of your relationship with your boss. After you have taken the job and think you have negotiated your role and prerogatives, you might very well have surprises in store for you. In Chapter 3, we discussed a number of issues. By now, you will have faced a few more.

Besides a full range of professional areas that could be ripe for disagreement, some of your personal habits may annoy your boss. He or she might value an office or desktop that is orderly and neat, a reflection of organization and good planning. Your boss might not think the way you dress, the length or style of your hair, or your habits of speech reflect the image he or she wants to project.

Your boss may be a late starter who stays late. If you are an early starter who leaves early, you may not score many points for your hours. Your boss isn't there to see your 6:30 a.m. arrival, only your 4 or 4:30 p.m. departure to be home for dinner with your family or to coach a neighborhood team. Check it out with your boss.

You can try to be stubborn and do these things your way. You may not lose, but you will not win. Whatever your boss's annoyances, they will crop up again and again, and they will color his or her perception of your performance.

Keep the things your boss disapproves of in your lifestyle out of sight. Don't bring them to work. Don't talk about them with coworkers, fellow managers, or even with friends at work. For the time you are in the office, they don't exist.

Pay attention to the hints your boss makes, to how he or she may gently tease you. Remember that there is frequently at least some, if not a lot, of truth in humor. If you have a suspicion about how your boss feels, raise issues of style directly. The more issues put responsibly on the table between you, the smoother the relationship.

Being Overdependent on an Advocate or Mentor

Overdependence on your mentor can lessen your effectiveness. Lisa, a junior manager serving on a corporate task force, impressed Sheila, a senior task force member, and shortly thereafter Lisa received a major promotion to a job in Sheila's organization. Sheila appropriately rewarded Lisa's drive, organization, group skills, problem-solving ability, and determination, all of which she had observed on Lisa's task force assignments. Working closely together, Sheila rapidly became Lisa's mentor and her strong advocate.

But Lisa developed problems later that stemmed not from her working for Sheila but from doing Sheila's bidding on some difficult assignments. For example, Sheila was dissatisfied with the pace of new product testing, and she asked Lisa to oversee new project management. As director of project management, Lisa was in the position to push product development very hard, which she did. She shared Sheila's feeling that products were developing too slowly. By doing Sheila's bidding, however, four things, all bad, could happen to Lisa:

1. Sheila's enemies could become Lisa's.
2. Lisa, politically much weaker than Sheila, would now be tied to Sheila's successes. Should Sheila's career falter, or should she leave for another job, Lisa would be gone too because she would lose her advocate.
3. Lisa might not be perceived as independent or capable in her own right. Her close association with her mentor may deny her the ability to demonstrate her capabilities in her own right and establish herself on her own. She would earn few opportunities that were not linked to Sheila. She would be seen as Sheila's representative in whatever she did.
4. Others in the organization may perceive that Sheila was propping Lisa up, a perception that would further weaken Lisa's effectiveness.

The effective leader has to acknowledge and benefit from the support of other leaders and mentors. Without people who recognize our talents and nurture us, few of us would move beyond our first job in a company. At the same time, we must attempt to remain reasonably independent of the people who sponsor us, and be self-reliant, a difficult balancing act.

Surviving and thriving in an organization is a complex, risky, and sometimes temporary business. It requires continuous attention. To succeed in a leadership role, at a minimum, you have to be smart, creative, and hardworking. Business and organizations of all types are so very dynamic. There is always something new with which to contend. In leadership you must simultaneously manage a complex of human, work flow, technology, planning, and competitive pressures that make leadership at once the most difficult, maddeningly complex and perhaps the most challenging and rewarding thing you will ever do.

Never Fail to Develop as a Leader

Never fail to achieve your goals to develop as a leader. We spoke earlier about the importance of improving your technical, professional, leadership, and personal competencies. Your knowledge, skills, and attitudes are the "qualifiers," the tickets to get in the door and stay there. Managers mature into superior leaders partly by setting challenging self-development goals. Leaders on the rise who follow through with such plans develop their own skills and abilities while communicating a clear message to their people about personal and professional growth.

We suggest updating and reviewing your executive development plans with your boss every six months and using every resource at your disposal in and outside of your organization.

Gain an Understanding of the Impact of Moving Up on Your Family, Health, and Time

The seventh and final principle in SOARING is to gain an understanding of the impact of moving up on your family, health, and time. The importance of this principle is so great that we have dedicated the entire last chapter of the book to it. Managing your personal life can be the quintessence of tap dancing on marbles. It is slippery, complex, elusive, and full of difficulties. Just when you think things have settled down, you will discover a new set of difficulties. Chapter 10 looks at suggested approaches to the challenge of successfully integrating your professional and personal life.

Quick Reminders to Keep You on Track

- Since planned organizational growth takes a toll in time, effort, and money, there comes a point when it is best to pull the reins in and slow the pace of change. This usually occurs after some of the major change goals have been achieved, while enthusiasm for the new vision and direction is still strong.

- Managing the pace of change will be a difficult challenge. Here are some helpful hints:
  1. Try to achieve the very difficult balance between the forces of stagnation and overextending people, so that both the ongoing work and the change process can succeed.
  2. If you miscalculate the speed of change, err on the side of overpacing, enthusiasm, and high levels of communication. It is much easier to throttle back than to throttle up in moving an organization forward.
  3. Be attentive and react as necessary to the business-as-usual mentality that typically impedes organizational growth.
  4. There are times to slow down or back off on the pace of change. During these periods, concentrate on the work at hand.
  5. Keep your ear to the ground and eyes wide open. Maintain your approach to solving problems through careful diagnosis.
  6. Remember that what you gained in the year of renewal can be lost in a few weeks if you allow old habits to return.
- Toward the end of your first year, step back from your day-to-day responsibilities to reflect on your new role. Review your performance, get ideas and input from others, and determine how you really feel about your job. Use the SOARING model as a way to view yourself, your job, your family, and your friends. Remain in regular communication with your boss; stay in his mental inbox; keep his expectations of you high.

PART III

Managing the Impact of Moving Up on Your Family and Personal Life

CREATING YOUR
NEW LIFE INTEGRATION

*Let us endeavor so to live that when we come to die, even the
undertaker will be sorry.*
— Mark Twain

*Time is at once the most valuable and the most perishable of all
our possessions.*
— John Randolph, member of
Congress 1799 to 1827

As women entered the workforce in greater numbers, *work/life balance*
became a popular term. It was meant to convey the relationship between
work and the rest of an employee's life. Today, with the advent of cell
phones, PDAs, mobile computing, and globalization, the term no longer
applies. *Work/life balance* implies that both work and the rest of your life
are equal—equal in time and equal in importance. Since the lines
between work and home have been blurred substantially, you can be
working 24 hours a day, from anywhere. There is no such thing as
work/life balance. That is why we now use the more appropriate term
work/life integration.

At various times in your life, different aspects of your life are more
important, require greater investments of your time, your energy, and
your focus. Many young professionals entering their careers are very
focused on their work. They need to invest significant amounts of time
in learning their new jobs and preparing for their professional careers.

When people form marital or partner relationships, some of their attention and focus generally shifts to accommodate that relationship. The birth of children dramatically changes how we spend our time and our focus, and more of our energy moves to family.

For almost everyone, moving up means changes at work and your overall management and leadership responsibilities. In turn, this usually means changes at home and in other areas of your life. New leadership responsibility affects how you use your time and your ability to act on what is important to you. Some handle these changes well. Many, if not most, find the changes a challenge. You will need to accomplish the following:

- Help those close to you understand the personal impact of moving up on your work and life systems.
- Use the six principles in this chapter to strengthen and complement the personal aspects of your life.

In this chapter, there is useful information about the following:

- The personal basis of moving up into a new leadership role
- Six principles of managing the impact of moving up on your family, health, and time:

  1. There is a profound relationship between personal wellness, family, health, and executive work effectiveness as you move up the ladder.
  2. Major job changes can often trigger major life changes.
  3. Leaders who are moving up are in a state of transition that can be understood and managed.
  4. Health and well-being in one's personal, family, and work lives affect, and are affected by, stress and distress.
  5. Mutual understanding, support, and responsible collaboration within dual-career families or with partners are essential for leaders on the rise.
  6. The goal is to achieve a new life integration.

THE PERSONAL BASIS OF MOVING UP

Today the composition of the workforce is considerably different than it was even 20 years ago. One of the most stunning social changes has been the number of women who have entered the workforce. Women are now half of the workforce in the United States, and they hold slightly more than half the supervisory, managerial, and leadership jobs.[1] In some cases women are now earning more than their spouses, and the decision about who stays home to care for the children becomes an economic decision about who has the greater earning power. The majority of women still bear the major responsibilities for the care of children even though increasingly men are sharing more of the responsibility.

Whether a leader is male or female, single or married, or has children or not, moving up to accept a new leadership position is a major life transition that spawns events seemingly unrelated to career advancement. Many of the pleasant and unpleasant by-products of career advancement are, however, predictable parts of a total life system. Job changes affect many things:

- Where you live
- The lifestyle of immediate family members
- Your community affiliations and activities
- Your relationship with your spouse
- Your relationship with your children
- The amount of time that you spend at work, at home, or with friends
- Your salary and expenses
- Your commuting time
- Available energy and time to maintain your health
- Your friends, colleagues, or associates
- Access to your church, synagogue, or religious and spiritual anchors
- Access to parents, brothers, sisters, or your "roots" in general
- Free time to vacation or do things you love

There are trade-offs and payoffs to every career decision. Moving up will challenge you to minimize the disadvantages and maximize the pluses. Your ability to identify and achieve your desired life integration will be tested and tested again. The stories of Bob and Linda Doyle and Susan and John Sterling are good examples.

Bob and Linda Doyle

CASE STUDY

Bob and Linda's experience is quite typical. One partner, Bob, targeted and achieved a major career goal. Neither Bob nor Linda anticipated or planned for the impact of his promotion on their professional and personal lives. Bob's selection to head the research division for a large international corporation changed their lives markedly. Unknowingly, they quickly lost control over several important areas of their lives, with regrettable consequences.

Bob had an excellent record as a researcher. Over a 12-year period he had proven himself as a scientist and project team leader, developing several new products and successfully tackling every challenge set before him. For the first 6 years after graduate school, Bob was primarily a bench researcher, participating in the important discoveries that led to the development of several important products. For the next 3 years, as a project team leader in charge of five researchers, his team developed new applications for several company products, increasing the profitability and market reach of those products.

At year 10, a change in companies allowed Bob to take over a research department of about 25 professionals, an opportunity that broadened his scientific background. While he continued to enjoy the time he devoted to his research projects, he now had broader leadership and managerial responsibilities.

He did very well at his science and managing his team. He inherited experienced, highly motivated people who presented very few personnel or administrative problems. They rarely tested his ability as a manager. The work was well planned and well organized; his teams were productive and well managed. Bob, now one of his company's shining lights, enjoyed management and looked forward to increased management responsibility. Then came his big opportunity.

Bob's promotion to vice president of research was, as he described it, "a high point" in his life. He now directed a division critical to the company's future, and he and the division were responsible for bringing innovative products to the market in the shortest possible period of time. Bob knew his new division had some problems.

- Research and development had evolved into small empires with little interdependence, little coordination, and few shared procedures, resources, or policies.
- His division had a generally mediocre track record of getting new products to market. The new product pipeline was barely filled. Most new product development consisted of so-called line extensions, which were actually new uses or analogs of old products. There had been four vice presidents in about 10 years, with little stability at the top. All were solid researchers, but none was an effective leader. With inefficient work flow and adequate but not cutting-edge information technology systems, product planning and development were slow, inefficient, and too expensive.
- There were inadequate numbers and types of researchers and support staff to meet the goals established by Bob's boss. Quality was lacking in several key areas. Hiring was unsystematic. Good candidates were often snatched up by more aggressive competitors. Training was virtually nonexistent.

Bob's charge, presented clearly to him, was to significantly improve the division's performance. He was to bring more and better-differentiated products to the marketplace faster and more efficiently. Given the authority to hire and fire and to restructure the department as he deemed appropriate, his boss's parting words upon Bob's appointment as vice president were, "Revitalize this group once and for all. It has dragged us down for long enough. My job and yours depend on it."

At the time of his appointment, Bob and Linda had been happily married for 11 years. They had a bright son who was 10 years old and a well-adjusted but visually impaired daughter who was 8 years old. The children attended good public schools. Their daughter was in an excellent program headed by a caring and experienced special education teacher. Both children loved school and were heavily involved in sports, scouts, and church activities in their midsized suburban town.

Linda had worked as a teacher in a private school for 12 years. She enjoyed her job and was popular with students and staff alike. She was fond of her students, and she was respected by parents and fellow teachers. Linda had learned to juggle the difficult task of being a mother, wife, and teacher, and she received great family and professional satisfaction. Religious worship, involvement in their children's activities, and physical activities were strongly shared family values.

The family was comfortable with their upper-middle-class lifestyle. Their five-year-old suburban tract home had a manageable monthly mortgage payment, and Linda's late model car was paid for. Finances were managed carefully, but there was enough money to allow for vacations, a tennis club membership, and a growing trust fund to cover the children's college education. Overall, Bob and Linda's marriage was going well. They lived in a comfortable house, were raising two well-adjusted children, they had enough money and job security, and both found their jobs satisfying. They shared many common activities, had time for each other, and had time for the things they valued and enjoyed. Theirs was a loving, happy marriage.

The promotion to vice president was Bob's big career opportunity. He had prepared himself, interviewed well, and was ultimately selected from four finalists. He was offered the job on a Friday, and he all but accepted the position on the spot. The company wanted Bob to start within a month. He said that he would like the weekend to discuss it with his family and he would give a final decision on Monday.

Bob and Linda had discussed the possibility of a job change and promotion on two occasions. Bob didn't think that he would get the position ("I don't have all the management tickets"), but, ever supportive, Linda encouraged him to interview. "If you get the position, we will worry about the details then." As so often happens with an unexpected opportunity, events occurred more quickly.

Professionally and personally, Bob, Linda, and their children were unprepared for the consequences of their decision. What was seemingly an excellent career opportunity turned into a family nightmare. Bob and Linda did not appreciate the negative effects the change would have on their family system.

A critical family decision was the one to relocate. The new job was 100 miles away, and neither Bob nor Linda liked the idea of Bob's commuting over two hours a day each way. He would be home few evenings before 8 p.m., and he would have to leave the house by 6 a.m. He would see little of the children, whose bedtime was 9 to 10 p.m., and evening dinner, an important family ritual, would be without Bob. So they decided against commuting. Unforeseen implications of the decision to relocate included the following:

- *They had to sell an affordable, comfortable home they enjoyed.* Even though their company paid for the move, took over the selling of their old home, and helped them find a new home, it was nonetheless a time-consuming and arduous task. Linda spent a lot of time looking for the right place that was within their price range. Homes in the new area were much more expensive, taxes were higher, and the mortgage payment, with higher interest rates, was substantially higher.
- *Their daughter lost the very supportive situation in which she was comfortable and successful, and she had to work out a new set of relationships with teachers.* She had to find new friends who could accept her disability. Their son was old enough to have strong feelings about leaving his buddies who had been his friends since kindergarten, his scouting group, Little League, and his church group. He was very unhappy with the move.
- *Linda lost a job she loved, her status as a respected professional, and the income that had made her feel that she was contributing to her family.* Giving up her job also reinforced feelings of her own vulnerability, that now she was totally dependent on Bob for her support, a feeling that made her angry and engendered feelings of dependency and powerlessness, which she resented. To make matters worse, Linda had difficulty finding a new job in the tight job market in the new area.
- *Bob, Linda, and their children surrendered strong community ties with their longtime neighbors and with friends they had made through the local parent-teachers' organization, Little League, and their church.* They moved away from friends they had known for years, as well as away from parents and close relatives. For years

these people had provided emotional support, help with babysitting and child rearing, and other types of daily assistance that had made life easier for Bob and Linda's dual-career family.

■ *As if the relocation by itself were not difficult enough, Bob's difficulties on the job made things worse.* He was not developing the momentum needed to change the organization. The jump from director of a small, smoothly functioning research group to vice president of a much larger, more troubled group was proving to be a bit much to handle. Never professionally trained in leadership, he was not familiar with the formal planning, financial management, and human resources systems necessary to effectively direct such a large organization.

The organization was elusive for Bob. Direct reports gave him verbal assurances, but they rarely committed things to paper. Thus, he had no clear information about project planning, product development timelines, product strengths and weaknesses, or possible problems that might require more time or more money to solve. He couldn't nail his direct reports down. He couldn't get them to make commitments backed by full accountability. Everything "depends," nothing was firm. He felt controlled, manipulated, and impotent.

He felt he was failing, and he shared his frustration with his boss. In his disappointment in his own performance, he began to press. He was less approachable, had a shorter fuse, found himself getting angry more often. He felt manipulated by his employees and resented it. He brought that resentment home with him, and he felt he was more short tempered with his children.

The part of the job he most resented was managing and leading others. As vice president, responsible for a division of over $50 million, he found he was giving most of his time to others—planning, monitoring, and troubleshooting the work of others, overseeing the work of the organization. He had no time for the science he enjoyed, no time to "do his own work." He was finding that managing a large organization under stress required that 100 percent of the time he would pay attention to the work of others, something he wasn't finding very satisfying.

Bob had not fully anticipated that this job change was, in fact, a major career switch from that of being a strong scientist with some management responsibility to that of being a research executive with considerable divisional and corporate administrative responsibilities. Because he lacked the experience of leading a larger organization, Bob underestimated how his time would be spent. He lacked good models that would allow him to creatively attack management problems with the skill and fervor that he had previously applied to scientific challenges.

The myriad problems that had plagued the division for years were now his. His game plan was rather scattershot, riddled with gaps and inconsistencies. Within two months after starting, Bob began to question the wisdom of his decision to have accepted his new role. Pressures built at work and were compounded by the difficulties of establishing roots in a new community. In a matter of less than a year, the Doyles' fulfilling and tidy world was coming undone.

Susan and Doug Sterling

Let's take another example of a family that successfully navigated a major career transition, Susan and Doug Sterling. Susan was a nurse with many years of both clinical and administrative experience. Susan and Doug had two young sons, ages two and four. Susan was acting as an interim chief nursing officer (CNO) for a major university hospital when a recruiter called with the prospects of a job that Susan had long thought about.

Susan was encouraged to apply for the job of chief nursing officer at one of the premier hospitals in the country. She was excited about the opportunity, but she understood quickly that taking this job would involve major changes for the family. The job would be a significant promotion for her. While she was an interim CNO, she was really maintaining the function until her boss was able to return to work after an illness. Now she would have the chance to advance to the position of CNO, a position that she had set her sights on for quite some time.

However, her new job was in another metropolitan city, and it meant the family would have to relocate. Doug was a litigation attorney with a prestigious law firm, and he had developed a substantial practice over the years. Doug enjoyed his work, liked the law firm, and had colleagues he valued. The Sterlings decided that the family would relocate to the new city, and once the relocation was complete, Doug would get a small apartment in the city where they were currently living and would commute back and forth. It wasn't an ideal arrangement, especially with young children, but this arrangement met both of their career aspirations.

Finding a new house was much more difficult than the couple imagined. They were making this move in winter when very few houses were on the market. The search for a new house took five months. During that time, Susan commuted to her new job while her husband and sons stayed in their current home. Susan had anticipated that the relocation would be a strain on her, the boys, and her husband. It was particularly complicated during the period once Susan began her role in the new city and Doug and the boys were still in their original home. Susan had arranged for additional support for the children and her husband while she was commuting to her new job. She had arranged for additional child-care hours for the boys and extra cleaning help in the house so that Doug could spend the little time he had caring for the boys. This was a bit of a financial strain for Susan and Doug, but they decided that it was a short-term cost for a longer-term gain.

Doug and Susan both negotiated more flexible work arrangements. Doug planned his schedule to work in the office from Tuesday through Friday once they had moved. Susan negotiated a schedule with the hospital during her relocation that allowed her to commute from their current home to the hospital on Monday morning and work at home on Fridays. However, even with all of the extra support Susan had arranged and with the extra support from Doug, Susan said that the relocation was very hard on her. Leaving the boys and working long hours during the week to get established in her new role was difficult. She planned the time she was away from the family carefully so that she could have more free time over the weekends when they were all together.

Susan knew that as the CNO, she needed time with her key stakeholders and to be visible in her new role. She worked with her direct reports to conduct an early organizational assessment with the help of an outside consultant. Susan used the time she was in the new city without her family to do administrative work at night so she could be more visible during the day or meet with stakeholders and establish these critical relationships.

The first year was very hard on Doug, Susan, and their sons. Susan realized that she wasn't taking good care of herself. She was frequently eating on the run and not getting enough exercise. She was also feeling additional stress because of the jump she had made in leading a much larger staff and learning her new role. Fortunately for Susan, she had developed a strong relationship with her boss, the COO of the hospital, who kept expectations high but made every effort to support Susan. The COO of her new hospital saw Susan as a real asset to the hospital and wanted to retain her. As Susan got more comfortable with her job and the family relocated, life became more "normal" for the Sterling family. Susan began to get more exercise by walking more with the boys, and she became more focused on taking better care of herself. The first year of her new assignment was stressful not only for Susan but her entire family. However, because of the planning they had done and the fact that they had worked together to make the transition successful, they were able to reap the benefits of the new opportunity.

In the remainder of this chapter, we will suggest principles that can help you, your spouse or partner, and family through the experience of navigating a new leadership role. These principles can increase your ability to anticipate the personal and family life implications of being a leader on the rise. Before looking at the principles, let's look at the issues that help and challenge you to successfully integrate your new leadership role and your family and personal life outside of work.

Typical Areas of Personal Conflict

Earlier in this chapter we listed important considerations related to your personal and family life that you should look at very closely as you think about moving up. The following is an expanded list of the areas most frequently affected when you take on bigger and tougher responsibilities.[2] You might want to create your own checklist or use the list below to help you anticipate and plan the management of issues that could become troublesome:

- Housing: Location, type, cost
- Family members: Spouse, children, parents, siblings
- Time: At work, home, traveling, commuting, vacation, leisure
- Finances: Income, expenses, investments
- Friendships: At work, home
- Lifestyle
- Recreation, hobbies
- Education, schools
- Marriage, love relationships with significant others
- Material possessions
- Work style
- Religious affiliations
- Community activity
- Health, fitness
- Are there others that fit your personal circumstances?

THE SIX KEY PRINCIPLES OF MANAGING THE IMPACT OF MOVING UP ON YOUR FAMILY, HEALTH, AND TIME

1. Personal wellness, family health, and work effectiveness are strongly interdependent. Understanding personal/family and work systems will help you better manage the process of navigating your leadership transition.

2. Major job changes often trigger major life changes. The impacts of these changes are best addressed through careful individual and family reflection, communication, and clarification of personal/family priorities and values.
3. Leaders who are moving up are in a state of personal transition. The process of personal transition can be understood and effectively managed by individuals and by families.
4. Health and well-being in one's personal, family, and work life affect and are affected by stress and distress.
5. Mutual understanding, support, and responsible collaboration within dual-career families or with partners are essential for leaders on the rise.
6. The goal is to achieve a new life integration.

Principle 1. Personal Wellness, Family Health, and Work Effectiveness Are Highly Interdependent

Understanding how personal/family and work systems interact will help you better manage the process of moving up. A system is any complex of elements in which each element has an affect on the others. Computer systems, machines, weather systems, rocket systems, body systems, and environmental systems are each composed of multiple elements, each one affecting the others within the system. Borrowing this concept, social scientists have, for several decades, studied the integrated nature and importance of personal, family, and work organizational systems. Importantly, the actions taken by one person in a system have the potential to affect others who belong to the system.

Social scientists have found that human systems are similar to technological systems, with one critical difference: technological systems can generally function independently of each other. An information technology system does not affect a weather system or body system unless they are deliberately or naturally linked (such as a computer system and a machine, a machine and a person, the body systems and the ecosystem). Human systems, on the other hand, are integrally linked. They are highly interdependent. What happens in one system of a person's life has a very high likelihood of affecting the others. What happens at home affects your work and your well-being; and what happens to you personally affects your family life and work. Human systems are highly interdependent, try as we may to keep them separate.

For both Bob and Linda Doyle as well as Doug and Susan Sterling, as one of the spouses experienced a leadership transition in his or her respective work systems, it affected other important areas of their lives. Changes in their work system dramatically affected their personal and family system. The Doyle and Sterling family cases can serve as examples as you navigate your own leadership, family, and personal transitions.

Figure 10.1 illustrates the interrelationships between your systems. During a transition, each system ebbs and flows as you manage the transition through your successes and problems. Also represented are forces in the environment that help or hinder you. These forces are dynamic, constantly tug-

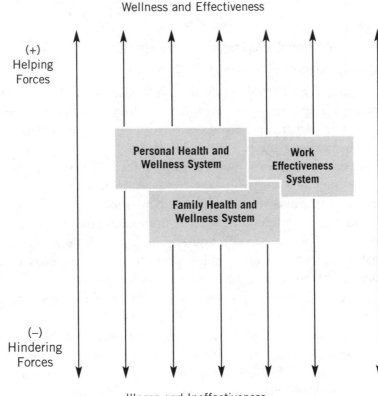

Figure 10.1 Personal Systems Interrelationships

ging and pulling each individual system, its subsets, and the relationships between systems.

Figure 10.2 illustrates Bob Doyle in his first year following a major promotion successfully plowing tremendous effort, attention, and energy into his work system, to the detriment of his family and personal systems.

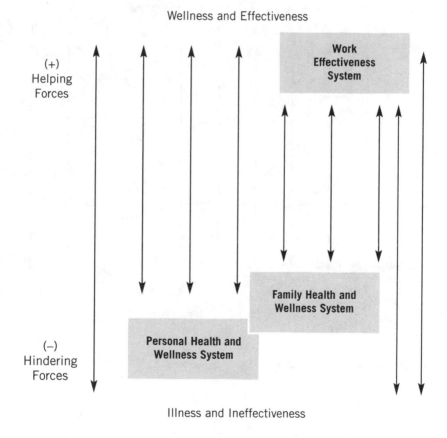

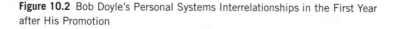

Figure 10.2 Bob Doyle's Personal Systems Interrelationships in the First Year after His Promotion

Figure 10.3 shows a transitioning leader keeping all systems under control at a high level of wellness and effectiveness. Things are going very well.

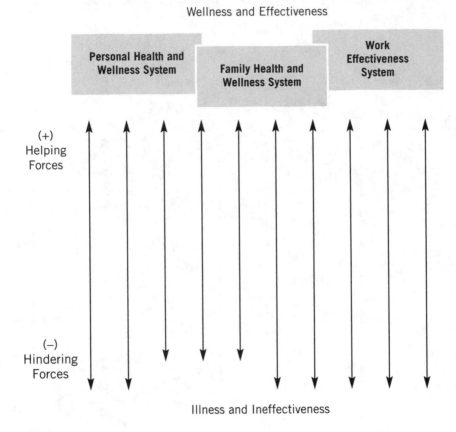

Figure 10.3 Bob Doyle's Personal Systems Interrelationships Transitioning to Being under Control

JUST PROMOTED LEADER TOOL 11
Your Work/Life Integration Assessment

Using the assessment in Figure 10.4, approximate your present situation. Draw your own boxes in relation to the scales for wellness and effectiveness and illness and ineffectiveness.

What can you conclude about your own systems' effectiveness?

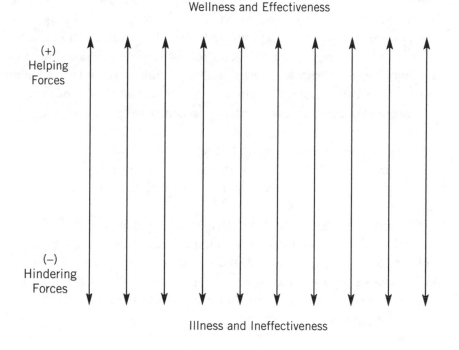

Wellness and Effectiveness

(+)
Helping
Forces

(–)
Hindering
Forces

Illness and Ineffectiveness

Figure 10.4 Your Work/Life Integration Assessment

The following guidelines will help you effectively manage the relationship between your personal, family, and work effectiveness systems:

1. *Know what is important to you, what you value, and what has priority at any given time.* Consciously strive to gain consistency and congruence between what you *say* is important and what you actually *do*.

Think about the Doyles and the Sterlings as families of individuals. What was most important to them? In Doyles' case, in what ways were their most important values compromised by Bob's job change? What preventive steps could they have taken to minimize the negatives? Job changes are times for heightened family communication and for creatively addressing opportunities and problems. The key is to know what should and shouldn't be changed and how to compensate effectively when compromises are unavoidable.

The Sterling family consciously planned how they would ease the transition for Linda, Doug, and the children. They purchased additional services (housecleaning, cooking, and babysitting) so that the family felt supported while Linda was away from the house until they relocated. They also planned a series of activities to learn about the opportunities and recreational resources in their new community. They did this together over many weekends for several months until they made new connections. It is wise to continue certain rituals and customs that have great meaning to your marriage and family, such as these:

- Playing and reading with young children at their usual times.
- Arranging special "alone time" with children and spouse.
- Making arrangements for frequent reunions with friends and family.
- Structuring time to ensure that cherished activities are maintained. Whether it is religious worship, working on a car, bowling, aerobics, playing tennis or golf, or volunteer community service, schedule what is of value to you and do it.
- As parents and partners, ensure that you preserve your own rituals and time together.

2. *Realize that you have a finite amount of time and energy.* Heighten your awareness about how you use your time and energy. Engineer your time. Take charge of your time and energy by taking care of real priorities, not simple urgencies. You can't do everything you are asked to do. Protect your real priorities, and learn to say no to the rest.

If you need help with managing your time better, talk with people who seem to use their time well. Get at least one new idea per week. Read books and articles written on this subject, and adopt a few of these ideas to your situation. Never accept that you have no alternatives. A group of friends can help each other generate ideas and alternatives to their problems when they seem to be stuck. Don't forget to assign work to your children. For example, a sixth and third grader who pack their lunches for the next school day with minimal supervision save at least 20 minutes of time for mom or dad and become more responsible in the process.

Select your child-care support carefully from among the several options available. Do you need someone to come to your home and be available in the evening? Can either you or someone else take a child to day care and then pick the child up? Do you want your child to have a nursery school experience in addition to having a babysitter? There are pros and cons to each of the day-care alternatives. Which one best meets your family's needs? Make sure your child-care provider knows your expectations and needs. Be sure that your child-care provider is being paid a fair and competitive salary and receives recognition and reinforcement for a job well done so you can count on his or her long-term help.

3. *Avoid spreading yourself too thin.* Too many commitments ultimately reduce your effectiveness. Check the number of have-tos in your life. High achievers often overextend themselves. This is often because of enthusiasm and involvement in their job, but it is also because of ineffective delegation skills, unwillingness to say no, and lack of a support network. Sometimes people just feel guilty and do too many things themselves. It is not uncommon to see managers and executives of both genders trying to be all things to all people. Our contemporary lexicon includes the terms *superwoman* and *superman,* *supermom* and *superdad.* Do it all, want it all, have it all, lose it all. Delegate some of the work at home as well. Buy some of the services you need such as housecleaning, lawn mowing, and clothes cleaning so that when you are at home, you have time to relax and enjoy your family.

4. *Realize that every choice you make has payoffs and trade-offs.* Every action has pluses and minuses. When priorities are in conflict between self, family, and work, make the best decision possible, and don't criticize yourself for what you are unable to do. Make yourself a mental or written note to catch up with someone or something at a subsequent time if you can't spend the time now.

Our society is supercharged with options. Obligations weigh heavily on our choices. Try to make your best choices, and avoid the tendency to try to be perfect and satisfy everyone.

5. *Use your diagnostic skills at home and at work.* Be aware that spending extra time and energy in one area of your life likely has implications in another area. When work is dominating, something else (often spouse, children, favorite activities, personal wellness, or alone time) is usually suffering. *Recognize early warning signs.* Try to be aware of signals around and within you. Are you spending quality time in what you do, or are your efforts and relationships superficial? Do you see as many smiles as before? Do you give and get as many heartfelt hugs from your spouse, partner, children? Are you offering or accepting offers to spend special time with those who are really important to you, or are you always too busy?

6. *Don't let hobbies and interests go unattended.* How long has it been since you've done things that you really enjoy? Are you laughing and enjoying life as much as you used to or you would like to?

Hobbies and recreation serve as life's cushions. They not only help to absorb the stress of daily life but they also provide an energy reserve. They aid in preparing for the tougher challenges we face. But hobbies and recreational activities are often the first to go under pressure. This creates a troublesome cycle since leisure time provides for necessary relaxation and unwinding. Do your best to preserve and respect your leisure time.

7. *Maintain a high trust and supportive relationship with at least one other person or group.* Mutually beneficial relationships characterized by trust, sharing, and good listening are invariably healthy and therapeutic. Life is tough enough. To go it alone is to miss much of what life is about. Most managers who are successful at work and in other aspects of their lives are quick to credit their life partners, family, and close friends as essential for their success.

8. *Build frequent "pit stops" into your work and lifestyle.* No racer has ever won the Indianapolis 500 without periodic stops to refuel and check key parts. The same is true with people. Envision the balance that you desire in your life, and then design ways for it to happen. Taking the time to catch your breath and gain perspective increases your clarity, commitment, and energy to achieve your goals.

Principle 2. Major Job Changes Often Trigger Major Life Changes

The potential and actual impact of these changes is best addressed through careful individual and family reflection, communication, and clarification of personal and family priorities and values. This principle is closely related to principle 1. Think about the Doyle family and the Sterling family. One decision resulted in shaking the basic foundation on which the family system existed. Bob Doyle's promotion was, on the surface, a peak event, the high point of his career. But Bob, Linda, and their children did not take the time to consider the effects of this promotion on each individual family member and on the family as a whole. If they had, the Doyles might have anticipated many potential problems. The decision affected key areas of their lives. With reflection, they might have made a clearer choice whether to pursue and then accept (or not accept) the promotion. The entire family could have been involved in thinking through the pros and cons, the trade-offs and payoffs, and they might have discovered creative ways to deal with anticipated problems. Communication and involvement dramatically increase the possibility of commitment and buy-in.

While the first year of Susan's new job was challenging for the Sterling family, they lessened the stress by anticipating some of the difficulties. They took time to think about what they each needed and worked together to make the best of a difficult situation. Although having Doug keep an apartment near his law firm in their originating city was not ideal, it allowed him to continue the work he loved. Susan was able to take on the challenge she had been looking for as the next step in her career. By hiring extra help until they could relocate the children, Doug could attend to his work without worrying about having to do extra household chores that would have taken away from the time he could spend with his sons. Susan used the time she was away from the family during the relocation to be visible in her new role and spend time with her key stakeholders. Yes, the transition was stressful, but the Sterlings felt they came out of it even stronger as professionals, as a couple, and as a family.

Here are some additional guidelines:

- Confide in and involve those that you love and who love you in how, when, and if you will accept an opportunity to take on new leadership responsibility. Even when answers are not clear, keep talking and working on good solutions. They will come.
- Diagnose, plan, and solve problems both individually and as a family.
- Be sensitive to the hopes, fears, and concerns of a mate and of children, particularly if a relocation is required. This will be a time of adjustment. It will include broken, new, and interrupted relationships. It will be strange and can be very scary.

- If the downside of your management appointment appears too great, be careful that your ego and need for "stroking" are not the overriding factors in making your decision to accept a new leadership role. Get input and feedback from those you trust.

- When relocations, expatriations, and repatriations are involved, be certain to think through what it would really mean for everyone affected. Anticipate potential issues. Revisit typical areas of personal conflict.

- Rehearse the move. What needs to be anticipated? Talk to others who have experienced relocations and learn from them. Research good books and guides (available from Realtors, corporate relocation services, and contemporary bookstores).

- Identify and respond to the needs of each family member. Investigate the new geographic area ahead of time and repeatedly, if possible. Involve the family. Go there to shop, go to movies, visit recreational facilities, and visit other places that you are likely to frequent or rely on.

- Ask questions, questions, and more questions. Minimize your surprises.

- Maintain emotional bridges to your old home. This could include taking items of emotional meaning from your existing home or staying in touch with those who are important to you.

- Plan and then make the move as a family.

- Anticipate the costs and financial realities of a move. Relocations are expensive. There are both obvious and hidden costs. Identify as many as possible in advance. Tap into books, local civic groups, and people who already live in the area.

- If needed and appropriate, request and negotiate exceptions to your company's relocation package to help cope with the many expenses of moving. These are sometimes granted if requested.

- Try to meet new colleagues and neighbors in advance. They can be very helpful to you and remove some unknowns.

- When a second career of a spouse or partner is involved, dedicate yourself to successfully reestablishing his or her career or make an accommodation so your spouse or partner can continue his or her career. In doing this, utilize your company's resources and connections with other organizations in the area. Many companies will allow you to make a flexible work arrangement during a transition period or on an ongoing arrangement. Negotiate a flexible work arrangement, if needed, during the interviewing or recruiting period.

Principle 3. Leaders Who Are Moving Up Are in a State of Transition

The process of transition can be understood and effectively managed by individuals and by families. We have examined some of the issues that both the Doyle and Sterling families faced and highlighted some of the family and work systems implications that upwardly mobile leaders can anticipate. We have begun to view executive change in different ways. William Bridges, in his masterful book *Transitions: Making Sense of Life's Changes,* points out that our lives are composed of hundreds, even thousands of transformations, changes, or transitions that shape who we are and where we are going. Quoting Oscar Wilde, Bridges notes, "The gods have two ways of dealing harshly with us—the first is to deny us our dreams, and the second is to grant them."[3]

Bob Doyle was granted his dream. He sighted the job that he wanted, went after it, and was selected for it. But Bob Doyle and his family did not appreciate the dynamics of personal transitions. People do not automatically change. Some have difficulty operating on any new channel. For others it is easier and essentially a matter of fine-tuning. Some have trouble letting go of what exists, while others imagine the catastrophe that will be. Many individuals seem to shift smoothly from the conclusion of one job to the beginning of another. For the many who encounter difficulty in moving up or in changing jobs, homes, or responsibilities, there is often a lack of understanding and subsequent difficulty in managing the transition process. Typically, there is a period of orientation, disorientation, and reorientation. Many of our life's anchors are uprooted or shaken. We are challenged to maintain or establish new support in our lives.

Bridges views life transitions as having three stages, which occur in a predictable sequence:

1. An ending
2. A period of confusion and sometimes distress, which he calls the "neutral zone"
3. A new beginning[4]

We have already seen that a seemingly single transition is usually connected to many other issues in our lives—work, love, family, friends, leisure time, material possessions, and so on. Bridges' sequence of phases helps to explain what is happening and how we can deal more constructively with it.

Endings

Every transition begins with an ending. Some endings are chosen. Others begin because of unavoidable circumstances or when something goes awry; job termination is an example. In all cases, there is a disembarking or leaving from something that was to something that is, whether anticipated or unknown. Before new roots can be established, old ones must come out. Even when you are looking forward to a new beginning, the effects of ending your previous situation (at work and at home) should not be underestimated.

What endings have you experienced recently in one of your own life transitions, and how did you deal with them? Did you effectively anticipate your reactions to the ending experience?

_____

_____

_____

_____

_____

How would you deal differently in the future with your endings? Write a self-prescription of at least two or three ideas that could work for you.

_____

_____

_____

_____

_____

The Neutral Zone

Bridges describes the neutral zone as a period of seemingly unproductive "time out" when we feel disconnected from events, people, activities, or things that we have come to know. This is an uncomfortable and confusing time. People frequently feel mixed up and disoriented. It is a particularly frustrating and sometimes depressing time because we aren't sure what will come next.

The neutral zone is frequently associated with heightened anxiety and anticipation. For leaders on the rise, it often occurs during that period between ending one position and starting the new and expanded role. During this period, many leaders slow down long enough to reflect and say, "My God, do I really know what I am getting into?" This is sometimes a period of self-doubt when our deepest fears emerge from our subconscious. In a moment of anxiety during a two-week hiatus before stepping into a new leadership role, one newly appointed branch leader said, "Why am I doing this? I was so happy doing my previous work. I'm not sure that I can handle this."

The neutral zone is an important time, and it is crucial that you anticipate it. It may be nature's way of signaling a time out. On the surface, it may be an unproductive period. Bridges calls it a "time of inattentive activity." Others have described it as a period of healing and a phase of developing new potential, energy, and direction. Its importance should not be underestimated; nor should its existence be unexpected.

Describe your experiences with your own neutral zone. Tap into recent endings and beginnings, and think about what was going on between these two stages. List a few of your personal observations:

_____

_____

_____

_____

_____

Bridges suggests how to find meaning in the neutral zone experience and how to shorten it:

1. Find a regular time and place to be alone.
2. Begin a personal log of neutral zone experiences.
3. Take this pause in the action of your life to write an autobiography or autobiographical thoughts. This may often lead to more reflection and clearer personal insights.
4. Take this opportunity to discover what you really want. This is an excellent period for clarifying what is really important in your life.
5. Think of what would be unlived in your life if it ended today.
6. Take a few days to go on your own journey, a personal rite of passage.[5]

New Beginnings

Bridges indicates that we come to new beginnings only after an end, and when activities are being started.[6] While this is a period of great challenge and questioning, it is also an opportunity for new energy, direction, and success.

Principle 4. Health and Well-Being in One's Personal, Family, and Work Life Affect and Are Affected by Stress and Distress

Worksheet

To consider the concepts of stress and distress, consider the following statements. Test yourself by indicating whether each statement is true or false.

1. *Stress* and *distress* have just about the same meaning.   T   F
2. People in management and leadership positions usually
   feel the effect of stress more than those in technical or
   clerical positions.   T   F
3. People work best when their stress levels are low.   T   F
4. Most causes of stress (stressors) and distress are unpleasant.   T   F
5. It is generally better to be under- rather than overstimulated.   T   F
6. Two clear indicators of stress are poor concentration and
   poor job performance.   T   F
7. Most stress is related to an uneasy feeling about things to come.   T   F
8. A good predictor of a person's long-term stress management
   is his or her ability to adjust and adapt to immediate
   challenges and unanticipated alarming agents.   T   F
9. From a health and fitness point of view, your body can
   separate stressful and distressful experiences at work from
   those at home.   T   F
10. The primary way to manage daily stressors is to have
    releases, such as exercise, hobbies, and outside interests.   T   F

Although it may surprise you, all 10 of these statements are false.

Let's start by looking at the nature of stress. Stress is any reaction of the mind, body, and sometimes behavior to stressors or causes of stress. Everyone needs a certain amount of stress or stimulation. Without it we would not be alive. Thus, a key to understanding stress is becoming aware of our stress and using it constructively.

Each of us has an ideal stress level. We also have a range or "stress comfort zone" in which we function best and are most comfortable.[7]

The comfort zone has two endpoints. One point is the level that, when exceeded, indicates that we are too busy or too involved or the intensity of our experiences is too great. In short, we are overstimulated in either the number or seriousness of our present life and work events. Conversely, when we fall below our minimal endpoint in our stress comfort zone, we usually are not challenged enough, we are bored, or we are involved in activities that are not important to us.

When we go over the edges of our personal comfort zone, we experience distress. Too much or too little stimulation equals distress. Contrary to stress, which can mobilize us and is often a useful reaction of the mind or body, distress has negative aspects. When we are aware of our stressors and use them well, we feel challenged, alert, and alive. As we approach the endpoints of our comfort zone, we usually begin to have different feelings. They are not necessarily bad, but they often act as warnings that we are not at our peak. As we slide past our comfort zone, from either end, many telltale symptoms begin to appear.

As you can see in Figure 10.5, Steve, Joan, and Judy all have different hypothetical comfort zones. Joan has the largest range and shares the highest upper limit with Judy. Steve is comfortable within very limited boundaries. Judy has a fairly large range with a very high limit.

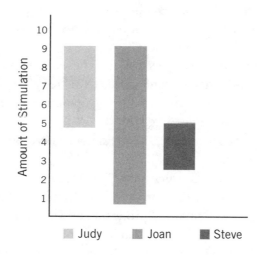

Figure 10.5 Hypothetical Comfort Zones for Judy, Joan, and Steve

A Further Look at Stressors[8]

We mentioned previously that stressors are the cause of stress or potential distress. The following are characteristics of stressors:

1. They can be generated from within yourself (undue worry or fear) or from outside sources (pressure or conflict involving a new job or boss).

2. They can be pleasant (an appealing, challenging work promotion or work assignment) or unpleasant (little hope of meeting a tight time schedule).
3. They can be few in number, or they can build up and be many.
4. They can be low or high in intensity.
5. They can be short (a major project with a short time frame) or long in duration (ongoing work or home responsibilities).
6. They can be old (have been with you for a long period) or new and less familiar to you.
7. They are changeable. A stressor with certain characteristics can affect us dramatically sometimes but not much or at all at other times.

What Leads to Distress?

Let's look at circumstances that typically cause a person to move from effective use of optimal stress levels toward distress:

1. Transitions of all types are likely to be associated with distress. A job change is a prime example. Increases in management responsibility; changes in colleagues, direct reports, or boss; relocations; loss of respect; and alterations in schedules are others.
2. Doing too much. Overtaxing or overloading yourself in either the number of events or intensity of tasks often leads to distress. This can occur at work or home. Individuals who are moving up in management are especially susceptible to overloading.
3. A person can be very busy but feel understimulated because the work or life in general is boring.
4. Doing work of little perceived value, being involved in activities that are unimportant to you or for which you do not understand the purpose, can lead to distress. A percentage of professionals who become leaders for the first time frequently are criticized by peers for leaving their professional roots and joining management. In certain technical and scientific professions, people often identify more with their profession than with their employer. Distress often occurs when individuals feel they will lose their expertise when they have taken on management and leadership responsibility.
5. Role confusion or conflict can lead to distress. The person feels down because of differences in perceived ability and actual responsibility or authority level (either too high or too low). Distress also occurs when there are unresolved conflicts in responsibility and authority with others.

This often happens to newly appointed managers in organizations that do not effectively define responsibilities and accountability.

6. A loss of someone personally or professionally important can lead to distress. This is true even in positive situations when an individual is promoted or takes a better job in a different organization.

7. Unresolved issues are the residual feelings we all carry with us when emotional issues are left unfinished. These can be current issues such as recent unresolved disagreements with coworkers or issues from the past that remain bothersome.

8. Perceived differences between what should be and what is can lead to distress. We previously discussed cognitive dissonance, the feeling of tension, when we realize that there is a difference between what we really value and what we actually do. Losing out on a promotion creates dissonance between your own and others' beliefs about you. Having less money than you need to support the lifestyle you want creates a discrepancy between your real and the ideal income needs. If you are a leader moving up and in transition, there will be differences between what you are experiencing and what you expected would occur.

Living with Chronic Stress

Too much stress leads to distress. As we move toward a state of distress, there are indicators or signals to be aware of, such as the following:

Headaches, neckaches, and backaches
Sore and tense muscles
Feelings of anger, even rage
Generalized feelings of anxiety
Loss of sleep and feeling chronically tired
Dental problems
Abnormal levels of perspiration
Constipation or diarrhea
High blood pressure
Violent behavior
Problems with perception, thinking, and concentration
Difficulty in getting along with others and generally being touchy
Boredom with activities that used to be enjoyable
Health issues such as diabetes
Depression

Identifying these areas enables you to recognize them, identify their causes, and realize your own comfort zone. To use stress more constructively, try the following activity.

JUST PROMOTED LEADER TOOL 12

Your Personal Stress Inventory

1. Look at Figure 10.6 to get the "big picture" of this activity.
2. List up to 15 significant personal stressors (at work, home, big or small).
3. Place the appropriate information next to the stressors on your list that matches the topics on the top of the form. If you have no response to

	List up to 15 Significant Personal Stressors	Who Is Involved in Stress?	Where in Your Body Do You Feel the Effects of Stress?
1.			
2.			
3.			
4.			
5.			
6.			
7.			
8.			
9.			
10.			
11.			
12.			
13.			
14.			
15.			

Figure 10.6 Your Personal Stress Inventory

a topic, leave it blank. After listing your stressors, work on one inventory topic at a time.

4. After completing your stressor listing and filling in the various columns, look for unique situations or patterns. For example, how many of your

When? Always? Often? Seldom?	When the Stressor Occurs, Do You Feel In or Out of Control? Scale of 1 for In Control to 10 for Out of Control	Yes or No: Is There at Least a Glimmer of Hope for Handling This Well?	What Are the 3 Highest-Priority Stressors That You Feel You Should Work On?

stressors have existed for a long time, or how many are work related versus home related?

5. Take 10 minutes to summarize your thoughts and feelings. Complete as many sentence stems as you would like. You may use any one stem as many times as you wish.

I learned

_____

_____

_____

I relearned

_____

_____

_____

I realized

_____

_____

_____

I was surprised

_____

_____

_____

6. Finally, think about the positive and negative implications of your inventory as it relates to the quality of your work, your life outside of work, and its impact on how you work and relate to others.

Combating Chronic Stress Leading to Distress[9]

The three major strategies for stress management are reducing your stressors, managing your stress filter, and building your resiliency to avoid the harmful aspects of chronic stress. Used in concert, this combination can be the cornerstone for better health and fitness as well as personal and professional effectiveness.

Managing Your Stressors. Figuring out how to reduce your stressors is an important task. Many factors, including your personal needs, the number of events, and responsibilities in your life, are important when managing stressors. Here are some suggestions:

1. Take personal responsibility for your pace of life and for major life changes. Do not blame circumstances or other people.
2. Be aware of your comfort zone and your minimal, optimal, and maximum levels of stimulation. Know your low and high limits.
3. Continually work to attain a good fit between your needs, your work challenges, and your home environment. Try to reduce the gaps and discrepancies between what you want to do, need to do, and have to do.
4. Try to predict the effects of major life changes, including job changes. Remember that transitions are often stressful.
5. If you can, avoid clustering too many major life changes within a short period of time. Too many changes overload and reduce your ability to cope effectively.
6. Engineer your time and effort. Provide yourself enough time to regroup after big events.
7. Do not let emotional issues go unresolved for long periods of time. Therapists call unresolved issues "unfinished business." Important unresolved issues have a gnawing, debilitating effect on us.
8. Be clear about what is important to you and what takes highest priority in your life. Take time for introspection. Strive for consistency between your values and your actions.
9. Choose the tasks and challenges that are most important to you. There will be more than enough—you don't need to handle those that have little or no meaning. Learn to say no to the things you "should" do that you don't really want to do.
10. Work on improving your stress awareness through introspective and reflective activities (such as Your Personal Stress Inventory), discussions with people you trust, spiritual or religious activity, and seminars and workshops on personal development.

Managing Your Stress Filter. Try as we might to reduce our stressors, the unpredictable nature of life and the charged pace of our world force us into trying situations. You can sometimes reduce their harmful effects by developing a good stress filter. A personal stress filter consists of the qualities that reduce the negative effects of stressors on your physical, mental, and emotional well-being. How many items from the following list do you already do? How many could you do more effectively?

1. Maintain good health habits in relation to eating, resting, and exercising. People who are worn down, physically weak, or constantly tired are more susceptible to stressors.
2. Assume a take-charge approach to your life. Be personally responsible for who you are, how you feel, what you are thinking, and the way you act. Believe that you can change aspects of yourself that need changing.
3. Each week come up with at least one additional way to build your psychological, emotional, and spiritual strength.
4. Learn to express your feelings. With your spouse or a trusted friend, open up. Don't sit on a powder keg of feelings. Stored negative feelings, old and new, are very unhealthy.
5. Be patient with your own and others' imperfections. Many high achievers try to be perfect. It is okay to make mistakes. Perfection and striving to improve yourself are two very different concepts.
6. Surround yourself with people whom you trust as friends and intimates. Be open to help and support. Be there for others.

Building Your Personal Resiliency. Here are a few examples of effective coping responses:

1. Energize with good stress. Take enough risks so you are challenged but not so many that you are overwhelmed. Set goals just out of reach, but not out of sight.
2. Balance stressful times with activities to repair and heal.
3. Find new ways to renew energy.
4. Get support from others.
5. Eat well and choose medium or low glycemic index foods.
6. Exercise using aerobic, flexibility, strength building, and conditioning activities.
7. Regularly use stress reduction techniques such as yoga, meditation, or breathing exercises.
8. Make sure to take vacations and plan periods of time to rest and renew.
9. Change how you relate to the stressor. Experiment with new behaviors.
10. Change the stressor. Sometimes you can change what is bothering you. Modify one or more stressful features of your immediate environment. For example, fix or replace something that is bothering you about your

new job, through discussions with your boss, peers, or those working for you.

11. Accept the situation and work to reduce the stress. When the situation cannot be changed, use stress-reducing options such as exercise, a talk with someone important to you, counseling or therapy, more sleep, or relaxation techniques such as meditation, biofeedback, brief solitude, or a religious activity.

Stress can have a positive effect on your life unless it reaches the point of becoming distress. Stress is a natural part of living in our complex society. As we pointed out previously, everyone needs a certain degree of stress to be stimulated, motivated, and challenged. The key is to have stress without distress, to keep the positive effects of stress working for you.

Principle 5. Mutual Understanding, Support, Fairness, and Responsible Collaboration within Dual-Career Families or with Partners Are Essential for Leaders on the Rise

Think back to the case studies of Bob and Linda Doyle and Susan and Doug Sterling. Try to recall some of the issues that the couples faced. Describe how their decisions helped or hindered each of their careers and their family cohesiveness. What could the Doyles have done more effectively to manage their dilemma?

In a dual-career couple, the individuals pursue separate careers alongside a commitment to their loving relationship. The following are the most common mistakes when facing major changes in either partner's career:

- Partners think and act in a self-centered manner and lack concern for the effects of change on others in the family. Or they ignore their own needs and do what they think others need.
- They do not take time to anticipate the effects and decide if they are willing to accept the predictable pros and cons of events. As we have seen, these include important issues such as uprooting children from school, loss of friends and key relationships, or loss of one partner's job. They don't ask each other for help, assistance, and support. They figure things out alone and often act without the other's support and counsel.
- They take on too many obligations and changes at one time, trying to do too much in too short a period of time.
- They don't clarify expectations, goals, and needs with each other. It is all too common for one spouse (traditionally the husband) to announce a

job change to his or her mate, with so much pressure that the spouse or partner feels obligated to go along, despite how he or she may feel.

- They fail to get help from outside the family for domestic maintenance and children's needs. Third-party help often becomes essential to help families cope with the change in the household's day-to-day operations.
- They don't plan for emergencies and don't have backup plans for situations that are not part of regular (and almost always harried) schedules. Typical disrupting events are sickness, trips out of town, and unanticipated late days at the office.
- They don't take time to get away from the pressures and recharge their relationship together.

Suggestions for Helping Dual-Career Families Cope during Periods of Transition

- The cornerstone of successful dual-career families is mutual respect for each other's careers and collaboration and support between the partners.
- Maintaining dual careers requires cooperation, not competition.
- Communication needs to be free of secret agendas. It should be open and clear. If one is feeling something, it should be said, no matter how trivial or selfish it may seem. Better to state feelings before the transition than afterward and in the eye of the storm.
- Uprooting often causes guilt. Guilt is predictable. Face it head on and talk it out.
- Keep the emphasis on flexibility, creativity, innovation, compromise, and commitment to problem solving. Look for win-win solutions.
- If relocation is necessary, carefully plan a process to reestablish both careers as part of the decision for one partner to accept a new position. Progressive employers know this is an issue today, and they often help the spouse or partner make a successful move.
- In advance, agree not to accept new positions, despite the benefits for one partner, if the disadvantages for the other partner or for other family members are too severe.
- Explore the new community together.
- If children are involved in relocation, or if one or both parents are going to be spending more time on work because of a promotion, plan for special time with children, individually and together with brothers and sisters.
- Provide for outside help with household, maintenance, and child-rearing needs.

- Plan to spend extra time taking care of your personal health and fitness during periods of transition.
- Plan for a special vacation with your loved ones after the initial peak work period following a promotion.
- Build backup or contingency plans for emergencies, for those periods when your packed schedules begin to fall apart.

Principle 6. The Goal Is to Achieve a New Life Integration

How we *intend* to use time and how we *actually* spend it are the primary measures of the integration in our lives. Using time as we wish is one of the biggest challenges in successfully navigating the personal side of leadership transitions. After all, the point of managing a career is learning how to plan and work toward a lifestyle that has professional and personal meaning to you and those closest to you.

Achieving your ideal lifestyle integration among career, family, and personal goals is a challenge that, left unresolved, will leave you confused and unhappy. More importantly, a lifestyle dominated by work can be unhealthy and hurtful to those you love and care about, your family and friends. The challenge of management will stress your daily schedule and the way you use your time.

Leaders are increasingly under the stress of deadlines, responsibilities, and quotas. As never before, you must learn to balance your "wannabes" with your "haftabes," what you want to do with what you have to do. It is a journey that only few survive unscathed, with marriage intact, children secure, body healthy, self at peace, and career assured.

JUST PROMOTED LEADER TOOL 13
Your Personal Pie Chart

Try the following activity, Your Personal Pie Chart. The chart reflects how you spend your time and how you would like to allocate time in key life areas. This is a self-assessment activity that is especially valuable to help you appraise how well your ideal self and real self are in sync. Try this activity several times in your first year as a leader. It is not uncommon to see the graphic change from the beginning to the end of a major career transition.

Step 1. Rank the following key aspects of your life in order of relative importance. No ties are allowed. Force yourself to distinguish and rank from first to last, starting with what is of highest value to you:

Work time ____
Family time ____
Religious and spiritual time ____
Recreational and vacation time ____
Unplanned and spontaneous time ____
Community time ____
Self-maintenance time ____
Sleep ____
Other time (your choice) ____

For even finer tuning, you might want to take any one of the areas and break it down (including a forced ranking) further for a closer view. The following are examples:

Family Time
Spouse
Daughters and sons
Parents, brothers, and sisters
Extended family
Close friends

Maintenance Time
Home repairs
Shopping
Doctors
Cleaners, repair shops, bill paying, finances, cooking, cleaning

Work Time
Time on own tasks
Managing others
Product development
Client and customer time

Community

Church activities, neighborhood activities, associations, children's
    school activities, children's recreation, scouts, clubs
Politics

Recreation

Reading, sports, and hobbies
Relaxing
Traveling
Listening to or playing music

Step 2. Using the blank pie graph in Figure 10.7, draw your best estimate of
how you would ideally like to spend your time. Use either a typical week or
month as your frame of reference. An example is shown in Figure 10.8. Start
by counting actual hours, and then translate hours into percentages. You might
wish to keep a daily time log for two or three weeks to determine an average
over that period.

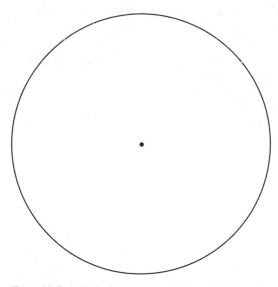

Figure 10.7 A Blank Chart for Your Personal Pie Chart:
How You Would Ideally Spend Your Time

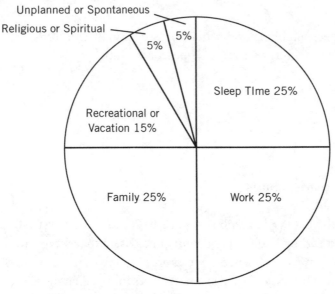

Figure 10.8 A Hypothetical Personal Pie Chart for a
Person's Ideal Use of Time

Step 3. On the blank graph in Figure 10.9, draw your best estimate of how
you are presently spending your time. An example is shown in Figure 10.10.
Use either a week or a month as your frame of reference.

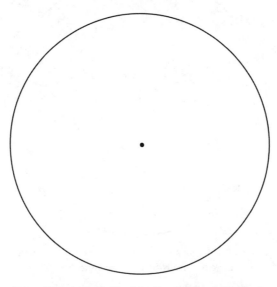

Figure 10.9 A Blank Chart for Your Personal Pie Chart:
How You Actually Spend Your Time

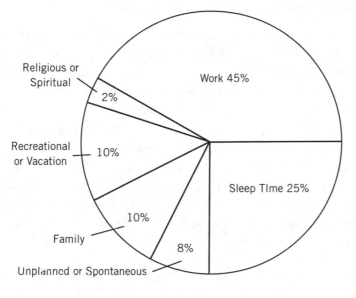

Figure 10.10 A Hypothetical Personal Pie Chart for a Person's Actual Use of Time

Step 4. Compare your graphs. As you contrast your ideal (Figure 10.7) and real (Figure 10.9) use of time, consider the following questions:

- What are the major differences between the two?
- Are you pleased with the way you are allocating your time? What seems right?
- Are there discrepancies between what you believe or say is important and the way your time is apportioned?
- As you review your charts, ask yourself about the quality of the time that you spend. For example, are you really attending to what you are doing, or are you going through the motions? When are you at your best? Your worst? What, if anything, would you change? As you concentrate on your new leadership position, are there important elements in other parts of your life that you are letting go? If so, can you think of ways to remedy the imbalance?
- Where might you add time to one activity by taking time from another?

By reflecting on your actual and ideal graphs, your view of how you balance your personal life should be getting clearer.

YOUR PERSONAL IMPLICATIONS CHECK

You have now had the opportunity to inventory, diagnose, and compare your life's time in both a real and ideal manner in the form of graphs and a customized personal time inventory. You have looked at what is important to you and how you are actually using your precious, finite time. You have reviewed your most important values. Because of the tremendous time pressures when assuming new leadership responsibility, most leaders develop discrepancies or imbalances between what is most important to them and the way they actually use their time. Our desire to integrate our life is constantly taxed, especially when more than one area of high personal value is compromised by work requirements. Your Personal Implications Check examines the interplay among the various aspects of your life, consistency between ideal and real use of time, and your most important values.

Worksheet: Your Personal Implications Check

Step 1. Review information from your time graphs (Figures 10.7 and 10.9) in terms of key information as well as important discoveries.

Step 2. List at least three points that you like about how your life is presently structured and how you use your time. State them in the form of concise statements beginning with any of the following sentence stems:

I am aware _____

I realize _____

I am pleased that _____

I am clear that _____

I plan to continue _____

For example:
- I am aware that I have been able to pay a lot of attention to my children.
- I am happy that my wife and I have continued our Sunday morning time together.
- I am pleased that I haven't gained any additional weight since I moved up to my new job.

Step 3. This is similar to step 2, but look only at what you regard to be negative trade-offs in your present lifestyle and how you use your time. Use the following sentence stems, and identify at least three issues.

I am aware _____

I realize _____

I am disappointed that _____

I am concerned that _____

I plan to discontinue _____

For example:

- I am aware that I am not giving enough time to my spouse.
- I am concerned that we will not like our new home and community as much as our last.
- I am disappointed that I don't have enough time to take walks with my spouse or play tennis with my foursome.

Step 4. Identify a key word or phrase to represent each of the positive and negative sentences that you completed in steps 2 and 3. Then write that word or phrase in the first column (Figure 10.11, Positive Personal Implications Check, and Figure 10.12, Negative Personal Implications Check).

Column 1 Positive Awareness	Column 2 Positive Implications	Column 3 Negative Implications
Example: Attention to children		
Example: Sunday		
Example: Steady weight		

Figure 10.11 Positive Personal Implications Check

Column 1 Negative Awareness	Column 2 Positive Implications	Column 3 Negative Implications
Example: Time with spouse		
Example: New community		
Example: Time for walks or tennis		

Figure 10.12 Negative Personal Implications Check

This activity can be done alone or shared with trusted family members or friends. It is intended to help you examine the implications (positive and negative consequences) of some of the key actions in your present life and work style. Take your time, and use your best diagnostic and predictive skills. Use logic, but listen to your feelings above all.

CREATING YOUR NEW LIFE INTEGRATION: YOUR PERSONAL ACTION PLAN

Having completed the previous activities, you are now equipped to pull together your awareness and insights in the form of a personal action plan. In so doing, you will have completed a cycle that includes the following:

- Heightened awareness of important work and life values as well as the way you are allocating your time in regard to these personally relevant areas
- Increased insight into the positive and negative implications of your work and life styles in comparison to a desired ideal situation
- Made decisions about what is important for you to maintain, change, or possibly remove from your work or life style to achieve a desired life balance
- Committed to actions that should align your work and nonwork life

In short, you are striving for a self-prescribed integration between your work and life styles. Doing so requires that your wisdom, logic, intuition, and feelings are working as one. In this way, you can focus more attention and assign higher priority to those areas of your life that are important to you, and over which you choose to exert control.

Worksheet: Your Personal Action Plan

Step 1. Review your conclusions from this chapter's three activities: Your Personal Pie Chart, Your Personal Stress Inventory, and Your Personal Implications Check.

Step 2.
- Crystallize your insights from these previous activities into clearly stated objectives.
- Identify one or two work and/or life value areas that you wish to change. Your primary criterion should be, "Is this important to me in bringing my life closer to the integration that I desire?" Remember to work on no more than two at a time. Go for success, and guard against doing too much in too little time.

As examples, we will use the following work and life factors:

- Extended hours of work
- Not having time to coach your son's baseball team
- Very little time alone with your spouse

Use the SMART formula for writing your personal behavioral objective:

S *Specific:* The objective should be to the point and should be behavioral in nature.

M *Measurable:* You should be able to observe clearly when the objective is achieved.

A *Attainable:* The objective should be possible to attain. Stretch yourself. A good guideline is "just out of reach but not out of sight."

R *Results oriented:* The objective is truly worth taking on; it is of value to you.

T *Time bound:* There should be a clearly identified time element involved. Goals and objectives without a tight time standard generally become unfulfilled wishes.

Personal objectives generally can be written in one sentence, two at the most. For example:

By June 1 of this year, I am going to leave the office by 6 p.m. every day.

Beginning this spring season, I am going to be the assistant coach for Steve's baseball team and miss no more than one practice every two weeks and no more than two games the entire season.

By December 1 of this year, my spouse and I will take a one-week vacation together without business calls, briefcases, or the children.

I will be home for dinner with the family every day that I am not out of town.

Write your personal work and life integration objectives here (remember, two at the most):

1. _____
   _____
   _____

2. _____
   _____
   _____

Step 3. Identify what keeps you from doing this now (barriers), and write down how you are going to overcome these barriers (enablers). What might help you to achieve your objective (for example, people, commitment, money, creative approach, or information)?

Barriers   Enablers

_____   _____

_____   _____

_____   _____

_____   _____

Be honest with yourself. Is this goal a "should" or a "want"? Do you feel you should (ought to) do it, or is it really an important value to you (want to)? Check one of the following three categories of personal motivation:

- ☐ *High motivation:* I am determined to achieve this objective, no matter what.
- ☐ *Medium motivation:* I'll do better, and I'll do the best I can.
- ☐ *Low motivation:* It is something I think I should do, but my feelings aren't really there.

Go back to your barriers, and, after reflection, answer four more questions:

Who can help and support my efforts?

_____

_____

What other factors or resources could help me?

_____

_____

Can I mobilize myself? What are my next immediate steps?

_____

_____

What additional actions will I take to help myself?

_____

_____

Step 4. Write a contract with yourself to help strengthen your commitment and resolve. It can usually be written in one or two paragraphs. In its shortest form, it is a restatement of the personal change objective that you wrote in step 1.

Address the contract to yourself, and indicate the date that you write it at the top. Be sure to be specific in terms of what and how you wish to change the work and life factor that you have identified. Remember to state the date by which your important change will be made.

Step 5. Give the contract to someone you trust, and ask that person to give it or mail it back to you on your designated due date. Doing so helps you stick to your goal. For some it works because of the added support, and for others it works because of the added pressure.

The personal change model that we have outlined is not new. It has been adapted over the years. We know it works. We present it here because leaders on the rise are simultaneously strong and vulnerable. They are in new leadership positions because they have either forged their own course or they have been handpicked to take on tough, important challenges and responsibilities. Leaders in positions of increased responsibilities are typically highly committed and dogged in their determination to be successful in their new roles.

In this chapter, we have examined the possible impact of assuming new or increased leadership responsibilities on the personal aspects of your life. In so doing, we have described the six principles that can aid the just promoted manager in finding success at work, at home, and in other important life areas.

Quick Reminders to Keep You on Track

- Being promoted, the process of moving up is a major life transition that spawns events that are seemingly unrelated to your career advancement. Many aspects of your life can be affected by job changes, and as a result there are trade-offs and payoffs to every career decision.

  The cases of Bob and Linda Doyle and Susan and Doug Sterling point out the many, and often predictable, areas of personal conflict that may arise when one assumes a new leadership role. These areas of personal conflict can occur even if you remain in your present work site and home. The situation often becomes more complex when significant lifestyle factors such as dual careers and relocations come into play. The good news is that you can take many steps to manage personal and family problems that surface as a result of your leadership role.

  There are six key principles of managing the impact of moving up on your family, health, and time:

1. Personal wellness, family health, and work effectiveness are strongly interdependent. Understanding personal/family and work systems will help you better manage the process of moving up.
2. Major role changes often trigger major life changes. The impact of these changes can be addressed through careful individual and family reflection, communication, and clarification of personal/family priorities and values.
3. Leaders who are moving up are in a state of transition. The process of transition can be understood and effectively managed by individuals and by families. Transitions usually begin with an *ending,* then move to a period of confusion and sometimes distress called the *neutral zone.* The transition period ends with a *new beginning.* Completing Your Personal Stress Inventory and applying accepted stress management strategies and techniques can add a lot of strength and resiliency as you work through the first 12 months of your new role.
4. Health and well-being in one's personal, family, and work life affect and are affected by stress and distress. Understanding concepts such as stress, distress, your personal comfort zone, and what leads to distress can help you effectively manage the work, personal, and family aspects of being promoted.
5. Mutual understanding, support, fairness, and responsible collaboration within dual-career families or with partners are essential for leaders on the rise. Relationships and families can either be weakened or strengthened, depending on how well you work together to solve problems that may arise during the first year of your new job.
6. The goal is to achieve a new life integration.

- People feel best about themselves when what they value most in life is consistent with the way they actually live. Using time as you wish is one of the biggest challenges in successfully managing the personal side of moving up.
- Some key personal values have great importance to you but mean less to others. During periods of intense work, such as that experienced during the first year of increased leadership responsibility, important areas of your life outside of work might be compromised.
- What is seemingly a short-term strain because of the transition into your new responsibilities can easily and inadvertently become a long-term

imbalance that can negatively impact your attention to family, health, and other activities you highly value.

- Completing an activity like Your Personal Implication Check can help you examine the interplay between your ideal and real time use, and your most important values.
- Completing and adhering to Your Personal Action Plan can help you achieve the kind of work and life integration you desire.

SUMMARY

This book has addressed the three major aspects of moving up into a new level of leadership responsibility:

Part I. Moving In: Establishing Yourself in Your New Management
 Assignment
Part II. Achieving an Impact on the Organization
Part III. Managing the Impact of Moving Up on Your Family and
 Personal Life

We hope that as you work through the difficult and unfamiliar challenges of the first year in a new leadership position, you will function effectively from the outset and achieve success in other vital parts of your life by using the principles and suggestions in this book.

ENDNOTES

Chapter 1

1. Unpublished study by Manchester Partners International, 1997 to 1998. See also the Corporate Executive Board, Learning and Development Roundtable, Leadership Transition Series, 2005, which is a valuable point of reference about the risk of underperformance of new leaders and the ripple effect that underperformance has on others and their organization. See also the results of a study by the Center for Creative Leadership, as cited in the June 22, 1998, *Fortune* magazine article "Don't Blow Your New Job," by Anne Fisher. Polling of participants in our seminars entitled "Navigating Your Leadership Transitions" that we taught throughout the United States from January 2009 through February 2010.
2. The expression "for which forgiveness will not be granted" was coined by Raymond Harrison, Ph.D., in describing the importance of delivering on the several most important objectives during your first year in a leadership role.
3. Jim Collins, *Good to Great*, HarperCollins, New York, 2001, p. 41.
4. Comments by Dick Clark, CEO, Merck and Co., in an article from Management Today.com by John Weeks, INSEAD, June, 1, 2006; www.russellreynolds.com/content/corporate-culture-becoming-science.
5. See "Top Companies for Leaders," Fortune-Hewitt Study, 2009.

Chapter 2

1. "A Timeline for Ford Motor Company," NPR Web site, January 23, 2006.
2. "Ford Cut Deal on Health Care Benefits," *The Washington Post*, February 24, 2009.

Chapter 4

1. Jim Collins, *Good to Great*, HarperCollins, New York, 2001, p. 41.
2. Adapted with permission from the original work completed by Martin Seldman, Ph.D.
3. Adapted from James H. Shonk, *Working in Teams*, Amacom, New York, 1982, pp. 8–16. Used with permission.
4. See Patrick Lencioni, *The Five Dysfunctions of a Team*, Jossey-Bass, San Francisco, 2002.
5. See Conference Board, *I Can't Get No . . . Job Satisfaction, That Is: America's Unhappy Workers*, Conference Board Research Report R-1459-09-RR, January 5, 2010.

Chapter 5

1. The source of this parable is not known. The authors first encountered it as part of course material at F. Hoffman-La Roche Ltd., Nutley, N.J.

2. See Rosamund Stone Zander and Benjamin Zander, *The Art of Possibility*, Harvard Business School Press, Boston, 1994.
3. See the International Business Machines Corp. (IBM) Web site at www.company-statements-slogans.ino/list.of.companies-i/ibm-international-business-machines.html.
4. See the Southwest Airlines Co. Web site at www.southwest.com/about-swa/mission.htm;/?Int+GFOOTER-About-Mission.
5. See the Colgate-Palmolive Company (Colgate) Web site at www.colgate.com/app/Colgate/US/Corp/LivingOurValues/CoreValues.cvsp.
6. See the McKinsey & Company Web site at www.mckinsey.com/aboutus/whatwebelieve.
7. See the Amgen Inc. Web site at www.amgen.com/about/mission_values.html.
8. Dr. Bernard Gifford, "Apple's Vision: The Learning Society," a speech delivered during the Apple K-12 Solutions Forum, February 1991, p. 1.
9. See the Apple Inc. Web site.

Chapter 7

1. See the P&G Web site at www.pg.com/en_US/company/purpose-people/pvp.shtml.
2. See the Bill & Melinda Gates Foundation Web site at www.gatesfoundation.org/about/PAges/guiding-principles.aspx.
3. See the Becton, Dickinson and Co. (BD) Web site at www.bd.com/aboutbd/values/.

Chapter 9

1. Adapted from Michael M. Lombardo and Cynthia D. McCauley, The Dynamics of Management Derailment, Technical Report 34, Center for Creative Leadership, Greensboro, N.C., July 1988.

Chapter 10

1. "We Did It!" *Economist*, vol. 394, no. 8663, January 2, 2010, p. 7.
2. Adapted from Sidney B. Simon, Leland Howe, and Howard Kirschenbaum, *Values Clarification,* Hart Publishing, New York, 1972, p. 15.
3. William Bridges, *Transitions: Making Sense of Life's Changes,* Addison-Wesley, Reading, Mass., 1980, p. 43. Reprinted with permission of the publisher.
4. Ibid., p. 9.
5. Ibid., pp. 121–131.
6. Ibid., pp.134–150.
7. Adapted from Walt Schafer, *Stress, Distress and Health,* Responsible Action, Chico, Calif., 1978, p. 47. Used with permission of the author.
8. Ibid., pp. 27–65.
9. Ibid., pp. 149–179.

INDEX

ABOUT THE AUTHORS

Edward Betof, Ed.D., is an executive coach, an Aresty Institute Fellow at the University of Pennsylvania's Wharton Executive Education, a faculty member at the Institute for Management Studies, and the executive director of the Corporate University Xchange's Leaders as Teachers Institute. Ed is the author of *Leaders as Teachers*.

Nila Betof, Ph.D., is the chief operating officer of and a senior executive coach at The Leader's Edge, an international leadership development and executive coaching company, headquartered in Bala Cynwyd, Pennsylvania. Nila was a senior business executive for over 30 years at several major corporations and currently sits on several boards.